MICROSOFT® OFFICE POWERPOINT® 2007

QuickSteps

CAROLE MATTHEWS

New York Chicago San Francisco
Lisbon London Madrid Mexico City
Milan New Delhi San Juan
Seoul Singapore Sydney Toronto

D1397794

MICROSOFT® OFFICE POWERPOINT® 2007 QUICKSTEPS

234567890 CCI CCI 01987

ISBN-13:   978-0-07-226370-1
ISBN-10:   0-07-226370-9

SPONSORING EDITOR / Roger Stewart

EDITORIAL SUPERVISOR / Jody McKenzie

PROJECT MANAGER / Samik Roy Chowdhury

SERIES CREATORS AND EDITORS / Marty and Carole Matthews

ACQUISITIONS COORDINATOR / Carly Stapleton

TECHNICAL EDITOR / John Cronan

COPY EDITOR / Lisa McCoy

PROOFREADER / Joette Lynch

INDEXER / Valerie Perry

PRODUCTION SUPERVISOR / Jim Kussow

COMPOSITION / International Typesetting and Composition

ILLUSTRATION / International Typesetting and Composition

SERIES DESIGN / Bailey Cunningham

ART DIRECTOR, COVER / Jeff Weeks

COVER DESIGN / Pattie Lee

To Marty, with love and admiration for my remarkable partner

About the Author

Carole Boggs Matthews has been connected to computers for over 35 years. During that time, she has been a programmer; systems analyst; technical consultant; and founder, co-owner, and vice president of a software company. She has been on all sides of computer software products, from designer and builder to an accomplished user of software in her business. She has authored or co-authored over 40 books, including *Microsoft Office PowerPoint 2003 QuickSteps, Photoshop CS2 QuickSteps, Microsoft Office Outlook 2007 QuickSteps*, and *Photoshop Elements QuickSteps*.

Carole lives on an island with her husband, Marty; son, Michael; cats, Domino and Tortoise; and dog, Tank.

Acknowledgments

Many thanks to my technical editor extraordinaire, John Cronan, for keeping text accurate and providing reliable and astute observations in his pursuit of the truth!

Also thanks to my copy editor, Lisa McCoy, who did wonderful things to my writing, making it more readable and easier to understand.

Thanks also to Valerie Perry, who excellently indexed this book to make it more accessible.

Thanks also to the McGraw-Hill team, to Samik Roy Chowdhury, project manager; Jody McKenzie, editorial supervisor; and many others unknown to me who helped to produce this book. And a special thanks to Roger Stewart, sponsoring editor, who continues to have faith in our writing.

Thanks to all of you!

Contents at a Glance

Contents

5

6

Chapter 7 Using Charts in a Presentation 129

Chapter 8 Using Special Effects and Drawing in PowerPoint 149

Chapter 9 Working with Multimedia and the Internet 175

10

Introduction

QuickSteps books are recipe books for computer users. They answer the question "how do I..." by providing a quick set of steps to accomplish the most common tasks with a particular operating system or application.

The sets of steps are the central focus of the book. QuickSteps sidebars show how to quickly perform many small functions or tasks that support the primary functions. Notes, Tips, and Cautions augment the steps, and are presented in a separate column so as not to interrupt the flow of the steps. The introductions are minimal, and other narrative is kept brief. Numerous full-color illustrations and figures, many with callouts, support the steps.

QuickSteps books are organized by function and the tasks needed to perform that function. Each function is a chapter. Each task, or "How To," contains the steps needed for accomplishing the function, along with the relevant Notes, Tips, Cautions, and screenshots. You can easily find the tasks you want to perform through:

- The table of contents, which lists the functional areas (chapters) and tasks in the order they are presented

- A How To list of tasks on the opening page of each chapter

- The index, which provides an alphabetical list of the terms that are used to describe the functions and tasks

- Color-coded tabs for each chapter or functional area, with an index to the tabs in the Contents at a Glance (just before the table of contents)

Conventions Used in This Book

Microsoft Office PowerPoint 2007 QuickSteps uses several conventions designed to make the book easier for you to follow. Among these are:

- A 🔍 or a 🧭 in the table of contents or the How To list in each chapter references a QuickSteps or QuickFacts sidebar in a chapter.

- **Bold type** is used for words on the screen that you are to do something with, like "...click the **File** menu, and click **Save As**."

- *Italic type* is used for a word or phrase that is being defined or otherwise deserves special emphasis.

- Underlined type is used for text that you are to type from the keyboard.

- SMALL CAPITAL LETTERS are used for keys on the keyboard, such as ENTER and SHIFT.

- When you are expected to enter a command, you are told to press the key(s). If you are to enter text or numbers, you are told to type them.

Chapter 1

Stepping into PowerPoint

PowerPoint 2007 is Microsoft Office's slide show offering. While maintaining the core features and functionality of PowerPoint from years past, this version adds many features to support anyone, from the casual user who wants to set up a simple slide show to the high-end user who wants to create a sophisticated Web–oriented presentation. When first looking at this version of PowerPoint, you may have quickly realized that things have changed from previous versions. Your first look at the new *ribbon* and other user interface items (those collection of screen elements that allow you to use and navigate the program) signal that the familiar menu structure you may have grown accustomed to with Microsoft Office programs is gone, replaced with a new organizational scheme.

QUICKSTEPS

STARTING POWERPOINT

In addition to using the mouse to access the Windows menu, you can start PowerPoint using the keyboard and shortcuts on your desktop

START POWERPOINT FROM THE KEYBOARD

1. Press the Windows flag key on your keyboard to open the Start menu, or press **CTRL+ESC**.

2. Press the **DOWN ARROW** key until **All Programs** is selected, and press **RIGHT ARROW** to open it.

3. Press **UP ARROW** or **DOWN ARROW** until **Microsoft Office** is selected; press **RIGHT ARROW** to display the list of programs.

4. Press **DOWN ARROW** until **Microsoft Office PowerPoint 2007** is selected; press **ENTER** to start it.

CREATE A SHORTCUT TO START POWERPOINT

Another way to start PowerPoint is from a shortcut icon you place on your desktop.

1. Click **Start** and select **All Programs**.

2. Click **Microsoft Office** and right-click **Microsoft Office PowerPoint 2007**.

3. Click **Send To** and click **Desktop (Create Shortcut)**.

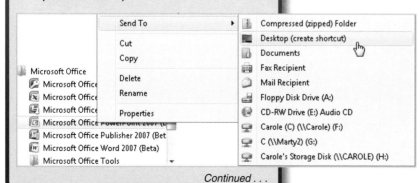

Continued . . .

Chapter 1 explains how to open PowerPoint, interpret the ribbon and new user interface, and configure them according to your personal needs. You will learn how to get help from Microsoft's Office online Help, from offline Help, and by using the Internet. You will learn how to manage your task panes and ribbon parts, and even how to customize your opening pane. This chapter will also show you how to close your presentation and exit a PowerPoint session.

Start PowerPoint

Assuming that you already know how to turn on the computer and load Windows, and that PowerPoint has been installed on your computer, you may start it as you would any other program. The quickest way may be to simply double-click the PowerPoint icon on your desktop (see the "Starting PowerPoint" QuickSteps). However, the most common way is to use the Start menu.

Use the Start Menu to Load PowerPoint

To load PowerPoint using the Start menu on the Windows taskbar:

1. Start your computer and log on to Windows, if necessary.

2. Click **Start**. The Start menu opens.

3. Click **All Programs**, click **Microsoft Office**, and click **Microsoft Office PowerPoint 2007**. The PowerPoint window will open, as shown in Figure 1-1.

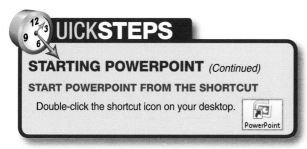

STARTING POWERPOINT *(Continued)*

START POWERPOINT FROM THE SHORTCUT

Double-click the shortcut icon on your desktop.

Explore the PowerPoint Window

The PowerPoint window offers many features to aid you in creating and editing presentations. Here are the main components of the window, as shown in Figure 1-1:

- The *Slide pane* is the container for PowerPoint slides. It is where you create a layout and design, type headings and text, and insert graphs, diagrams, and other design or informational elements to make your presentation look exactly how you want it.

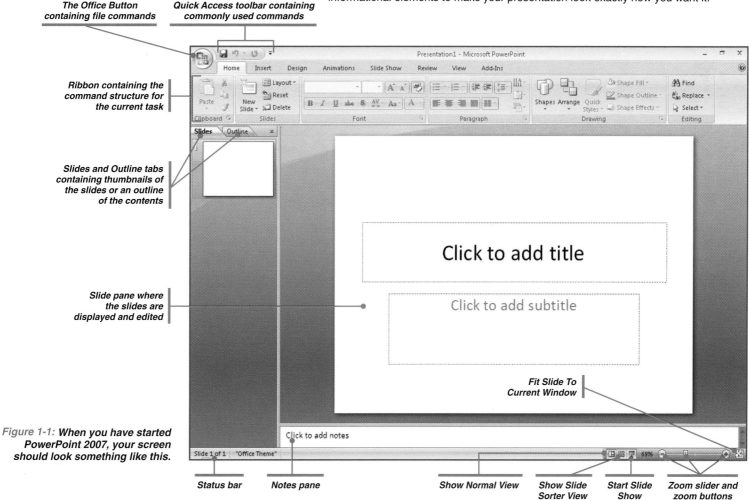

Figure 1-1: **When you have started PowerPoint 2007, your screen should look something like this.**

To see the shortcut keyboard commands for accessing the ribbon, press either **ALT** or **F10** to toggle the commands on or off. Small squares showing letters will appear. When you press **ALT** (or **F10**) and press the appropriate letter or number key, you will be executing the command. Once you begin a letter command using this mode, subsequent screens for that command or tool will continue to display the letter commands.

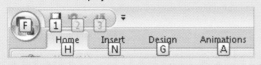

UNDERSTANDING THE RIBBON

So where are the familiar menus from previous versions of PowerPoint? They've gone the way of black-and-white televisions and 40-MB hard drives. The original menu structure used in earlier Office products (File, Edit, Format, Window, Help, and other menus) were designed to accommodate fewer tasks and features. That menu structure has simply outgrown its usefulness. Microsoft's solution to the increased number of feature enhancements is the *ribbon*, the container at the top of most Office program windows that holds the tools and features you are most likely to use to use (see Figure 1-2). The ribbon collects tools for a given function into *groups*—for example, the Font group provides the tools to work with text. Groups are then organized into tabs for working on likely tasks. For example, the Insert tab contains groups for adding components, such as tables, links, and charts to your slide (or spreadsheet or document). Each Office program has a default set of tabs with additional *contextual* tabs that appear as the context of your

Continued . . .

- The *Office Button* is in the upper-right area, and contains the file commands and PowerPoint options for manipulating the presentation document.

- The *Quick Access toolbar*, to the right of the Office Button, is where the most commonly used commands are displayed. By default, these are Save, Undo, and Repeat. You can customize this toolbar by right-clicking it to add or remove commands.

- The *ribbon*, located beneath the Quick Access toolbar, contains the commands and tools for working with the presentation (see "Understanding the Ribbon" QuickFacts). The rest of this book explores and explains how to use the ribbon commands.

- The *Slides* and *Outline tabs* pane, to the left of the slide pane, contains either thumbnails of the slides or the text of the presentation shown in outline format, respectively. You click either **Slides** or **Outline** to select the view you want (the Slides tab is shown in Figure 1-1).

- The *Notes pane*, located beneath the presentation pane, is where you can type notes that will be invisible to the viewer but that are available to the presenter.

- The *Status bar*, located at the bottom of the window, contains the status of the active slide, as well as some additional tools.

- The *View toolbar*, located on the right of the status bar, contains commands to vary the view from Normal view (seen in Figure 1-1) to Slide Sorter view to Slide Show view. See "Show Views" later in this chapter to see the other views.

- The *Zoom slider* allows you to zoom in and out using a slider or using the plus and minus (+ and −) buttons on either side of the slider.

- The *Fit Slide To Current Window* button resizes the slide to fit the size of the presentation pane.

Notice that the appearance of your ribbon may differ somewhat from that in this book if your Windows Display resolution is set to a different value. In that case, for example, you may see just an icon rather than both an icon and text identifying a button.

Open a Presentation

The initial PowerPoint window, shown in Figure 1-1, gives you a blank slide with the Home tab displayed. From here, you can open an existing presentation, begin creating a new one from scratch, create a presentation from one you want to modify, or create one from a template.

UNDERSTANDING THE RIBBON

(Continued)

work changes. For instance, when you select a placeholder (or objects within it—such as text or a graphic), a Format tab containing shapes and drawing tools that you can use with the particular object appears beneath the defining tools tab (such as the Drawing Tools tab); when the object is unselected, the Format tab disappears. The ribbon contains labeled buttons you can click to use a given command or tool. Depending on the tool, you are then presented with additional options in the form of a list of commands, a dialog box or task pane, or galleries of choices that reflect what you'll see in your work. Groups that contain several more tools than can be displayed in the ribbon include a *Dialog Box Launcher* icon that takes you directly to these other choices. The ribbon also takes advantage of new Office 2007 features, including a live preview of many potential changes (for example, you can select text and see it change color as you point to various colors in the Font Color gallery). See the accompanying sections and figures for more information on the ribbon and other elements of the PowerPoint window.

CREATE A NEW PRESENTATION

Although you can create a new presentation by just typing in the title and subtitle placeholder boxes of the blank slide, shown in Figure 1-1, and then creating a presentation from scratch, you have more options available to you with the Office Button.

1. Click the **Office Button**, and click **New**. The New Presentation dialog box appears, as shown in Figure 1-3.

2. Under New, select the type of presentation you want:

- **Blank And Recent** allows you to create a slide show from scratch or from a recently used presentation.

- **Installed Templates** presents a list of preset templates that come with PowerPoint and can be used to create a similar slide show, such as Corporate Presentation or Classic Photo Album templates.

- **Installed Themes** provides many standard themes from which to choose, allowing you to create your own slide design, with coordinated color, fonts, and design elements.

- **My Templates** brings up a New Presentation dialog box that allows you to find an existing template that you have created. Once you have found and opened the template, you can use it as is (for a standard company look, for example) or modify it to suit your purposes.

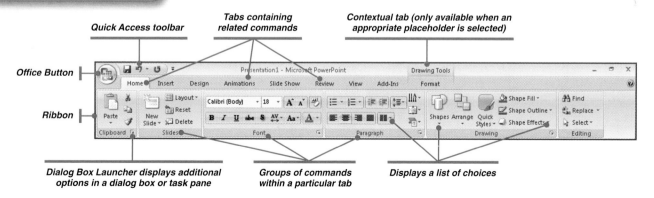

Figure 1-2: The Office Button, the Quick Access toolbar, and the ribbon containing groups of commands and tools are the means to create and modify a presentation.

*Figure 1-3: **In addition to preset themes for selected types of slides, the New Presentation dialog box allows you to create a new presentation starting with a blank slide, from a template, or from another existing presentation.***

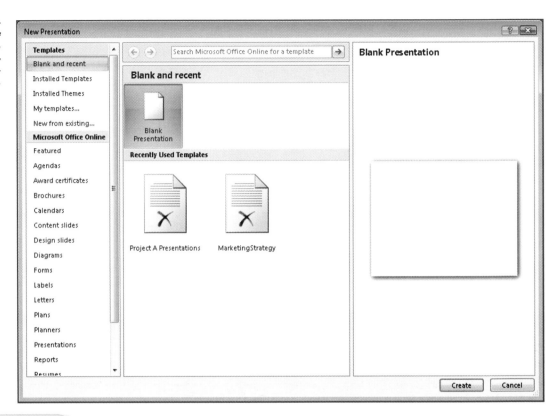

To gain working space in the Slide pane, you can minimize the size of the ribbon. To do this, double-click the active tab name. Click it again to restore the size of the ribbon. You can also press **CTRL+F1** to toggle the size of the ribbon.

If you place the pointer over a ribbon button but do not click it, you will see a ScreenTip describing the command or tool.

- **New From Existing** brings up a New From Existing Presentation dialog box that allows you to find an existing presentation. Once you have found and opened the presentation, you can modify it to suit your purposes.

- **Microsoft Office Online** displays a list of template options. When you click one, you can download a template created by Microsoft for specific documents, such as agendas, award certificates, brochures, calendars, etc.

3. Select the option you want, and follow the prompts. Chapter 2 explains how to create a presentation.

OPEN AN EXISTING PRESENTATION

Once you have created a presentation, you will have to find it and reopen it to make changes, print, or display it. To open an existing presentation:

To Set the Opening Page Default, click the **Office** button, click **PowerPoint Options**, and select **Advanced** from the list of options. Under Display, click the **Open All Documents Using This View** down arrow and click the view you want from the list displayed. Click **OK** when finished.

1. Click the **Office Button**, and click **Open**.

2. In the Open dialog box, find the location of the PowerPoint presentation. Use the techniques in Windows Explorer or Windows Vista that you normally use to find files.

3. When you have located and opened the folder containing the presentation, double-click the presentation itself to open it. You should see the presentation appear, as shown in Figure 1-4.

Show Views

In addition to the Slide Show view (which shows the current presentation you are building), there are two primary views in PowerPoint: Normal view and Slide Sorter view.

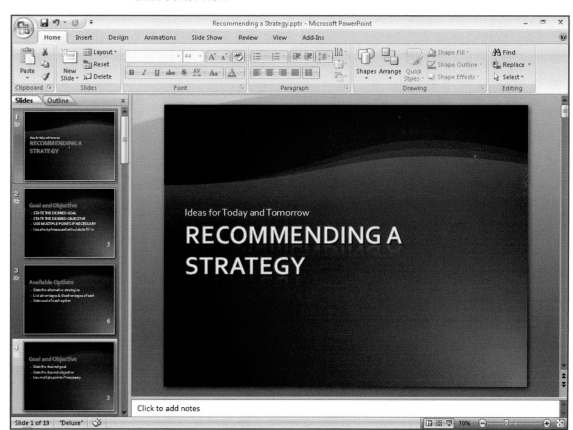

*Figure 1-4: **The PowerPoint window and panes will look similar to this when filled by an existing presentation.***

NOTE

To get back to the Normal view from another view, you can either click the **Normal** view button on the View toolbar or select **Normal** from the Presentations View group in the View tab.

OPEN NORMAL VIEW

The Normal view displays a larger view of the slide show, with a side pane containing the Slides and Outline tabs, as seen in Figure 1-4. Either:

- Click the **Normal** icon on the View toolbar, located on the lower- right area of the status bar.

  –Or–

- Click the **View** tab on the ribbon. In the Presentation View group, click **Normal**.

OPEN SLIDE SORTER VIEW

The Slide Sorter view displays thumbnails of the slides in your presentation, as shown in Figure 1-5, and allows you to rearrange them. Either:

*Figure 1-5: **You can easily rearrange and manipulate slides in the Slide Sorter view.***

- Click the **Slide Sorter** icon on the View toolbar, located in the lower-right area of the screen.

  –Or–

- Click the **View** tab, and, in the Presentation View group, click **Slide Sorter**.

Start a Slide Show

Start a slide show in one of three ways:

- In the current view, click the **Slide Show** icon on the View toolbar, located on the right of the status bar.

  –Or–

- Click the **View** tab, and, in the Presentation View group, click **Slide Show**.

  –Or–

- Press **F5**.

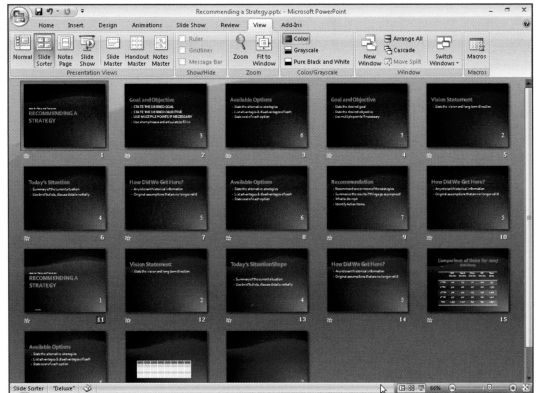

TIP

While you are in Slide Show mode, you may need to click the display of the current slide to advance the presentation to the next slide. To close the slide show and return to the previous view, press **ESC** on your keyboard.

NOTE

You can start a slide show using Windows Explorer without starting PowerPoint. Find the file in Windows Explorer, right-click the presentation's file name, and click **Show** from the context menu.

NOTE

You can increase the size of any pane (such as the Notes pane or the Slides or Outline tabs pane) by dragging its borders. Point at the border until you see a two-headed arrow separated by parallel lines, and then drag the border to increase the pane size.

Click to add notes

NOTE

You can add a command to the Quick Access toolbar from the ribbon by right-clicking the command and choosing **Add To Quick Access Toolbar**.

> Add to Quick Access Toolbar
> Customize Quick Access Toolbar...
> Show Quick Access Toolbar Below the Ribbon
> Minimize the Ribbon

Personalize PowerPoint

You can personalize PowerPoint by changing the default PowerPoint settings and by customizing the Quick Access toolbar.

Work with the Quick Access Toolbar

The Quick Access toolbar can become a "best friend" if you modify it so that it fits your way of working.

ADD TO THE QUICK ACCESS TOOLBAR

The Quick Access toolbar contains the commands most commonly used in a given program. You can add other commands to it that you regularly use.

1. Click the **Office Button**, and click the **PowerPoint Options** button.
2. Click the **Customize** option, and you will see the dialog box shown in Figure 1-6.
3. Click the **Choose Commands From** down arrow and select the type of command you want from the listed options.
4. In the leftmost list box, click the command you want to add to the toolbar, and then click **Add** to move its name to the list box on the right. Repeat this for all the commands you want on the toolbar.
5. Click **OK** when you are finished.

MOVE THE QUICK ACCESS TOOLBAR

To move the Quick Access toolbar beneath the ribbon, right-click the Quick Access toolbar, and choose **Show Quick Access Toolbar Below The Ribbon**.

Show Quick Access Toolbar Below the Ribbon

Show or Hide ScreenTips

When you hold your pointer over a command or tool, a ScreenTip is displayed. The tip may be just the name of the feature, or it may be enhanced with a small description. You can hide the tips or cause them to show feature descriptions or not.

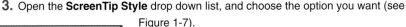

1. Click the **Office Button**, and click the **PowerPoint Options** button.

2. Click the **Popular** option.

3. Open the **ScreenTip Style** drop down list, and choose the option you want (see Figure 1-7).

4. Click **OK** to finalize your choice.

Figure 1-6: You can add commands to the Quick Access toolbar for quick access using the PowerPoint Options dialog box, and the Customize option.

Display the Mini Toolbar

When you highlight or select text, a small mini toolbar appears with commands for working with text. Highlight the text and move the pointer over the selection until the toolbar appears. You can hide the toolbar by changing the default setting.

1. Click the **Office Button**, and click the **PowerPoint Options** button.

2. Click the **Popular** option.

3. Click the **Show Mini Toolbar On Selection** check box to remove the check mark.

4. Click **OK** to finalize the choice.

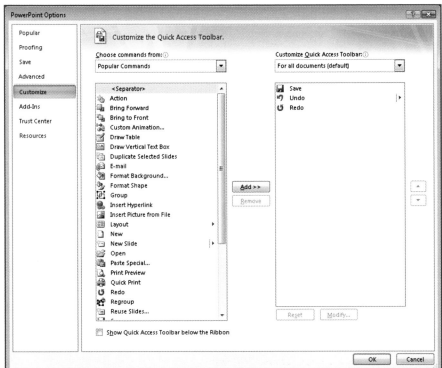

The screenshot shows the PowerPoint Options dialog box with the following:

Popular
Proofing
Save
Advanced
Customize
Add-Ins
Trust Center
Resources

Change the most popular options in PowerPoint.

Top options for working with PowerPoint

☑ Show Mini Toolbar on selection ⓘ
☑ Enable Live Preview ⓘ
☐ Show Developer tab in the Ribbon ⓘ
Color scheme: Blue ▼
ScreenTip style: Show feature descriptions in ScreenTips ▼
Show feature descriptions in ScreenTips
Don't show feature descriptions in ScreenTips
Don't show ScreenTips

Personalize your c...

User name: Carole
Initials: CBM

Choose the languages you want to use with Microsoft Office: Language Settings...

*Figure 1-7: **You can choose whether to show ScreenTips or not, as well as make other choices in the Popular section of the PowerPoint Options dialog box.***

Add Identifying Information

You can add identifying information to a presentation to make it easier to organize your information and to find presentations during searches, especially in a shared environment.

1. Click the **Office Button**, click **Prepare**, and select **Properties** from the context menu. A document information panel containing standard identifiers displays under the ribbon. An example is shown in Figure 1-8.

2. Type identifying information, such as a title, subject, and keywords (words or phrases that are associated with the presentation), a category, and the status of the presentation, and any comments.

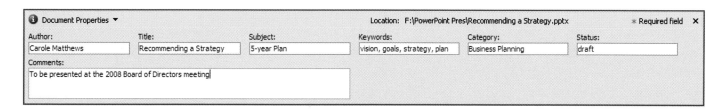

ⓘ Document Properties ▼   Location: F:\PowerPoint Pres\Recommending a Strategy.pptx   * Required field ✕

Author:	Title:	Subject:	Keywords:	Category:	Status:
Carole Matthews	Recommending a Strategy	5-year Plan	vision, goals, strategy, plan	Business Planning	draft

Comments:
To be presented at the 2008 Board of Directors meeting

*Figure 1-8: **You can more easily locate a presentation using search tools if you add identifying data.***

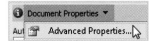

3. To view more information about the workbook, click **the Document Properties** down arrow on the panel's title bar, and click **Advanced Properties**. Review each tab in the Properties dialog box to see the information available, and make any changes or additions.

- **General** tab displays dates and times when the presentation was created, modified and last accessed.
- **Summary** tab displays information about the author, subject, company and manager, category of presentation, keywords, comments, and a hyperlink that might be included. You can include a preview picture to help identify the presentation if wanted.
- **Statistics** tab displays data about the presentation itself, such as number of slides, paragraphs, words, notes, etc. It reveals how many times it has been revised and the total amount of editing time.
- **Content** tab identifies the fonts, themes, and slide titles used in the presentation.
- **Custom** tab allows you to add new information about the presentation. You select a name for the new information, identify the type of data it is (text vs dates, for example), add a value, and identify the properties of the new information.

4. Close the Properties dialog box when finished by clicking **OK**.

5. When finished with the document information panel, click the **Close** button (the "X") at the rightmost end of the panel's title bar to close it.

Get Help

Help can be accessed from online Microsoft servers. A different kind of help, which provides the Thesaurus and Research features is also available.

Open Help

The PowerPoint Help system is maintained online at Microsoft. It is easily accessed.

1. Click the **Help** icon , and the PowerPoint Help window will open, shown in Figure 1-9.

NOTE

If you are not connected to the Internet, Help is also available offline.

ACCESSING MICROSOFT RESOURCES

Microsoft maintains an online resource center that you can easily access. This resource center allows you to communicate with Microsoft about Office and PowerPoint subjects.

1. Click the **Office Button**, and click the **PowerPoint Options** button.

2. Click the **Resources** option:

   - Click **Get Updates** to find out if updates are available for Microsoft Office.

   - Click **Run Microsoft Office Diagnostics** to run a diagnostic program if Microsoft Office seems to be operating incorrectly. The program will automatically capture data and send it to Microsoft to be diagnosed. No personal identifying information will be sent to Microsoft if this option is selected.

   - Click **Contact Us** to send a message to Microsoft experts. You may be seeking advice for a problem or making suggestions for improvements to the product.

   - Click **Activate Microsoft Office** if you cannot access all features within PowerPoint. If you have already activated Office, a message will be displayed telling you so.

   - Click **Go To Microsoft Office Online** to access new product information, tips for using products, downloads (for product updates, free demos, and third-party downloads), clip art, templates and so on.

   - Click **About Microsoft Office PowerPoint 2007** to open the About Microsoft Office PowerPoint dialog box, which gives the version, licensing information, and so on.

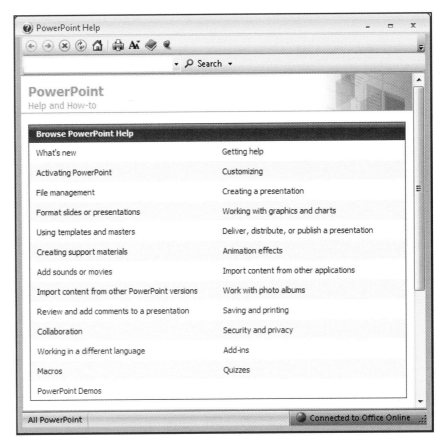

Figure 1-9: When you click the Help icon, you will see the PowerPoint Help dialog box, where you can click the topic you want or search for more specific words.

- Find the topic you want, and click it.

  –Or–

- Type keywords in the Search text box, and click **Search**.

UNDERSTANDING POWERPOINT XML FILE FORMATS

XML (eXtensible Markup Language) is rapidly becoming the de facto standard for a data-exchange format throughout modern computing. XML was introduced to Office in its 2003 release, but it is now fully embedded in Office 2007 programs. It is the default file type produced by PowerPoint and other Office programs.

XML does to data what HTML has done to the formatting of Web pages—it interprets or translates data, thereby making it known to other programs. By providing a consistent set of *tags* (or identifiers) to data, along with a road map of how that data is structured (a *schema*), and a file that *transforms* the data from one use to another, documents can easily interchange information with Web services, programs, and other documents.

A key feature of the new file formats (identified by the "x" in the file extension, such as .pptx) is how a file is now organized. Previously, a presentation was a single binary file, such as *filename*.ppt. Office 2007 XML files are actually a collection of several files and folders that all appear as a single file, such as the presentation, *filename*.pptx, or the template, *filename*.potx. XML provides several key advantages over binary files in addition to data parsing. XML files are:

- **Smaller**—They use ZIP compression to gain up to a 75-percent file size reduction.
- **More secure**—Executable code, such as VBA (Visual Basic for Applications), used in macros and ActiveX controls is segregated into more secure file packages, such as macro-enabled commands.
- **More easily recovered**—Individual XML files can be opened in text readers such as Notepad, so it's not an all-or-nothing proposition when opening a corrupted file.

Continued . . .

Conduct Research

You can conduct research on the Internet using PowerPoint's Research command. This displays a Research task pane that allows you to enter your search criteria and specify references to search.

1. Click the **Review** tab, and click **Research**. The Research task pane will appear to the right of the Slide pane.

2. Enter your search criteria in the **Search For** text box.

3. Beneath the text box is the reference source. To change the default reference (All Reference Books), click the down arrow to open the drop-down list, and click the reference you want to search.

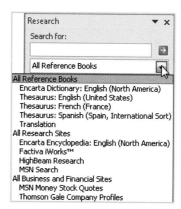

Close Your PowerPoint Presentation

When you have finished working on your presentation, you need to save it and exit PowerPoint. One way to make this more efficient is to have PowerPoint save it automatically while you work.

UNDERSTANDING POWERPOINT XML FILE FORMATS *(Continued)*

So what does all this have to do with you if you simply want to create a presentation to report your monthly status? Fortunately, very little. All this XML tagging and multiple file organizing is done behind the scenes. As far as you're concerned, you have one file per presentation to save, copy, delete, or perform any standard file-maintenance actions upon.

In the PowerPoint Options dialog box (which is displayed by clicking the Office Button), you can set a default location where your presentation files will be saved.

Save a Presentation Automatically

It is important to periodically save a presentation as you work. Having PowerPoint save it automatically will reduce the chance of losing data in case of a power failure or other interruption. To save your files automatically:

1. Click the **Office Button**, and click **PowerPoint Options**.
2. Click the **Save** option on the left.
3. Click **Save AutoRecover Information Every** to select it. A checkmark will appear in the checkbox.
4. In the **Minutes** box, type a time or use the spinner to set how often PowerPoint is to save your presentation.

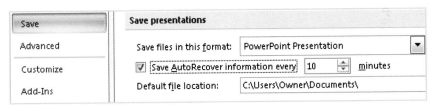

5. Click **OK** to close the dialog box.

Save a Presentation Manually

You can save a presentation manually or create a copy of it under a different file name.

SAVE A PRESENTATION

To save a file:

- Click the **Office Button**, and click **Save**.

  –Or–

- Click the **Save** button 💾 on the Quick Access toolbar.

  –Or–

- Press **CTRL+S**.

SAVE A COPY OF YOUR PRESENTATION

When you save a presentation under a different file name, you create a copy of it. Both the original presentation and the newly named one will remain. To create a copy with a new name:

1. Click the **Office Button**, and click **Save As**.

2. In the Save As dialog box, shown in Figure 1-10, type the file name.

3. To find the path to the folder you want, you can either click the down arrow beneath the title bar, or you can click **Browse Folders** in the lower-left area of the dialog box. If you do this, you will have available a Folders list and Favorite Links list that will facilitate finding the path to the folder.

4. Click **Save**.

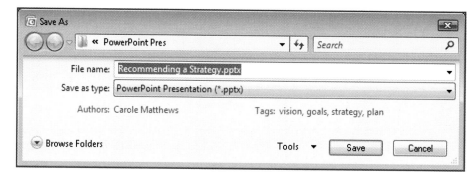

Figure 1-10: *The Save As command is a way to make a copy of your presentation so that you can modify it to meet new requirements without changing the original.*

SAVE A PRESENTATION AS A TEMPLATE

To save a newly created presentation as a template from which to create new presentations:

1. Click the **Office Button**, and click **Save As**.

2. Type a file name for your template, and locate the path to the folder under which it will be saved.

3. Click the **Save As Type** down arrow, and click **PowerPoint Template**.

4. Click **Save**.

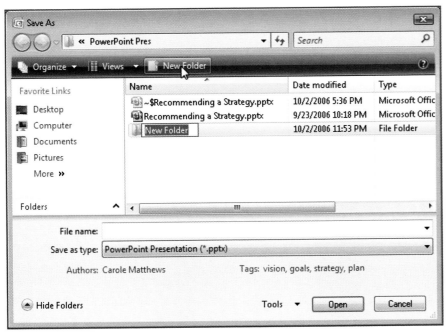

Figure 1-11: **You can create a new folder to store your presentation in while you are saving it.**

TIP

You can also create a folder using Windows Explorer.

Create a PowerPoint Folder

You prepare a folder to store your presentation in so that you won't have to search for it every time you need it. You may have a special need that requires storing your presentations in a unique location (for example, if you have a project or task folder where you want the presentation to be stored). Or you may want to create a folder within the common Folder list or Favorite Links list available in the Save As dialog box. You can direct PowerPoint to save your presentations by default to a given location.

SAVE TO A NEW FOLDER

1. When you save the presentation file for the first time, click the **Office Button**, and click **Save As**.

2. In the Save As dialog box, find the folder under which you want to create a new folder. (In Figure 1-11, the folder is named "PowerPoint Pres.")

3. Click the **Browse Folders** down arrow to display the whole dialog box. Click the **New Folder** button. A new folder with "New Folder" as the name will be inserted into the folder selected in step 2, as shown in Figure 1-11.

4. Type the name of the new folder, such as a project name or some other identifying name.

5. Type the file name, verify the type of file you are saving, and click **Save**.

CHANGE THE DEFAULT SAVE FOLDER

To store all your PowerPoint presentation files in one place, direct PowerPoint to save your files in a default folder.

1. Click the **Office Button**, and click **Save As**.

2. Click the **Tools** button to open the drop-down list, and click **Save Options**.

3. Type the path to the folder where all presentations will be saved in the **Default File Location** text box.

4. Click **OK** when finished.

Close a Presentation Session

When you have completed your work for the day, or if you want to use another application, you must "officially" close your presentation and then exit PowerPoint. Closing a presentation removes it from the PowerPoint window, and exiting PowerPoint stops the program from using your computer's memory. If the presentation has been saved, nothing will be lost. However, if you have not saved your work, you could lose all the work you have produced since the last time you saved your presentation (see "Save a Presentation Manually.")

CLOSE THE PRESENTATION

After you have saved all changes to your presentation, you can close your presentation and then exit PowerPoint.

- Click the **Office Button**, click **Close**, and click **Yes** to save the presentation. (If you have just saved the presentation, you will not be asked to do it again.)

–Or–

- Click **Close** [x] in the upper-right corner of the PowerPoint window.

EXIT POWERPOINT

- To exit PowerPoint, click the **Office Button**, and click the **Exit PowerPoint** button.

X Exit PowerPoint

–Or–

- Click **Close** in the upper-right corner of the PowerPoint window.

How to...

Chapter 2
Creating the Presentation

Chapter 2 describes how to create a presentation. You'll find that PowerPoint provides many methods for quickly and easily creating dramatic and effective presentations. Sometimes, you'll find what you need in the prepackaged themes and templates that are already designed with specific presentation types in mind (for instance, an academic or business presentation, or one for healthcare professionals). These may be available from the online gallery. Sometimes, you'll find what you need in previous presentations you've created, so that you can simply borrow slides or design elements from past successful efforts. And other times, nothing you have in your presentation library or that is offered by PowerPoint can fill your particular requirements. In this case, you can create your own template from scratch or using Office-wide themes and the styling assistance of PowerPoint. This chapter then

DEFINING THEMES, LAYOUTS, AND MASTER SLIDES

Themes in PowerPoint lend presentations color and design coordination. Up to 20 theme templates are available in a ribbon gallery in PowerPoint. Or, you can download additional choices from Microsoft's online templates. Chapter 3 explains how themes can be changed and customized to give you almost unlimited variations in how your presentation looks.

Layouts define where the objects of a slide (such as the text, spreadsheets or diagrams, pictures, or headings and footers) will be placed and formatted. Objects are positioned on a slide using *placeholders* that identify the specific object being inserted (a text placeholder versus a chart placeholder, for instance). PowerPoint has defined several standard layout templates that you can choose when you insert a new slide. When you insert a new slide into a given theme, the slide takes on the colors and design elements of the theme, with the chosen layout attributes and placeholder positioning.

When you want to create your own themes and layouts to use in a future presentation, you create your own templates by saving them with a special file extension: .potx. Figure 2-1 depicts some of the components of layouts and themes that you may have on a slide.

You can make your templates be *master slides*—see Chapter 3 for additional information. Master slides, another type of template, define the parts of a slide that you want to be the same for a whole presentation or a for group of contiguous slides.

Continued . . .

looks at how to organize and manage your slides by creating and working with a presentation outline. Finally, you will see how to protect your presentations with passwords.

Create a Presentation

There are three ways to begin creating your presentation: using a theme and standard layouts that define the design and layout of a slide, using another existing presentation and then modifying it, and starting from scratch—creating your own template in the process.

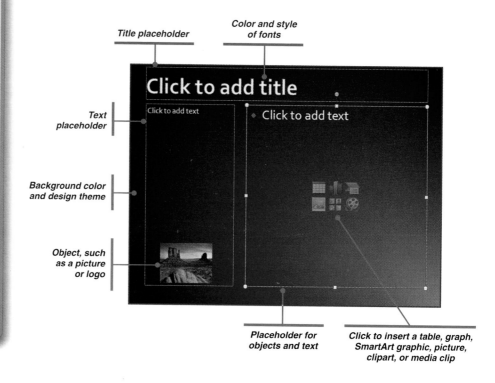

Figure 2-1: *These components make up the theme and layout of a slide and can be saved as a template.*

QUICK**FACTS**

DEFINING THEMES, LAYOUTS, AND MASTER SLIDES *(Continued)*

(You can have multiple master slides in a presentation.) In addition to any color and design elements (such as fonts) found in themes, master slides might include unique graphics (such as a logo), a specific header or footer, and options for placing placeholders for text and other objects while you are creating a presentation.

Create a Presentation from Another Presentation

The easiest and most direct way to create a new presentation is to start with an existing one. To copy a presentation, rename it, and then modify it according to your needs:

1. Click the **Office Button**, and click **New**.

2. On the New Presentation window, double click **New From Existing**.

3. Find the presentation or template you want to use, and click **Create New**, as displayed in Figure 2-2.

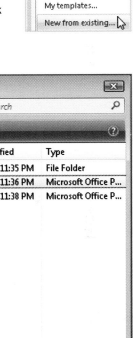

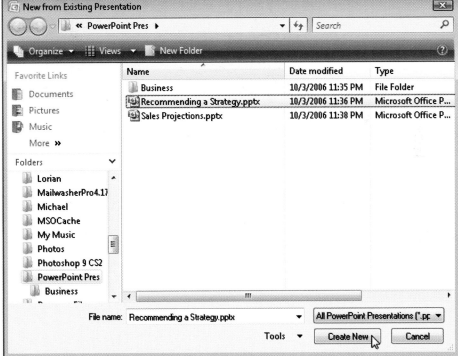

Figure 2-2: **In this window, you find the presentation you want to use as a model and create a new one.**

4. Modify the presentation by replacing the theme; highlighting text and replacing it with your own; deleting unnecessary slides; inserting new slides; inserting your own graphics, charts, and art; and rearranging the slides according to your needs (subsequent chapters in this book describe how to do these actions in detail).

5. Click the **Office Button**, and click **Save As**. Enter a name for the presentation, click the **Save As Type** down arrow and identify the file type, and click **Save**.

Create a Presentation Using a Standard Theme

Themes are used to give your presentation a unified and professional look. They provide background color and design, predefined fonts, and other elements that hold a presentation together. Once you have defined the overall theme, it is a simple task to add slides with the appropriate layout for the data you wish to present. You select a theme from a predefined gallery available on the ribbon. See "Defining Themes, Layouts, and Master Slides" QuickFacts. To use one of PowerPoint's standard themes:

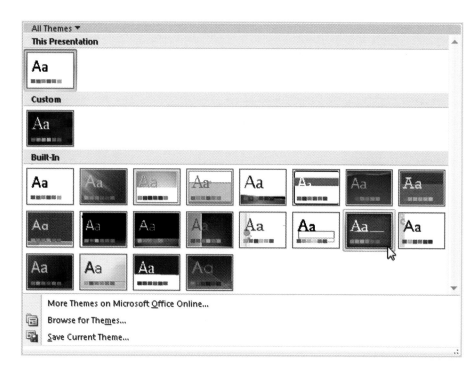

1. Click the **Office Button**, and click **New**. The New Presentation dialog box appears.

2. Double-click **Blank Presentation**, and a standard blank slide will open.

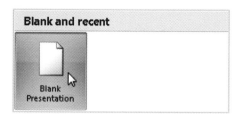

3. Click the **Design** tab, and, in the Themes group, click the **Themes More** down arrow to see thumbnails of color and design themes. Hold your mouse pointer over individual thumbnails to see their effects on the slide. When you find the theme you want to use, click its thumbnail.

4. At this point, you can either begin to add content to an actual presentation (see "Adding Content to a Slide" QuickSteps) or you can create a template for a presentation (see "Create a Template").

Create a Template

A template contains one or more slides with attributes of the colors, themes, and standard layouts you want to have available. First, you create the slide with the desired themes and layouts. Then you save it as a template so that it can be used when formatting and adding your own colors and design theme to new presentations. Template files have .potx extensions. When you create a new template, it will be displayed in the New Presentations dialog box under My Templates. To create a new presentation:

1. Click the **Office Button** and click **New**. Double-click **Blank Presentation** to see the basic slide layout.

2. To prepare your slide:

● Click the **Design** tab, and in the Themes group click the **Themes More** down arrow to select themes or design elements for the template.

● Click the **Home** tab, in the Slides group click the **New Slide** down arrow to list possible layouts, and then click the layout you want. Repeat this step to add one slide for each layout you want in the presentation.

3. When you have a template with the attributes you want the presentation to have, click the **Office Button**, and click **Save As**.

4. In the **File Name** box, type a name for the new template.

5. In the **Save As Type** drop-down list box, click **PowerPoint Template (.potx)**, as seen in Figure 2-3.

6. Click **Save**. The templates are now available under My Templates in the New Presentations dialog box.

QUICKSTEPS

WORKING WITH THEMES

You can search Microsoft Online resources to find other templates, apply a theme to selected or all slides in a presentation, or set a theme to be the default assigned to all future presentations, for a consistent business look, for example.

FIND OTHER MICROSOFT THEMES AND TEMPLATES

1. Click the **Design** tab, and in the Themes group click the **More** down arrow.

2. Scroll beneath the last thumbnail of the Built In list, and click **More Themes On Microsoft Office Online**.

3. Click the link to the template you want, or click the type of template under Browse Templates. Follow the download instructions to install the template. The new template will appear on a blank slide in PowerPoint. (If you don't immediately see templates, click the **Templates Home** link or type it in the search text box and click **Search**.)

APPLY A THEME TO ALL SLIDES

Use the context menu for the theme thumbnail to apply the theme to all slides.

1. Right-click the theme thumbnail.

2. Click **Apply To All Slides**.

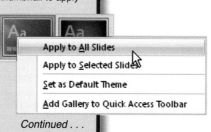

Continued . . .

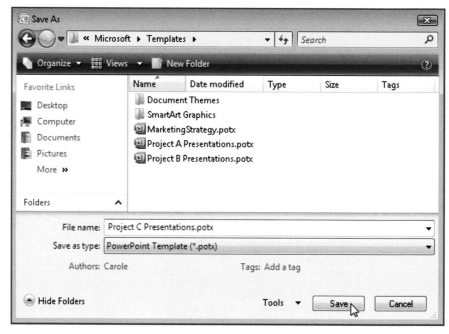

*Figure 2-3: **You can save a file containing themes and layouts as a template for future presentations.***

Create a Presentation from Scratch

When you create a presentation from scratch, you'll begin with blank slides and add layouts, color schemes, fonts, graphics and charts, other design elements, and text.

1. Click the **Office Button**, and click **New**. The New Presentation dialog box will appear.

2. Double-click **Blank Presentation**. A blank title page slide will be displayed.

WORKING WITH THEMES *(Continued)*

APPLY A THEME TO SELECTED SLIDES

1. First, select the slides to which the themes will be applied:

- Press **CTRL** and click the thumbnail in the Slides tab.

    –Or–

- Press **CTRL** and click slides in the Slide Sorter view.

2. On the Design tab, click the **More** down arrow on the Themes group, and right-click the theme thumbnail to be selectively applied.

3. Click **Apply To Selected Slides**.

SET A DEFAULT THEME FOR ALL FUTURE PRESENTATIONS

1. Under the Themes group in the Design tab, click the **More** down arrow, and right-click the thumbnail you want.

2. Click **Set As Default Theme**.

NOTE

A theme can be further modified by changing its constituent components, color, font, and graphic effects. Chapter 3 describes how to work with themes in more detail.

3. On the Design tab, select a theme for the background color and design for your presentation. If none of them are acceptable, click **More Themes On Microsoft Office Online** beneath the list of thumbnails to search the themes available online.

4. On the slide, click in **Click To Add Title**, and type the title of your presentation. If you want to add a subtitle, click in **Click To Add Subtitle** and type your subtitle.

5. When you are satisfied with that slide, click **New Slide** in the Slides group on the Home tab to insert another blank slide with the layout you want:

- Click the **New Slide** button itself to see a slide using the last layout.

- Click the **New Slide** down arrow to see a menu of layout choices.

6. Click the **Insert** tab, and click the relevant buttons to add text and other content to your slides. (See "Adding Content to a Slide" QuickSteps.)

7. Repeat steps 5 through 6 for as many slides as you have in your presentation.

8. Save the presentation. Click the **Office Button**, and click **Save As**. Enter a file name, and click **Save**.

Select a Layout

As mentioned earlier, you can add a slide and select a layout by clicking the New Slide button on the Home tab. However, there is another way. To add a slide and select a layout:

1. Right-click the slide immediately preceding the one you want to insert.

2. Click **New Slide**.

3. Right-click the new slide, and, on the context menu, click **Layout**. A submenu containing layout possibilities will be displayed, as seen in Figure 2-4.

4. Click the layout thumbnail you want.

QUICKSTEPS

ADDING CONTENT TO A SLIDE

The following elements are available to help you present the points you are making in the slide show. This is an overview of the procedures. Each element is covered in depth in later chapters of this book.

WORK WITH TEXT

Text can be added to placeholders, text boxes, and some shapes, or changed easily. Chapter 4 deals with text in detail. To add type, you click inside of a text box, some shapes, or placeholder and then begin to type.

1. To modify text attributes, highlight the text by dragging the pointer over it. A mini toolbar will appear that you can use for simple changes, such as font, font color, font size, boldface, italics, and other text attributes.

2. Click the **Home** tab, and click any of the Font group buttons. On this same tab are the paragraph setting options. (See Chapter 4 for additional information on using text.)

ADD OR CHANGE COLOR SCHEMES

Ask yourself what color schemes you might want to use. Are there company colors that you want to use or colors you want to stay away from?

1. To see your standard options, click the **Design** tab, and click the Themes group **More** down arrow to see thumbnails of the standard choices. These establish a design and color foundation for the presentation.

Continued . . .

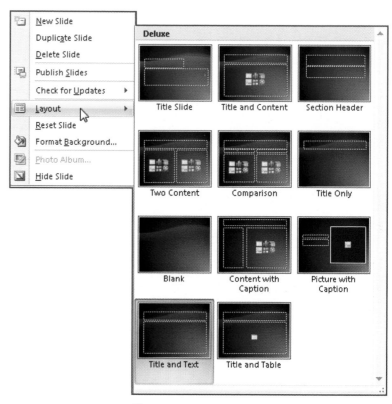

Figure 2-4: *You can select layouts from a gallery of choices.*

Outline a Presentation

Outlining a presentation is easy in PowerPoint. You simply display the Outline tab and begin typing. These sections explain how to create, manipulate, modify, and print an outline.

TIP

For more typing room in the Outline tab, expand the tab by dragging its inside edge into the Presentation pane.

UICKSTEPS

ADDING CONTENT TO A SLIDE *(Continued)*

2. To change the color grouping for a theme, click the **Theme Colors** button, and click the color group you want. (See Chapter 3 for more information.)

3. To change color and shading, keeping the design for slides, change the background style (see Chapter 3). Click **Background Styles** and click an option.

SELECT AN ANIMATION SCHEME

To display animated text on your slide, click the **Animations** tab. Click the animation scheme you want in the Animations or Transition To This Slide groups. (See Chapter 8 for more information.)

INSERT ART AND GRAPHICS

1. Click the **Insert** tab, and, in the Illustrations group, click the button for the art or graphic object you want to insert.

2. Drag the object where you want it on the slide, and resize it as needed.

   –Or–

   Create and insert your own drawing. (See Chapter 8 for additional information.)

INSERT A TABLE

Insert a table to present organized data. You can insert three types of tables: a PowerPoint-created table, one you draw, and one from Excel. On the Insert tab, click the **Table** down arrow, and select your choice. (See Chapter 5 for more information.)

Create an Outline

The outline is created, modified, and viewed using the Outline tab, shown in Figure 2-5. An outline is created from scratch or by inserting text from other sources. You create an outline by indenting subtopics under topics. When you create a subtopic, or indent it under the one above it, you *demote* the point, or make it a lower level than the previous topic. It is contained within the higher level. When you remove an indent, you *promote* the point, making it a new topic. It becomes a higher level, which may contain its own subtopics.

TIP

The name on the Outline and Slides tabs changes to an icon when the pane is too narrow for the words to appear.

CREATE AN OUTLINE FROM SCRATCH

To create an outline from scratch, type your text on the Outline tab.

1. To open a blank presentation, click the **Office Button**, and click **New**. Click the type of presentation you want: **Blank Presentation, From My Templates**, or **New From Existing**.

2. Click the **View** tab, and click **Normal** in the Presentation Views group. (You can also click the **Normal** view button on the View toolbar.)

3. Click the **Outline** tab so that the Outline view is available, as shown in Figure 2-5.

4. Click to the right of the Outline slide icon to place the insertion point.

5. Type the title (the title of your first slide is typically the title of your presentation). Press **ENTER** to insert a new slide.

Outline tab, where you create,
edit, and rearrange the slides

Presentation pane, where you create the look and feel of your
presentation with color, fonts, text, and design elements

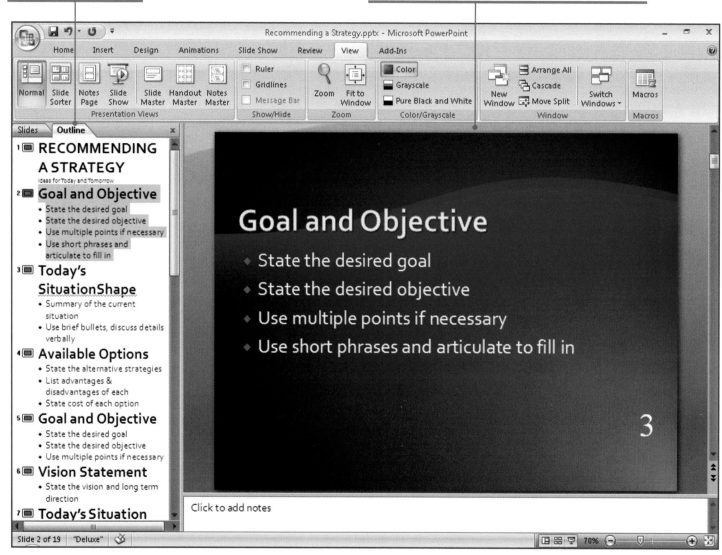

Figure 2-5: The Outline tab is an alternative way that you can work with your slides to organize, create, and modify your presentations.

QUICKFACTS

UNDERSTANDING THE OUTLINING FEATURE

PowerPoint's outlining feature is not only an organizational tool—it is also a quick way to create a cohesive and logical path for your presentation. As you type the outline, you are creating the actual slides in a presentation. This is an alternative way to create a presentation from scratch. If you like to outline your presentations prior to entering your information, you'll like this way of building your presentation. The outline should contain:

- The main points you want to make, which will become the titles of the slides

- Subsidiary points that support the main points, which will become the bulleted content of each slide

Your main and subsidiary points are essential to the presentation. Although not essential at this point, certain secondary considerations are beneficial in fleshing out your main points and the "feel" of your presentation. The more you think these through initially, the more smoothly your presentation will flow. What graphics will you want to use on each slide? Do you have charts or graphs that tell the story? Are there photos that will take up part of the slide? Will you have a logo or other mandated identification information on the slide?

6. Type your next title, typically the first topic or main point. Press **ENTER** when you are done. Another new slide will be inserted:

- To add points to the slide rather than to insert a new one, click the **Home** tab, and click **Increase List Level** in the Paragraph group to move the topic to the right. It will become a subtopic under the previous slide.

- To move points to the left, making them a higher level, click **Decrease List Level** on the Home tab Paragraph group to move the topic to the left. It will become either become a higher-level point or a new slide, depending on the original level.

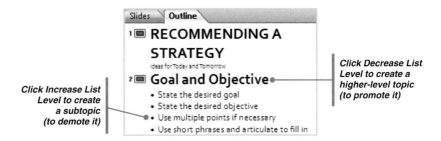

7. Continue typing and pressing **ENTER** and clicking **Increase List Level** or **Decrease List Level** to move the text into headings and bulleted points until the presentation is outlined.

You can create slides from an outline you have previously created in another document. Depending on the format of the text, the formatting retained and used by PowerPoint will differ:

Insert an Outline from Other Sources

- A **Microsoft Word (.doc) or Rich Text Format (.rtf)** outline will use paragraph breaks to mark the start of a new slide. Each paragraph will become a slide title. However, if the document is formatted with headings, Heading 1 will become the title of the slide, Heading 2 will be the second level, Heading 3 the third level, and so on (see Figure 2-6.)

- An **HTML** outline will retain its formatting; however, the text will appear in a text box on the slide and can only be edited in the Presentation pane, not in the Outline tab. In addition, you must create a separate HTML file for each slide. (To see the HTML file in the Insert Outline dialog box, you may have to select .htm as the file type.)

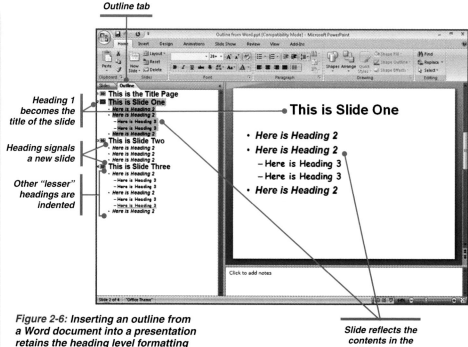

Outline tab

USING THE OUTLINING COMMANDS

Although some of the buttons available on the ribbon work well with the outlining function, you can display commands specifically for use with the Outline tab.

DISPLAY THE OUTLINING COMMANDS

1. Select the slide or line of text in the Outline tab.

2. Right-click and select one of the following commands.

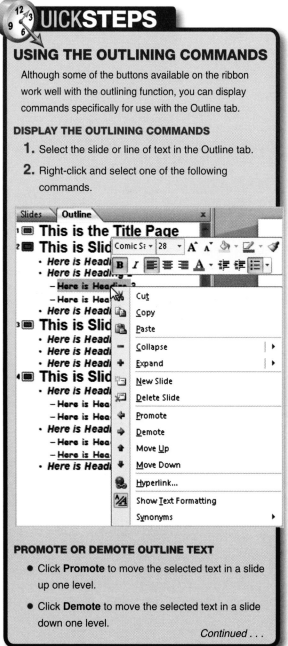

Heading 1 becomes the title of the slide

Heading signals a new slide

Other "lesser" headings are indented

Figure 2-6: Inserting an outline from a Word document into a presentation retains the heading level formatting to separate slides and bulleted items.

Slide reflects the contents in the Outline tab

- A **Plain Text (.txt)** outline will adopt the styles of the current presentation. PowerPoint will use paragraph separations to start a new slide.

To insert an outline from another source:

1. On the Home tab, in the Slides group, click the **New Slide** down arrow. On the bottom of the menu, click **Slides From Outline**.

2. In the Insert Outline dialog box, find and select the outline you want to use, and click **Insert**.

PROMOTE OR DEMOTE OUTLINE TEXT

- Click **Promote** to move the selected text in a slide up one level.

- Click **Demote** to move the selected text in a slide down one level.

Continued . . .

QUICKSTEPS

USING THE OUTLINING COMMANDS
(Continued)

MOVE OUTLINE TEXT UP OR DOWN

- Click **Move Up** to move the selected text of a slide up one line or item.

- Click **Move Down** to move the selected text of a slide down one line or item.

COLLAPSE OR EXPAND A SLIDE

- Click **Collapse** and from the menu, click **Collapse** to hide the detail beneath the title of a selected slide; or click **Collapse All** to hide all the detail lines in the outline.

- Click **Expand** and from the menu, click **Expand** to show the detail beneath a title of a selected slide, or click **Expand All** to show all the detail lines in the outline.

—	Collapse	▶	—	Collapse
✦	Expand	▶	🔼	Collapse All

SHOW FORMATTING

Click **Show Text Formatting** to toggle between showing and not showing the formatting in the outline text.

NOTE

Instead of using the Increase List Level or Decrease List Level buttons, you can also press **ENTER** to create a new bulleted line. Pressing **CTRL+ENTER** will create a new slide or the first subtopic line. Other options for working with outlines include specific key combinations (see "Indenting with the Keyboard" QuickSteps) and the right-click context menu (see "Using the Outlining Commands" QuickSteps).

Preview the Outline

To preview an outline and then print it:

1. Right-click the **Outline** tab, and click **Expand All** to expand the entire outline so that all detail is showing.

2. Click the **Office Button**, and click **Print**.

3. Click the **Print What** drop-down list box, and click **Outline View**, as seen in Figure 2-7.

4. Click **Preview**.

5. Click **Close Print Preview** to close the Preview view.

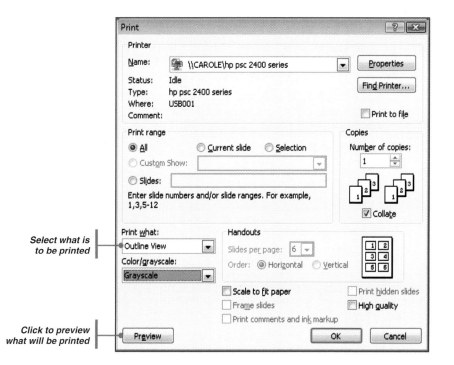

Figure 2-7: The Print dialog box allows you to preview the outline before you print it.

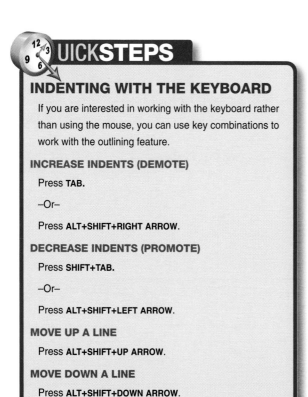

INDENTING WITH THE KEYBOARD

If you are interested in working with the keyboard rather than using the mouse, you can use key combinations to work with the outlining feature.

INCREASE INDENTS (DEMOTE)

Press **TAB**.

–Or–

Press **ALT+SHIFT+RIGHT ARROW**.

DECREASE INDENTS (PROMOTE)

Press **SHIFT+TAB**.

–Or–

Press **ALT+SHIFT+LEFT ARROW**.

MOVE UP A LINE

Press **ALT+SHIFT+UP ARROW**.

MOVE DOWN A LINE

Press **ALT+SHIFT+DOWN ARROW**.

Print the Outline

To print the outline without previewing it:

1. Click the **Office Button**, and click **Print**.
2. In the Print dialog box, click the **Print What** drop-down list box. Click **Outline** View.
3. Click **OK** to print.

Protecting Your Presentation

You can set two levels of passwords restricting access to your presentation: you can deny access to look at a presentation, and you can permit looking but deny modifying it. You can also strip personal information from the presentation—information that is automatically stored by PowerPoint, such as your name and certain file information.

Set Passwords for a Presentation

1. Open the presentation to be password-protected.
2. Click the **Office Button** and click **Save As**.
3. Click the **Tools** button, and then click **General Options**. The General Options dialog box will appear:

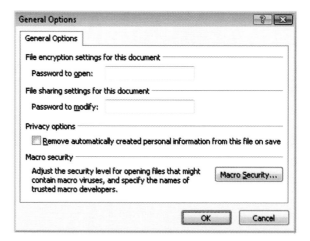

- To restrict anyone without a password from opening and looking at the presentation, type a password in the **Password To Open** text box.
- To restrict anyone from modifying the presentation, type a password in the **Password To Modify** text box.

4. Click **OK**.

5. In the Confirm Password dialog box, reenter the password and click **OK**.

6. Click **Save** to save the file.

When anyone tries to open or modify a protected file, they will see a message in the Password dialog box requesting a password.

Remove Password Restrictions

1. Click the **Office Button**, and click **Save As**.

2. Click **Tools** and click **General Options**.

3. Clear any passwords in the **Password To Open** or **Password To Modify** text boxes.

4. Click **OK**.

5. Click **Save** and, if saving an existing file, confirm that you want to replace the existing file.

Strip File Information from the Presentation

When you set PowerPoint to strip personal information from a presentation, it is done when you save the file. Once you set the option to strip personal information from a presentation, it will be done until you change the option.

1. Click the **Office Button**, and click **Save As**.

2. Click the **Tools button**, and then click **General Options**.

3. Under Privacy Options, click the **Remove Automatically Created Personal Information From This File On Save** check box.

4. Click **OK**.

5. Click **Save** and, if saving an existing file, confirm that you want to replace it.

Chapter 3

Working with Slides

3

Getting around in a presentation and being able to manipulate slides easily is a critical skill in becoming a capable PowerPoint user. In this chapter you will learn how to work with presentations at the slide level. In addition to navigating through the slides in various views of PowerPoint, you will learn to insert, delete, rearrange, and copy slides, as well as to change a presentation's basic components of themes, fonts, and colors.

Navigate and Manipulate Slides

Working with slides enables you to find your way around PowerPoint and to manipulate the slides, both individually and globally. This section addresses how to insert and delete slides, display slides in a variety of ways, and move and duplicate slides.

QUICKSTEPS

NAVIGATING WITH THE KEYBOARD

You can work with slides using the keyboard instead of the mouse if this method is more comfortable for you.

MOVE TO THE NEXT AND PREVIOUS SLIDES

You have two ways on the keyboard to move to the next or previous slide on the Slide pane and the Slides tab:

- To move to the previous slide, press **PAGE UP** or press **UP ARROW**.
- To move to the next slide, press **PAGE DOWN** or press **DOWN ARROW**.

MOVE TO FIRST AND LAST SLIDES

- Press **CTRL+HOME** to move to the first slide.
- Press **CTRL+END** to move to the last slide.

MOVE TO THE NEXT PLACEHOLDER (DOTTED BOX)

Press **CTRL+ENTER**. (Note that if you press this after the last placeholder is reached, a new slide will be inserted.)

OPEN AND CLOSE THE RIBBON

Press **CTRL+F1**.

START AND END SLIDE SHOWS

- To start a slide show on the current slide, press **SHIFT+F5**.
- To start a slide show beginning with the first slide, press **F5**.
- To close the slide show and return to Normal view, press **ESC**.

Continued . . .

Navigate from Slide to Slide

You can use the Slide pane, the Outline tab, or the Slides tab to select and move to the slide you want:

- On the Slides tab, click the thumbnail of the slide you want.
- On the Outline tab, click the icon of the slide you want.
- On the Slide pane or Slides and Outline tabs, click the vertical scroll bar to move to the next or previous slide.
- On the Slide Sorter view, click the vertical scroll bar to move to the next screen of thumbnails. Click the down arrow or up arrow on the scroll bar to move more slowly in increments. Click each slide to select it.

Insert a Slide

You can insert new slides in various ways in several places in PowerPoint. You can also insert slides from other presentations.

INSERT A NEW SLIDE

You can insert a new blank slide from several places in PowerPoint. The most common ways are:

- In the Home tab Slides group, click **New Slide** in the Slides group.
- In the Outline tab, when entering bulleted text, press **CTRL+ENTER**.
- In either the Slides or Outline tab, right-click the slide before the one you want to insert, and click **New Slide**.

  –Or–

  In either the Slides or Outline tab, click the slide before the one you want to insert, and press **ENTER**.

- In the Slide Sorter view, right-click the slide preceding the new one, and click **New Slide** or press **CTRL+M**.

NAVIGATING WITH THE KEYBOARD

(Continued)

- To switch to Normal view from Slide Show view, press **ALT+TAB**. (Must start with the slide show.)

TIP

To delete a slide from the Slide Sorter view, the Outline tab, or the Slides tab, click the thumbnail of the slide to select it, and press **DELETE**. You can also right-click the thumbnail slide, and click **Delete Slide** from the context menu.

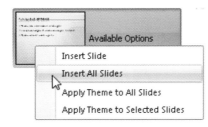

TIP

Before closing the task pane, you can browse for other files and insert slides without closing the task pane.

INSERT A SLIDE FROM ANOTHER FILE

To insert a slide copied from another presentation into the displayed presentation, you must display the slides from the source presentation and then select the slide or slides that you want to copy to your destination presentation.

1. Open your destination presentation and click the slide in the Slides tab immediately before the one to be inserted.

2. Click the **Home** tab, and in the Slides group click the **New Slide** down arrow. From the drop-down menu, click **Reuse Slides** (at the bottom of the menu). The Reuse Slides task pane will be displayed.

3. Click **Browse** to find the source file containing the slide to be copied. Choose **Browse Files** from the menu. Find and select the file you want, and click **Open**. The Reuse Slides task pane, illustrated in Figure 3-1, will contain thumbnails of the presentation.

4. To insert the slides into the presentation, you must work back and forth between the Slides tab (the destination) and the Reuse Slides (the source) task pane:

   - Scroll to the thumbnail of the image in the Reuse Slides task pane, and click the one you want to insert. It will be inserted when you click it.

   - To insert all the slides in the Reuse Slides task pane, right-click a thumbnail and click **Insert All Slides** from the context menu.

   - To apply the formatting of the source slides to those in the destination Slides tab, right-click and click **Apply Theme To All Slides** to copy the formatting to all of them, or click **Apply Theme To Selected Slides** to copy the format only to selected destination slides.

   - To retain the formatting of the source slides as you copy them, click the **Keep Source Formatting** check box at the bottom of the task pane.

   - To view a larger image of the Reuse Slide task pane, place the pointer over the slide thumbnail image but do not click.

5. When you have inserted all the slides you want, click **Close**.

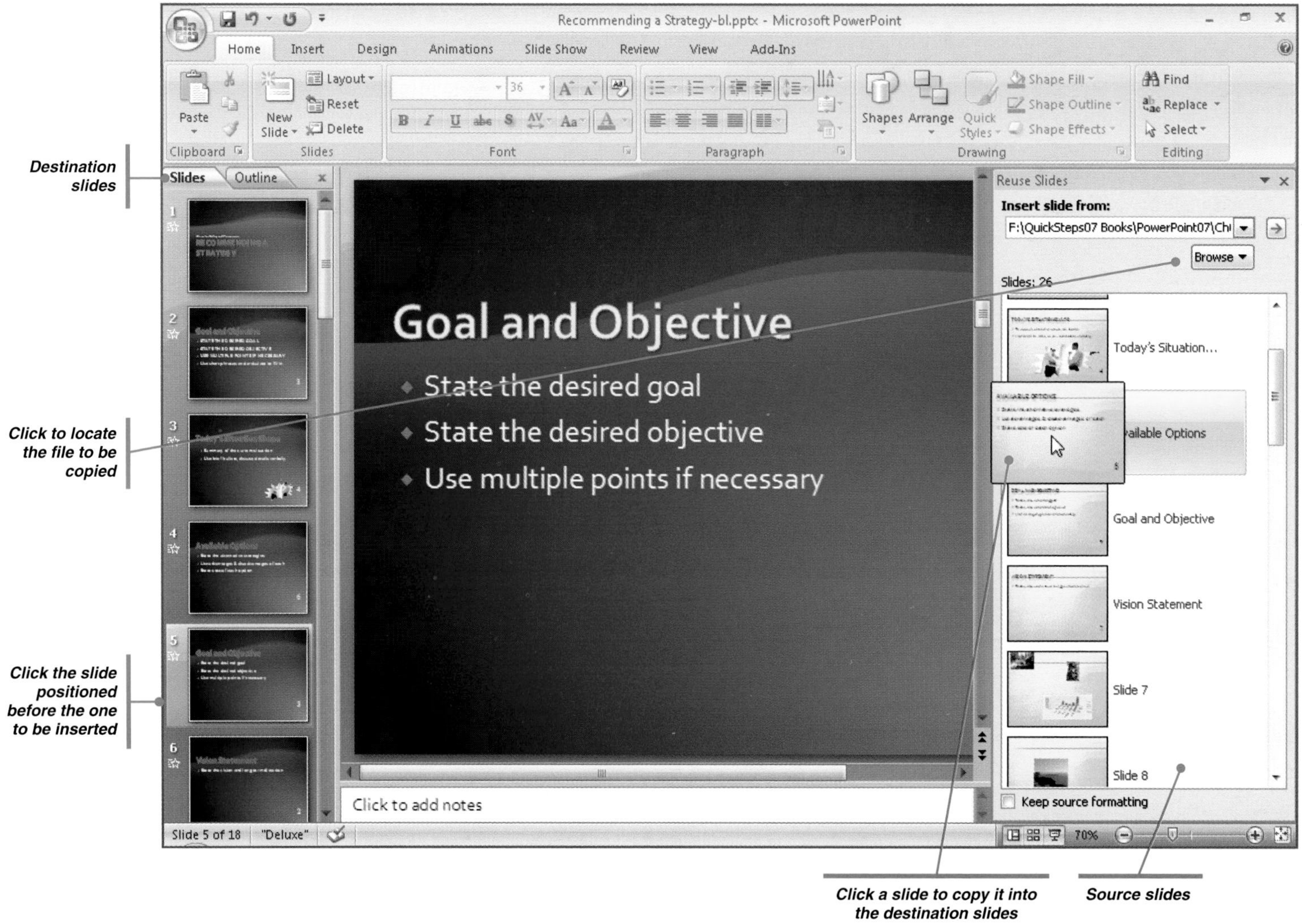

Figure 3-1: The Reuse Slides task pane allows you to find and copy one or more slides from another presentation into your current one.

Display Multiple Presentations at Once

Opening and displaying two or more presentations offers many possibilities for dragging a slide from one presentation to another, copying color or formatting from one slide or presentation to another, and comparing the presentations or slides side by side.

1. Open both presentations. Click the **Office Button**, click **Open**, and complete the sequence of locating and opening the presentations.

2. Click the **View** tab, and, from the Window group, choose one of the following views:

Tiles all open windows

Opens all windows in an "offset-stacked" view

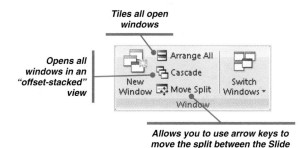

Allows you to use arrow keys to move the split between the Slide pane and the Notes pane

- Click the **Arrange All** button to display each presentation window side by side, as seen in Figure 3-2.

  –Or–

- Click the **Cascade Windows** button to see the windows cascading, as seen in Figure 3-3.

- Click **Move Split** and then press the **UP ARROW** or **DOWN ARROW** keys to move the split between Slide pane and the Notes pane. Press **ENTER** or **ESC** to exit the Move Split mode.

- Click **Switch Windows** to go back and forth between two or more presentations.

TIP

Another way to perform a move split action is to place the pointer over the border between the Slide pane and the Notes pane, and drag the two-headed arrow icon up or down to increase or decrease a pane, respectively.

TIP

To enlarge one of the presentations so that it occupies the whole window again, click its **Maximize** button.

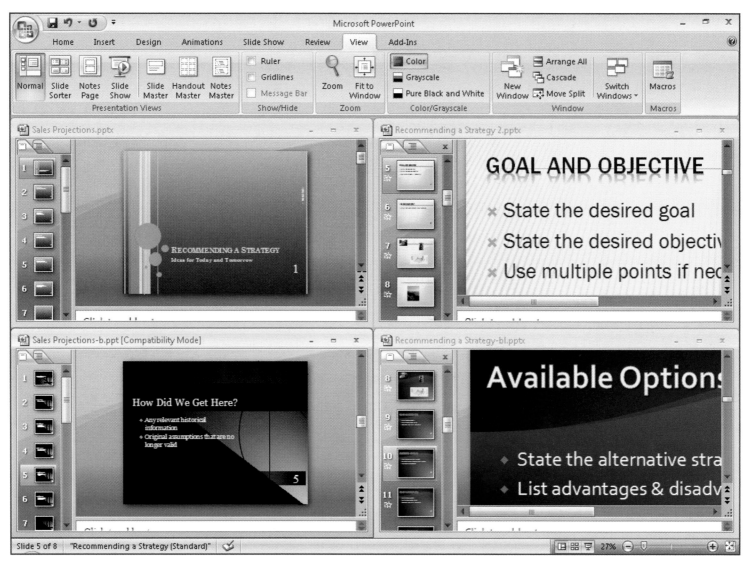

Figure 3-2: You can see each window separately by using the Arrange All command.

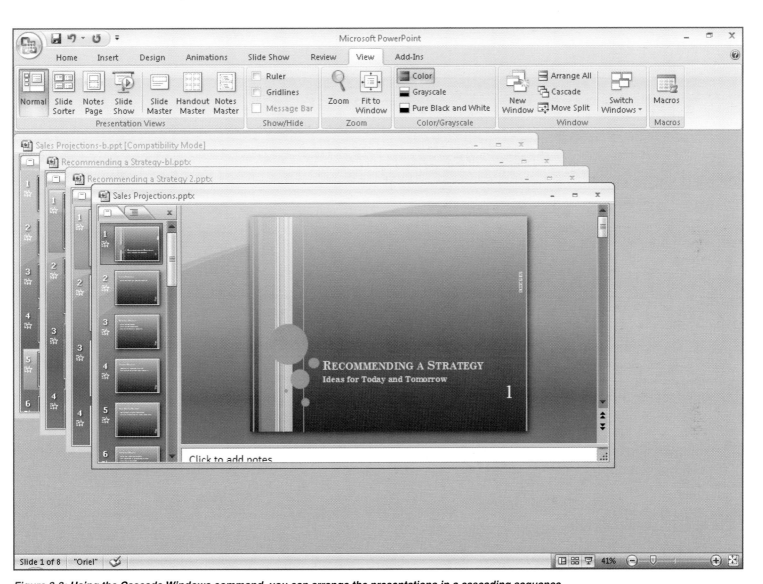

Figure 3-3: *Using the Cascade Windows command, you can arrange the presentations in a cascading sequence.*

NOTE

To copy rather than move on the Slides tab and Slide Sorter view using the thumbnails, right-click and drag the selected slides to the new location. When you release the pointer, click **Copy** on the context menu that appears.

CAUTION

When you are inserting a new slide, you need to be careful where you place the insertion point. That will determine where the new slide will be positioned. It's possible to insert a slide into the middle of another one, splitting its contents unintentionally. Make certain you place the insertion point precisely where you want the new slide to go.

NOTE

If you have more than one design theme applied to a presentation, the first one will be copied, and if you haven't opened the presentation recently, you will be asked if you want the remaining themes to be made available.

Duplicate a Slide

An alternate way to copy or duplicate a slide uses the Duplicate Slides command.

In the Slides tab, select the slide you want to copy. Right click the slide, and click **Duplicate Slide** from the context menu.

To duplicate multiple selected slides in the Slide Sorter view, the Outline tab, or the Slides tab, select the slides (press **CTRL** while you click the slides to select them, or for contiguous slides, you can press **SHIFT** and click the first and last slide in the range) click the **New Slide** down arrow (on the Home tab), and click **Duplicate Selected Slides**.

Copy a Design Using Browse

To copy just the design (and not the content) of a presentation, use the Browse command of the Design Themes feature.

1. Open in Normal view the presentation to which you will apply the design of another presentation.
2. Click the **Design** tab, click the **More** down arrow for the Themes group, and click **Browse For Themes**.

3. In the Choose Theme Or Themed Document dialog box, find the document or presentation containing the theme you want to copy, and click it.
4. Click **Apply**, and the theme will be copied to the original presentation.

Use Zoom

You can zoom in or out of a slide, which enables you to work at a detailed level or back off to see the total slide, respectively:

QUICKSTEPS

COPYING SLIDES BETWEEN PRESENTATIONS

To copy attributes, such as formatting, color, alignment, fonts, and so on, from one presentation to another, you must first display both presentations in the Slide pane.

1. Open the PowerPoint presentation in Normal view. Click the **Office Button**, and click **Open**. Choose the source presentation to be opened. Then repeat for the destination presentation. Continue for as many presentations as you need to have open.

2. In the View tab Window group, click **Arrange All**. The Slide pane will be divided into multiple windows, as shown earlier in Figure 3-2. In the Presentations View group, click **Normal** in the Presentations Views group in all displayed presentations

3. Right-click the slide you want to copy and click **Copy**.

4. Right-click the slide before the one to be inserted and click **Paste**.

5. A Paste Options icon will appear near to the destination slide. Click the down arrow of Paste Options and click **Keep Source Formatting** to copy all the formatting or click **Use Destination Theme** to copy just the slide content without the formatting.

Continued . . .

- To control the zoom with a specific percentage, click the **View** tab, and click the **Zoom** button in the Zoom group. When the Zoom dialog box appears, click the percentage you want displayed or use the Percent spinner. A smaller percentage will reduce the image; a larger percentage will increase it. Click **OK** when finished.

- To make the slide fit in the window, click the **View** tab, and then click the **Fit To Window** button in the Zoom group. The image will be reduced or increased in size to fit in the Slide pane. If you are not in the View tab, a quicker way to do this is to click the **Fit Slide To Current Window** button [icon], located on the right of the status bar.

- To increase or decrease the zoom effect with a slider, drag the **Zoom** slider on the right of the status bar, or click the **Zoom In** or **Zoom Out** buttons on either side of the slider to zoom in smaller increments. The percentage of the zoom will be shown to the left of the slider.

Change the Look and Feel of Slides

At some point, you will likely want to change the look and feel of slides in a presentation. The slides may have been created from another presentation, and you want this one to be unique. You may need to just tweak a few components of the presentation. You can change the theme, color, fonts, and special effects.

Change a Theme

As you learned in Chapter 2, you can select a built-in (or PowerPoint standard) theme for your slides. These themes themselves can be changed to fit your own presentation requirements. The theme can be changed for a single slide or for the whole presentation by altering the fonts, color, and design elements.

CHANGE THE COLOR OF A THEME

Each theme consists of a set of four colors for text and background, six colors for accents, and two colors for hyperlinks. You can change any single color element

COPYING SLIDES BETWEEN PRESENTATIONS *(Continued)*

You can move or copy slides most easily from the Outline tab, the Slides tab, or the Slide Sorter view:

- To copy a slide on the Outline tab, the Slides tab, or the Slide Sorter view, right-click the slide to be copied, and click **Copy** on the context menu. Right-click the slide preceding where you want the new slide to go, and click **Paste** on the context menu.

- To move a slide on the Slides tab, Outline tab, or the Slide Sorter view, click the slide icon or thumbnail to be moved, and drag it to the new location. The insertion point will indicate where the slide will be inserted.

- You can select and drag multiple slides at the same time if they are contiguous. To select more than one slide at a time on the Slides tab or the Slide Sorter view, press **SHIFT** and then click the first and last slide thumbnail. Drag the slides while pressing **SHIFT**.

TIP

You may have to drag your text placeholder to the right or left to see the effects of the fonts as you pass your pointer over them.

or all of them. When you change the colors, the font styles and design elements remain the same.

1. With your presentation open, click the **Design** tab.

2. If you want to change the theme colors on only some of the slides, select those slides. Hold down **CTRL** and select the noncontiguous slides you want, or hold down **SHIFT** and select the contiguous slides you want.

3. Click **Theme Colors**. The menu of color combinations will be displayed, as seen in Figure 3-4.

4. Run the pointer over the rows of color combinations to see which ones appeal to you.

5. When you find the one you want, right-click the row and click **Apply To All Slides** to change the colors throughout the whole presentation, or click **Apply To Selected Slides** to change the colors on selected slides.

CHANGE THEME FONTS

Each theme includes two fonts: the *body* font is used for general text entry and a *heading* font is used for headings. The default font used in PowerPoint for a new presentation without a theme is Calibri for headings and body text. Once a theme is assigned to slides, the fonts may be different, according to the design of the theme; however, they can be changed.

1. In the Design tab Themes group, click **Theme Fonts**. The drop-down list displays a list of theme fonts.

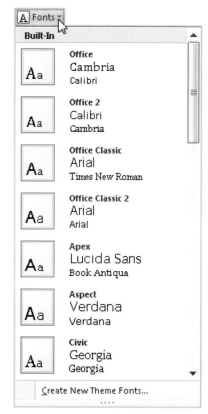

Figure 3-4: *The menu of color combinations offers alternatives for your theme colors.*

QUICKSTEPS

WORKING WITH SLIDES USING A KEYBOARD

If you are more comfortable using the keyboard rather than the mouse, several commands are available to you for working with slides. Some of them use a combination of mouse actions and keyboard commands, such as Copy.

START A NEW PRESENTATION

Press **CTRL+N**.

INSERT A NEW SLIDE

Press **ALT,** press **N**, press **I**, and then use the arrow keys to select a layout from the menu. Press **ENTER** when finished.

REMOVE A SLIDE

Press **DELETE** or press **CTRL+X**.

COPY A SLIDE

1. Click a thumbnail to select it, and press **CTRL+C**.

2. Click where you want the copied slide inserted, and press **CTRL+V**.

COPY THE CONTENTS OF A SLIDE

1. Click a thumbnail to select it, select the text to be copied, and press **CTRL+C**.

2. Move the insertion point to where you want the items copied, and press **CTRL+V**.

2. Point to each font combination to see how the fonts will appear in your presentation.

3. Click the font name combination you decide upon. The font will replace both the body and heading fonts in your presentation on one or selected slides.

CREATE A NEW SET OF THEME FONTS

You may also decide that you want a unique set of fonts for your presentation. You can create a custom font set that will then be available in the list of fonts for current and future presentations.

1. In the Design tab Themes group, click **Theme Fonts**.

2. Click **Create New Theme Fonts** at the bottom of the drop-down list.

3. In the Create New Theme Fonts dialog box (see Figure 3-5), click either or both the **Heading Font** and **Body Font** down arrows to select a new font combination. View the new combination in the Sample area.

4. Type a new name for the font combination you've selected, and click **Save**. Custom fonts themes are available at the top of the Theme Fonts drop-down list.

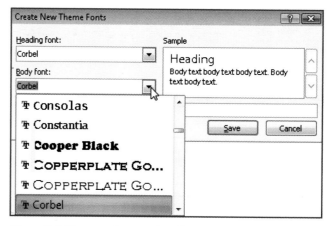

Figure 3-5: You can choose a heading or body font from the fonts available in your Windows system.

CHANGE THEMED GRAPHIC EFFECTS

Shapes, illustrations, pictures, and charts include graphic effects that are controlled by themes. Themed graphics are modulated in terms of their lines (borders), fills, and effects (such as shadowed, raised, and shaded). For example, some themes simply change an inserted rectangle's fill color, while other themes affect the color, the weight of the border, and whether it has a 3-D appearance.

1. In the Design tab Themes group, click **Theme Effects**. The drop-down list displays a gallery of effects combinations.

2. Point to each combination to see how the effects will appear on your presentation, assuming you have a graphic or chart inserted on the slide (see Chapters 5, 6, 7, and 8 for information on inserting tables, charts, graphics, and drawings, respectively).

3. Click the effects combination you want.

Create Custom Theme Colors

You can create a new theme, save it, and use it in your presentations. You select a group of text, background, accent, and hyperlink colors and then give them a name.

1. Click the **Design** tab, and then, in the Themes group, click **Theme Colors**.

2. At the bottom of the menu of colors, click the **Create New Theme Colors** link. The Create New Theme Colors dialog box will appear, a working example is shown in Figure 3-6.

3. To select a color for one of the color groups, click the down arrow for the Text/ background, accent, and/or hyperlink group, and then click the color you want to test. It will be displayed in the Sample area.

TIP

Click **Reset** to restore the original colors in the Create New Theme Colors dialog box Sample pane and start over.

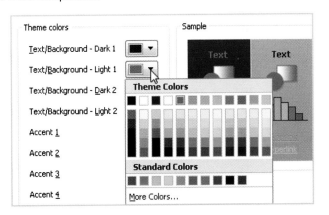

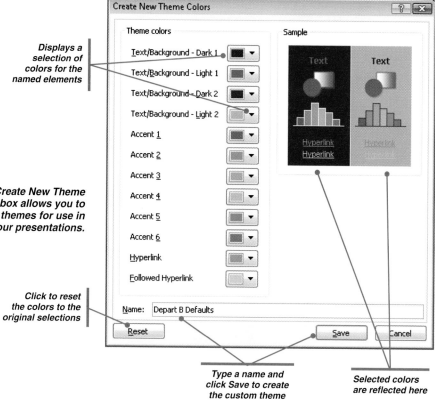

Displays a selection of colors for the named elements

Figure 3-6: *The Create New Theme Colors dialog box allows you to create new color themes for use in your presentations.*

Click to reset the colors to the original selections

Type a name and click Save to create the custom theme

Selected colors are reflected here

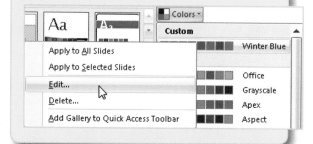

NOTE

You may find you want to change something in a custom theme after you've been using it for awhile. To edit a custom theme in Normal view, click the **Theme Colors** button in the Design tab Themes group, and right click the custom theme you want to edit. From the context menu, click **Edit**. The Edit Theme Colors dialog box, similar to that shown in Figure 3-6, will be displayed.

4. Go through each set of colors that you want to change.

5. When you find a group of colors that you like, type a name in the Name text box, and click **Save**.

USE CUSTOM COLORS

Using a similar technique, you can create your own unique color mix for text, background colors, accents, and hyperlinks.

1. Select the slides that you want to apply the new colors to.

2. Click the **Design** tab, and click **Theme Colors**. At the bottom of the rows of color combinations, click **Create New Theme Colors**. The Create New Theme Colors dialog box will appear.

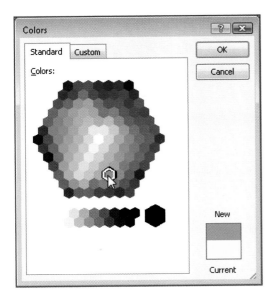

Figure 3-7: *You can precisely change the color by clicking the specific color shade you want.*

3. Click the theme color group that you want to work with. The Theme Colors submenu will be displayed. Click **More Colors**.

4. In the Colors dialog box, you have two options:

   ● Click the **Standard** tab to see the dialog box shown in Figure 3-7. Click the color unit you want to see displayed in the New preview pane. When you want to see it in the Sample pane, click **OK**.

   ● Click the **Custom** tab to see the dialog box shown in Figure 3-8. Click the approximate color you want on the color rainbow. Then drag the slider to get precisely the color you want. You will see it displayed in the New preview pane.

   –Or–

   Click the **Red**, **Green**, or **Blue** up arrows or down arrows to get the precise color mix you want. Displayed is the RGB color standard (Red, Green, Blue) color, but you can also select HSL color standard (Hue, Saturation, and Luminosity). When you are finished, click **OK**.

5. When you have the colors you want, type a name in the **Name** text box, and click **Save**.

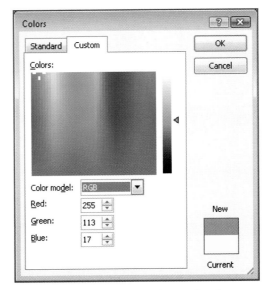

Figure 3-8: *You can create unique colors by "mixing" the combination of red, green, and blue.*

CHANGE THE BACKGROUND STYLE

You can change the slide background on one or all slides in a presentation. When you change the background style after you have a theme already assigned to the slides in your presentation, the design elements from the theme will remain—only the background color or shading changes.

1. If you want only some of the slides changed, select the ones to which you want to apply a new background style.

2. Click the **Design** tab, and, in the Background group, click **Background Styles**. A menu of styles is displayed.

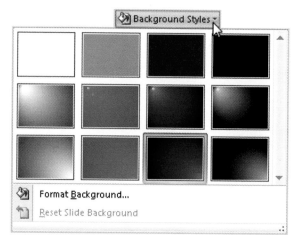

3. Run your pointer over the thumbnails to see which ones appeal to you. As you do this, the slides in the Slide pane will reflect the selection.

4. When you find the style you want, click it to change all the slides. Or right-click the thumbnail, and click **Apply To Selected Slides** to change only the selected slides. The menu will close and the slides in the presentation will be changed.

Save a Custom Theme

If you have worked on a presentation, customizing it to your own needs, you can save it as a custom theme. This will allow you to preserve the theme elements as a Custom theme, available to you in the Themes group gallery.

NOTE

See Chapter 8 for information on how to create gradient backgrounds, insert patterns or textures, or insert a picture into the background using fill effects.

TIP

To save changes to a theme, click the **More Themes** down arrow, and click **Save Current Theme** after making changes to the background, color, font, or effects in the current theme. Your altered theme will be saved as a custom theme and listed in the Themes group gallery for use in future presentations.

UICKSTEPS

USING FOOTERS ON SLIDES

To work with any aspect of footers, you need to display the Header and Footer dialog box (shown in Figure 3-9). (Headers are available for Notes and Handouts only—see Chapter 4.) To display and use this dialog box:

1. Select the slide or slides that need footers.

2. Click the **Insert** tab, and click **Header & Footer** in the Text group.

3. Click the **Slide** tab for footers (see Chapter 4).

4. When you have finished making your selections, described next, click **Apply** to apply the choices to selected slides only, or click **Apply To All** to apply the choices to all slides.

DISPLAY THE TIME OR DATE

You must first display the Header and Footer dialog box, as described in the preceding section, and then click the **Date And Time** check box:

- To apply a time or date that always reflects the actual time and date, click **Update Automatically**. From the drop-down list box, click the date only, time only, or time and date format you prefer.

Continued . . .

1. With your custom theme open, click the **Design** tab.

2. Click the **More** button for the Themes group and click **Save Current Theme**.

3. In the Save Current Theme dialog box, type the name you want for the theme, and click **Save**.

Copy Attributes with Format Painter

The Format Painter can be used to copy all attributes (such as font, alignment, bullet style, and color) from one slide to another, as well as from one presentation to another.

To copy text and graphic attributes between slides:

1. Display the source slide in the Slides tab or Slide Sorter view. Copy the object containing the attributes to be copied, such as the text or graphic.

2. Click the **Home** tab. Click **Format Painter** in the Clipboard group once to copy the source format to one slide. If you want to use the source slide to reformat several slides, double-click **Format Painter** to turn it on until you click it again to turn it off (or press **ESC**).

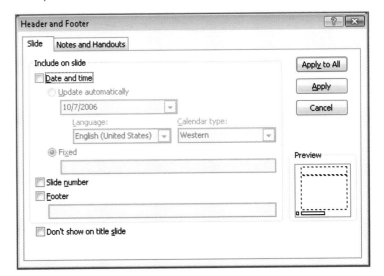

Figure 3-9: You can add footers to selected slides or to the whole presentation.

USING FOOTERS ON SLIDES

(Continued)

- To apply a fixed time or date or other text, click **Fixed**. In the Fixed text box, type the text that will always appear in the footer.

ENTER A FOOTER

After displaying the Header and Footer dialog box:

1. Click the **Footer** check box.

2. In the Footer text box, type the text for the footer.

> ☑ Footer
>
> CONFIDENTIAL

HIDE THE FOOTER ON THE TITLE PAGE

Once you have displayed the Header and Footer dialog box, click the **Don't Show On Title Slide** check box if you don't want the footer displayed on the title page.

> ☑ Don't show on title slide

REMOVE HEADERS OR FOOTERS

Once you have displayed the Header and Footer dialog box:

1. Clear the **Date And Time, Slide Number**, and **Footer** check boxes.

2. To remove the footer for selected slides, click **Apply**.

   –Or–

   To remove the footer for all slides, click **Apply To All**.

3. Find the destination slide, and select the text (drag over it) or graphic (click it) that will receive the new attributes.

4. If you are copying the source attributes to multiple slides, continue to select destination text or graphics on the slides.

5. When you are finished, click **Format Painter** to turn it off or press **ESC**.

Work with Hyperlinks

Inserting hyperlinks in a presentation allows you to link to other files or presentations, to a Web site, to an e-mail address, or to another slide within the current presentation.

INSERT A HYPERLINK

To insert a hyperlink in the presentation:

1. On your slide, highlight the text by dragging the pointer over the characters that you want to contain the hyperlink.

2. Click the **Insert** tab, and, in the Links group, click the **Hyperlink** button.

3. In the Insert Hyperlink dialog box, find the destination for the link:

   - If the destination is within the presentation itself, click **Place In This Document**, and click the destination slide, as seen in Figure 3-10.

   - If the destination is on an existing document or Web page, click **Existing File Or Web Page**, and follow the prompts to the destination.

   - If you must create a new document for the hyperlink to point to, click **Create New Document**, and proceed as directed.

   - If you want to place a hyperlink to an e-mail address, click **E-mail Address**.

4. Click **OK**.

REMOVE A HYPERLINK

To remove a hyperlink from text or an object:

1. Right-click the text or object containing the hyperlink.

2. Click **Remove Hyperlink** from the context menu.

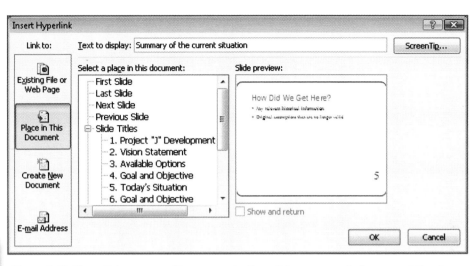

Figure 3-10: Hyperlinks can provide a means to "jump" from one part of a presentation to another.

To remove both the text and the hyperlink, select the text and press **DELETE**.

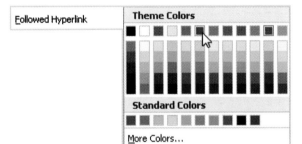

The hyperlink only works in Slide Show view.

CHANGE A HYPERLINK COLOR

To change the color of hyperlinks in a presentation:

1. Highlight the link to be changed.

2. Click the **Design** tab, and click the **Theme Colors** button on the Themes group.

3. At the bottom of the list of color combinations, click **Create New Theme Colors**. The Create New Theme Colors dialog box will appear with your current theme's color selected in each of the sets.

4. Click the hyperlink color you want to change to open the colors gallery, and click the new color.

5. Type a name for the custom theme color, and click **Save** to make the change to the hyperlinks in the presentation. Your changed color will be applied to the links in your presentation, and a custom theme color will be listed in the Theme Color list. By default, it will be named "Custom 1," unless you rename it. (Subsequent saved custom changes will be named using sequential numbers.)

Chapter 4

Working with Notes, Masters, and Slide Text

This chapter covers three important features that make a presentation more effective: notes, slide masters, and slide text. Using notes for preparing speaker and handout notes allows you to fully prepare a presentation so that you remember all you wanted to say and so that the audience remembers your important points as well. Slide masters allow you to make changes to your presentations that are reflected on each slide or on only some of them.

This chapter also addresses how to work with text, from selecting a layout or inserting a placeholder, to modifying text by editing, positioning, moving, copying, and deleting it. The Office Clipboard is covered, as is checking the spelling of standard and foreign languages. Special features, like AutoFit and AutoCorrect, are also discussed.

Work with Notes

Notes are used to create speaker notes that aid a speaker during a presentation and to create handouts given to the audience so that it can follow the presentation easily. The notes do not appear on the slides during a slide show presentation; they are only visible for the presenter's benefit.

Create a Note

To create speaker notes, which can also be used as handouts, you can either use the Notes pane in Normal view (as shown in Figure 4-1) or the Notes Page (shown in Figures 4-2 and 4-3). In both views, you can see a thumbnail of the slide with your notes pertaining to it. Each slide has its own Notes Page. You can also add charts, graphs, or pictures to the notes. To add or change attributes or text to all notes in a presentation, make changes to the notes master.

CREATE A NOTE IN THE NOTES PAGE

1. To open the Notes Page, click the **View** tab, and, in the Presentation Views group, click **Notes Page**. The Notes Page opens, as shown in Figure 4-2.
2. To increase the size of the notes area, click the **View** tab, and, in the Zoom group, click **Zoom**.
3. Click the zoom magnification you want, and click **OK**.
4. To move to another slide, click the scroll bar.

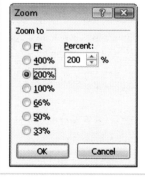

Preview Speaker Notes

To preview your notes:

1. Click the **Office Button**, and click **Print**. The Print dialog box appears.
2. Click the **Print What** down arrow, and click **Notes Pages**.

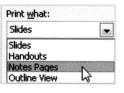

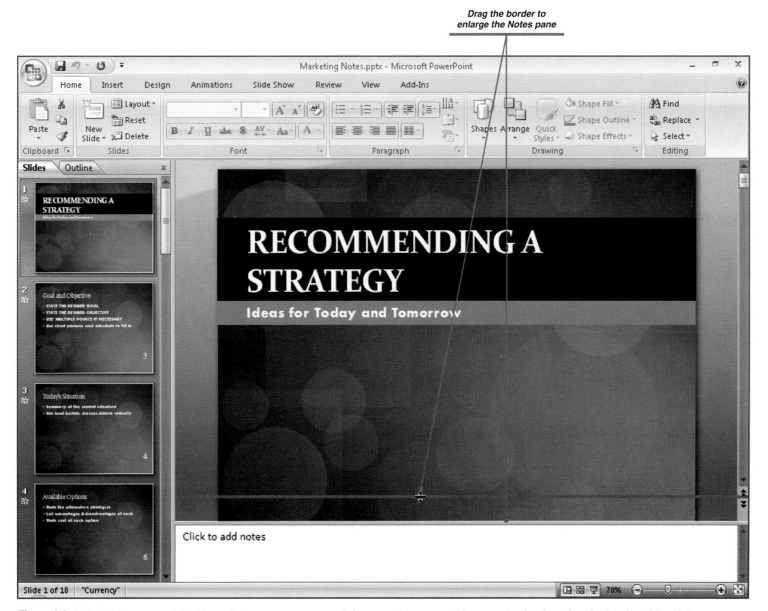

Drag the border to enlarge the Notes pane

Figure 4-1: In the Notes pane of the Normal view, you can expand the area where you add your notes by dragging the border of the Notes pane upward to increase its size.

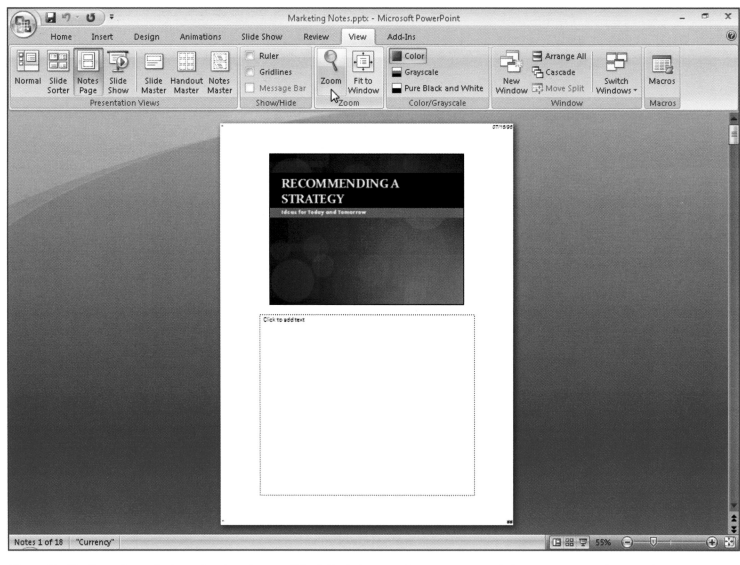

Figure 4-2: The Notes Page displays what the printout will look like before entering your notes and allows you to zoom in on the image to have more room for editing.

Figure 4-3: The Print Preview Notes Page displays speaker notes with the accompanying slide and allows you to print from this view.

3. Then click **Preview**. The Print Preview window, shown in Figure 4-3, opens with the slide and notes showing as they will be printed.

4. Click **Print** to print notes (see "Print Notes and Handouts"), or click **Close Print Preview** to return to the Notes Page.

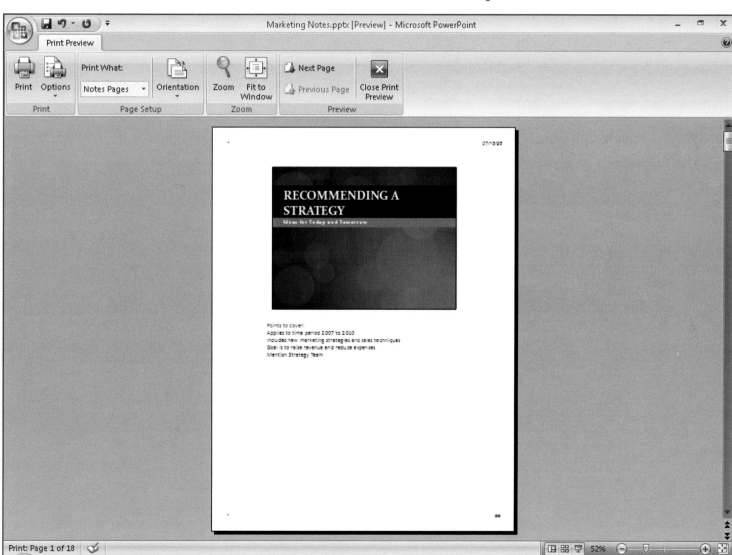

In the Print Preview window, the pointer will become a Zoom tool. Place the tool on an area of the slide image, and click. Click a second time to return the image to the original size.

Before Zoom applied

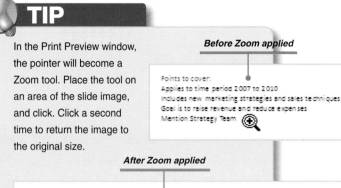

Points to cover:
Applies to time period 2007 to 2010
Includes new marketing strategies and sales techniques
Goal is to raise revenue and reduce expenses
Mention Strategy Team

After Zoom applied

Points to cover:
Applies to time period 2007 to 2010
Includes new marketing strategies and sales techniques
Goal is to raise revenue and reduce expenses
Mention Strategy Team

QUICKSTEPS

USING HEADERS AND FOOTERS ON NOTES AND HANDOUTS

To put headers and footers on Notes and Handouts:

1. Click the **View** tab, and, in the Presentation View group, click **Notes Page**.

2. Click the **Insert** tab, and then click **Header & Footer**.

3. Click the **Notes And Handouts** tab. The Header And Footer dialog box, shown in Figure 4-4, appears.

4. Choose the items you want by placing a check mark next to them:

Continued . . .

Print Notes and Handouts

Speaker notes and handouts are printed in a similar way.

PRINT SPEAKER NOTES

To print your notes:

1. Click the **Office Button**, and click **Print**. The Print dialog box will appear, an example of which is displayed in Figure 4-5.

2. Click the **Print What** down arrow, and click **Notes Pages**. You have these options:

   - Click **Preview** to see the Notes Page as it will be printed.
   - Under Print Range, click **All**, **Current Slide**, or **Selection**; or enter the slide numbers for specific slides or slide ranges.
   - Enter the number of copies.
   - Click the **Color/Grayscale** down arrow, and choose **Color**, **Grayscale**, or **Pure Black And White**.

3. Click **OK** to print.

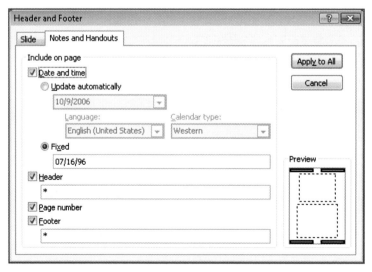

Figure 4-4: You can create a header and footer to display on note and handout pages.

QUICKSTEPS

USING HEADERS AND FOOTERS ON NOTES AND HANDOUTS *(Continued)*

- To include a date or time in the header, click **Date And Time**, and choose between **Update Automatically**, for a time/date that updates according to the current date, or **Fixed**, for a time/date or other text that remains the same each time it is printed.

- Click **Header**, click in the text box, and type the header text for notes and handouts.

- Click **Page Number** to place a page number on the note or handout page.

- Click **Footer**, click in the text box, and type footer text.

5. Click **Apply To All**.

TIP

To remove the borders that are automatically placed around the handout thumbnail slides, clear the **Frame Slides** check box in the Print dialog box. ☐ Frame slides

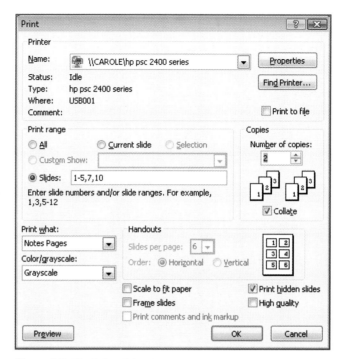

Figure 4-5: The Print dialog box allows you to select specific slides and speaker notes to print and to preview before printing.

PRINT HANDOUTS

A printed handout contains a number of thumbnail slides, an example of which is shown in Figure 4-6.

1. Click the **Office Button**, and click **Print**. The Print dialog box appears.

2. Click the **Print What** down arrow, and click **Handouts**.

3. To print only some of the slides, click **Slides** and enter the slide numbers or ranges.

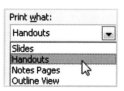

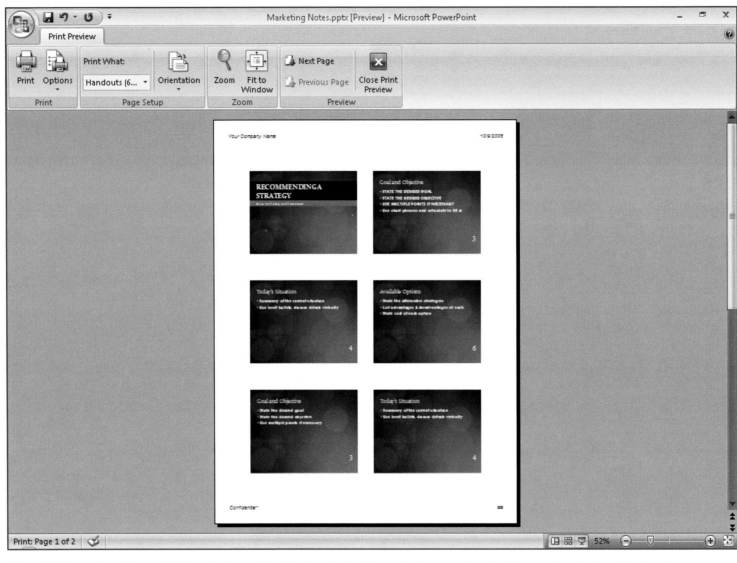

Figure 4-6: *A preview of the printed handouts contains thumbnails of slides and allows you to select the number of slides displayed on a page.*

In the Preview window, you can also set how many slides will appear on a handout page. Click the **Print What** down arrow, and choose one of the options.

Print What:

Handouts (6...

Slides
Handouts (1 Slide Per Page)
Handouts (2 Slides Per Page)
Handouts (3 Slides Per Page)
Handouts (4 Slides Per Page)
Handouts (6 Slides Per Page)
Handouts (9 Slides Per Page)
Notes Pages
Outline View

To specify what will be included on the printed page, use the Headers And Footers dialog box. (Click **Options** in the Print Preview window, Print group.) Click the **Notes And Handouts** tab, and click to remove the check mark next to the items you want to remove from the page. Click **Apply To All**.

Options

4. Click the **Slides Per Page** down arrow, and select a number to set the number of slides on a page if the default number is incorrect.

5. Set the number of copies, and make other adjustments as needed.

6. Click **Preview** to see what the printout will look like, and then click **Print** to return to the Print dialog box.

7. Click **OK** to print.

Work with Slide, Note, and Handout Masters

Working with masters gives you an opportunity to change a presentation globally. PowerPoint gives you a set of master slides for slides, notes, and handouts: the slide master controls the slides of a presentation; the notes master controls the global aspects of notes; and the handout master controls the handouts. Note and handout masters are not automatically created: they are only created if you want to use global attributes for them.

Manage Slide Appearance

A presentation has a *slide master* containing formatting and other design elements that apply to all slides in a presentation (or to a set of slides with the same "look"). Usually associated with that slide master are up to twelve *layout masters* that apply to other slides in a presentation. The title slide, for example, has a layout master for unique positioning of page components, formatting, headings, and design elements. The slide master may get its specific formatting from a theme template that you used, and you can change the master without changing the original template. This is one way that you can customize your presentation even after using a suggested theme to get you going. The original theme is not changed—only the theme as it is in your presentation. It becomes a custom theme.

CHANGING FONT ATTRIBUTES

You can change font attributes either by changing the fonts or by applying WordArt styles to title text, for example.

MAKE FONT CHANGES

You can change the attributes of text on only one type of slide by changing a layout master, or you can change attributes throughout the whole presentation by changing the font or character in the master slide. The following font commands are found in the Font group of the Home tab. (When you highlight text, a mini-toolbar appears with additional commands available.) Figure 4-7 shows the possibilities for changing font attributes.

Use these commands to change text attributes:

- **Font** changes the font face. Click the down arrow, and a list of font names is displayed.

- **Font Size** changes the point size of fonts. Click the down arrow, and select a point size.

- **Increase Font Size** increases the point size in increments. Click the button to increase it.

- **Decrease Font Size** decreases the point size in increments. Click the button to decrease it.

- **Clear All Formatting** removes all formatting from a selection and retains only plain text.

- **Bold** applies boldface to selected text.

- **Italic** applies italics to selected text.

- **Underline** applies an underline to selected text.

- **Shadow** applies a shadow effect to selected text.

- **Strikethrough** applies a strikethrough to selected text.

Continued . . .

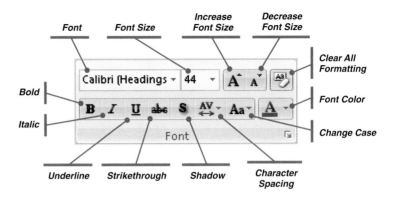

Figure 4-7: This group of text-editing commands can be found on the Home and Edit Master tabs or on the mini-toolbar.

EDIT A SLIDE MASTER OR MASTER LAYOUT

In a set of slide masters is one slide master that sets the standards for all slides in the presentation. Editing a slide master changes all the slides to which it applies. The set of associated layout masters, about twelve of them, will, by default, carry the slide master's theme and other formatting. The layout masters are specific to a type of layout that might be part of the presentation. For example, perhaps you will have one particular layout for all slides containing graphs. Another example for a specific type of layout is the title layout master. A layout master usually carries the same color, design elements, and formatting as the theme assigned to a master slide. You can change particular layouts to be different from the slide master, and then the overall theme will become a custom theme.

1. Click the **View** tab, and click **Slide Master**. The slide master is displayed (see Figure 4-8).

2. Add headings or subheadings and dates or slide numbers. Add graphics, themes, or background color. Add headers or footers or other elements of the master, just as you would a normal slide. Editing and formatting changes you can make include:

   - To change the overall font style, click the first thumbnail to select the slide master. Either click the placeholder for the text you want to change or highlight the actual heading or body text. Click the button in the Font group for the attribute you want to modify—for example, Font for the font face. See "Changing Font Attributes" QuickSteps.

CHANGING FONT ATTRIBUTES

(Continued)

- **Character Spacing** increases or decreases the space between the characters of a word. Choose Very Tight, Tight, Normal, Loose, Very Loose, or More Spacing—where you can set specific points between characters and set *kerning*, a more sophisticated method of setting the space between characters.

- **Change Case** changes the case of a word between several alternatives: Sentence Case, lowercase, UPPERCASE, Capitalize Each Word, and tOGGLE cASE.

- **Font Color** changes the color of the font. Point at each of the colors to see the effect on the background slide.

MAKE WORDART CHANGE

You can also change the text to WordArt styles. When you double-click a text or title placeholder, the Drawing Tools Format tab becomes available. On it are the WordArt Styles that can be applied to selected placeholders or text.

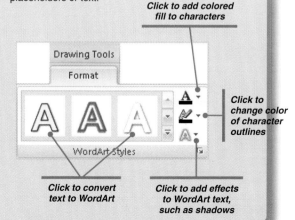

Click to add colored fill to characters

Click to change color of character outlines

Click to convert text to WordArt

Click to add effects to WordArt text, such as shadows

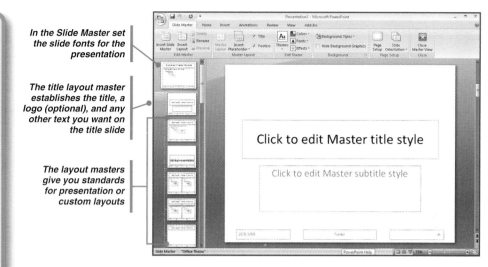

In the Slide Master set the slide fonts for the presentation

The title layout master establishes the title, a logo (optional), and any other text you want on the title slide

The layout masters give you standards for presentation or custom layouts

Figure 4-8: The masters for a new presentation contain a slide master (no. 1) and several layout slides, with the default "Office Theme."

- To change the bullets for bulleted text, double-click the placeholder containing the bullets to change them all, or select a specific level of bullet to change one level. Click the **Home** tab, and in the Paragraph group, click the **Bullets** down arrow, and click the style of bullets you like. You can point at each bullet type to see the results in the background master slide. To insert a picture that serves as a bullet, click **Bullets And Numbering** on the bottom of the list to display a dialog box. Click the **Bulleted** tab, click **Picture**, and click the bullet picture you want. To insert a new picture, click **Import** and then find the picture you want. Click **OK** on the Picture Bullet dialog box.

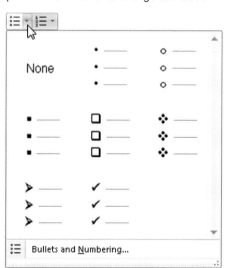

- To change the appearance of numbers for numbered lists, double-click the placeholder containing the numbered lists. Click the **Numbering** down arrow in the Paragraph group, and click the style of numbers you like. You can point at each item in the list to see the results in the background master slide. To get a size or color that isn't in the menu of choices, click **Bullets And Numbering** on the bottom of the list to display a dialog box. Click the **Numbered** tab, and click the **Size** spinner to increase or decrease the size. Click **Start At** to reset the beginning number. Click the **Color** down arrow to select a new color for the set of numbers. Click **OK** to close the Bullets and Numbering dialog box.

- By clicking the **Insert** tab and selecting **Header & Footer** in the Text group, you can include a footer, slide number, or time and date on the slide. Then, to change the format for the time or date, click a text placeholder to select it (you may have to click directly on the placeholder text to select it, such as on <date/time> in the Date Area placeholder). Then click the **Home** tab, and in the Font group, click the **Font** or **Font Size** down arrow, and select the font or size you want from the drop-down list.

CREATE MULTIPLE SLIDE AND TITLE MASTERS

Multiple slide masters and their associated sets of layout masters are used in a presentation to create different looks in layout or formatting for different sections of the presentation.

To create additional new slide masters:

1. Click the **View** tab, and click **Slide Master**.

2. Right-click the slide master, and click **Insert Slide Master**. A new slide master and its associated layout masters will be inserted.

WORKING WITH SLIDE MASTERS

You can duplicate masters, create title masters that vary from the other masters, protect your masters from being accidentally or intentionally changed, or create multiple new title and slide masters.

DUPLICATE A SLIDE MASTER

To duplicate a slide master:

1. Click the **View** tab, and click **Slide Master**.

2. Right-click the master slide thumbnail to be duplicated. It may be a master slide or a layout master slide. The options on the context menu will vary depending on the type of master you select:

   - For a slide master, click **Duplicate Slide Master**. The slide master and all the sets of layouts it carries will be duplicated.

   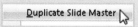

   - For a layout master, click **Duplicate Layout**, and just the layout master will be duplicated.

   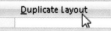

CREATE A TITLE MASTER

To make the format of your title page different from the rest of your slides, create a title master to contain its unique formatting or design elements.

1. Click the **View** tab, choose **Slide Master**, and click the layout thumbnail immediately beneath the slide master in the Slides tab. This is normally the title layout master.

Continued . . .

3. Make any changes or incorporate different design templates to the new masters as needed.

4. Click the **Slide Master** tab, and then click **Close Master View** in the Close group to close the Slide Master view.

Work with the Notes Master

To make global changes to all notes in a presentation, use the notes master. Here you can add a logo or other graphics, change the positioning of page components, change formats, and add headings and text design elements for all notes.

1. Click the **View** tab, and click **Notes Master**. The notes master will be displayed, as shown in Figure 4-9.

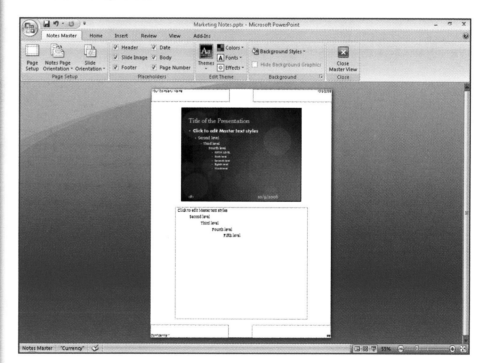

Figure 4-9: The notes master is used to globally change such note features as headers, footers, logos, graphics, note text formatting, and placement of note elements.

WORKING WITH SLIDE MASTERS

(Continued)

2. Click in the title placeholder, and type your title. Enter a subtitle if necessary.

3. Format the text as needed.

4. Insert a logo or other graphic by clicking the **Insert** tab and clicking the type of graphic you want. Follow the prompts to find what you want.

RETAIN A SLIDE MASTER

To retain a slide master within the presentation even if it is not being used, use the Preserve Master button.

1. Right-click the slide master to be retained.

2. From the context menu, click **Preserve Master** to retain the selected master. You will see gray thumbtacks or pushpins beside the master and title thumbnail slides.

TIP

To add a text placeholder to the Notes pane, click the **Insert** tab, and click the **Text Box** button. Then drag the icon where you want the text box to be created, and type in the box. You can drag the text box to another location.

---

2. To adjust the zoom so that you can see the notes area better, click the **View** tab, and click **Zoom**. Choose the magnification and click **OK**.

3. You can change the note master as follows:

- Change the formatting of the text elements, such as font size or style, or change the bullets or indents.

- Drag the position of the slide or note text placeholder (the dotted box) to a different location by placing the pointer over the border between handles until you see a four-headed arrow and then dragging.

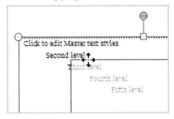

- Change the size of the slide or note text placeholder by placing the pointer over the border on the handles until you see a two-headed arrow and then dragging the border of the placeholder to resize it.

- Add a logo by clicking the **Insert** tab and clicking the **Picture**, **Shapes**, **Clip Art**, or other graphic button. Resize the graphic as needed, and drag it where you want it to appear on all notes.

- Add text that will appear on all notes, such as page number, date, or title.

4. Click the **Notes Master** tab, and then click **Close Master View** in the Close group to close the notes master.

Change the Handout Master

Handouts display thumbnails of the slides on a printed page. You can have one, two, three, four, six, or nine slides per page. To prepare your handouts for printing with titles and other formatting, use the handout master.

1. Click the **View** tab, and click **Handout Master**. The handout master will be displayed, as shown in Figure 4-10.

2. On the handout master ribbon in the Page Setup group, click **Slides Per Page** to set the number of slides to be displayed in the handout: one, two, three, four, six, or nine, or the slide outline.

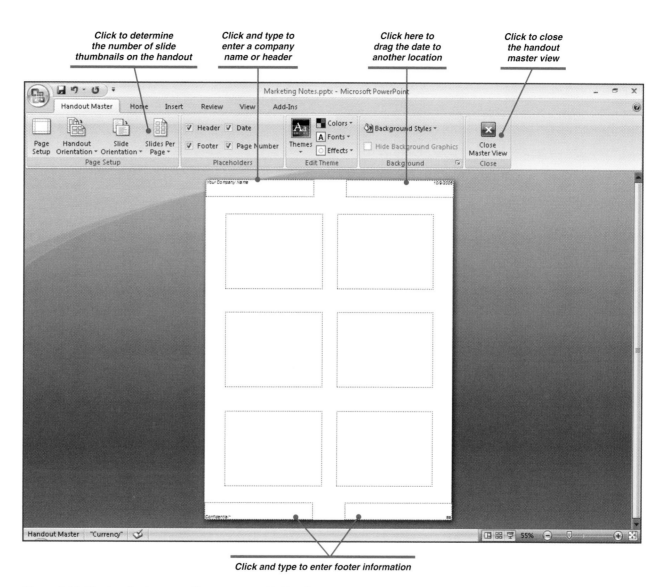

Click to determine the number of slide thumbnails on the handout

Click and type to enter a company name or header

Click here to drag the date to another location

Click to close the handout master view

Click and type to enter footer information

Figure 4-10: The handout master allows you to add titles for handouts, vary the number of slides displayed in the handout, and add other text or objects as needed.

3. Make changes to the handout master as needed:
- Click **Page Setup** in the Page Setup group to set the slide size, initial numbering of slides, and orientation or slides and notes, handouts, and outline.
- Click **Handout Orientation** in the Page Setup group to give the handout a portrait or landscape orientation.
- Click **Slide Orientation** in the Page Setup group to give the slides on the handout a portrait or landscape orientation
- Click **Header**, **Date**, **Footer**, or **Page Number** in the Placeholders group to remove the check marks if you do not want them to appear on the handouts. They are selected by default. If you choose for them to be there, enter the text in the text boxes for the header and footer information.
- To format the date, click in the date text box, click the **Insert** tab, and click **Date & Time**. Choose a format and click **OK**. Return to the Handout Master tab.
- To select a style for the background, click **Background Styles** in the Background group and choose one.
- If you want graphics to be hidden when printed, click the **Hide Background Graphics** check box in the Background group.

4. To close the handout master, click **Close Master View** in the Close group on the ribbon.

Work with Text

Entering and manipulating text is a major part of building a presentation. Text is not only titles and bulleted lists. It is also captions on a picture or a legend or labels on a chart. Text can be inside a shape or curved around it on the outside. Text communicates in a thousand ways. Here is how you work with text in PowerPoint.

Use a Text Layout

To create the "look" of your presentation, you will want to insert text, columns, graphics, charts, logos, and other pictures in a consistent way. PowerPoint

TIP

The text box will be applied to the current slide. If you have not created a new slide, the layout will be applied to whichever slide is selected.

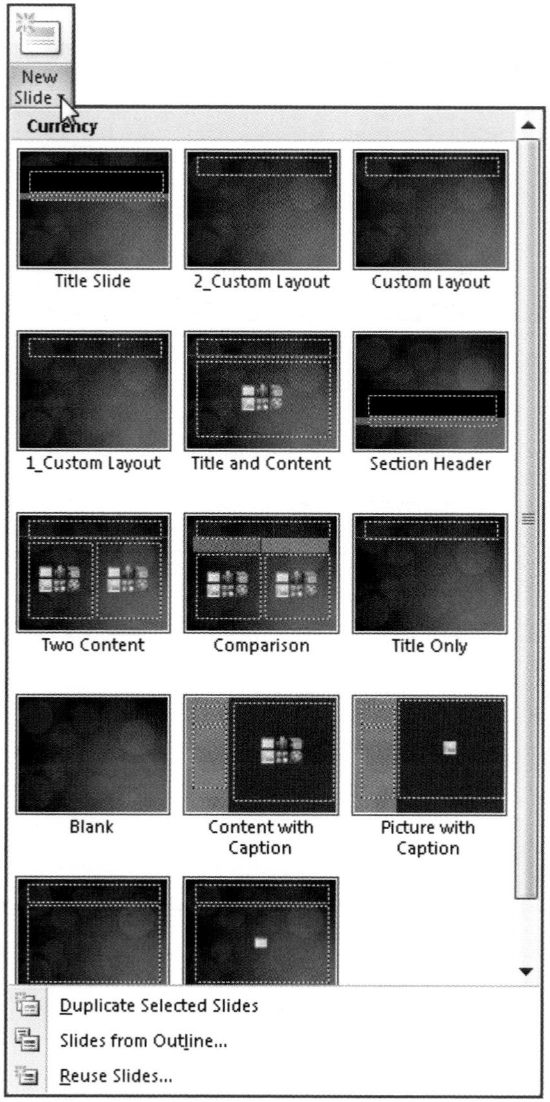

Figure 4-11: You can choose among several standard layouts containing text boxes.

provides standard layouts that position text or graphics in consistent ways. Chapters 1 and 2 discussed layouts in more detail. In this chapter, we are concerned with text layouts.

When you create a new blank slide, you must choose whether to use an existing layout that Microsoft provides (see Figure 4-11) or to create your own layout.

1. In Normal view, click the slide immediately preceding the one you want to insert.

2. Click the **Home** tab, and click the **New Slide** down arrow.

3. Look for the placement of text, titles, and content. Examples of text placeholders are shown in Figure 4-11.

4. Click the layout you want.

5. Click within the title or text placeholders to begin entering text. (See Chapters 5 through 8 for more information on working with other content placeholders.)

Insert a New Text Box

Even when you use a predefined layout that Microsoft provides, you will find times when you want to insert a new text box.

1. Display the slide within which you will place the text box.

2. Click the **Insert** tab, and click **Text Box** in the Text group. The pointer first turns into a line pointer.

3. Place the pointer where you want to locate the text box, and drag it into a text-box shape. As you drag, the pointer will morph into a crosshair shape. Don't worry about where the box is located; you can drag it to a precise location later. When you release the pointer, the insertion point within the text box indicates that you can begin to type text.

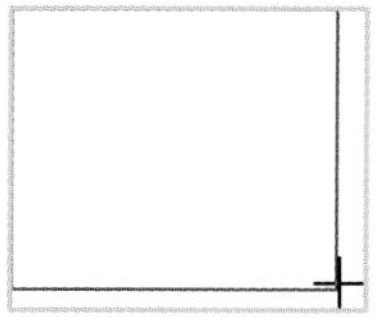

4. Type the text you want.

5. When you are finished, click outside the text box.

Work with Text Boxes

You work with text and text boxes by typing text into a text box, moving or copying the text box, resizing the text box, positioning the text box, deleting it, rotating it, filling it with color, and more.

ENTER TEXT INTO A TEXT BOX

To enter text into a text box, simply click inside the text box; the insertion point will appear in the text box, indicating that you can now type text. Begin to type.

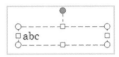

MOVE A TEXT BOX

To move a text box, you drag the border of the placeholder.

1. Click the text within a text box to display the text box outline.
2. Place the pointer over the border of the text box and between the handles. The pointer will be a four-headed arrow.
3. Drag the text box where you want.

RESIZE A PLACEHOLDER

To resize a placeholder, you drag the sizing handles of the text box.

1. Click the text to display the text box border.
2. Place the pointer on the border over the handles so that it becomes a two-headed arrow.
3. Drag the sizing handle in the direction you want the text box expanded or reduced. As you drag, the pointer will morph into a crosshair.

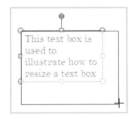

DELETE A TEXT BOX

To delete a text box:

1. Click the text within the text box to display the border.
2. Click the border of the text box again to select the text box, not the text (the insertion point will disappear and the border will be solid).
3. Press **DELETE**.

SETTING MARGINS, WORD WRAP, AUTOFIT, AND COLUMNS

All of the procedures in this section make use of the Drawing Tools Format Shape dialog box. To display it, right-click the text box and select **Format Shape**. Select **Text Box** from the menu on the left, as shown in Figure 4-12.

SET MARGINS IN A TEXT BOX

To change the margins in a text box, change the Internal Margin setting to **Left**, **Right**, **Top**, or **Bottom**.

DISABLE WORD WRAP FOR TEXT

To disable (or enable) the word wrap feature for text in a text box, click **Wrap Text In Shape**. A check mark in the check box indicates that word wrap is turned on.

☑ Wrap text in shape

ROTATE TEXT WITHIN A TEXT BOX

To rotate text within a text box, click the **Text Direction** down arrow, and choose an option: Horizontal, Rotate All Text 90°, Rotate All Text 270°, or Stacked.

ABC	Horizontal
ABC	Rotate all text 90°
ABC	Rotate all text 270°
A B C	Stacked

ANCHOR TEXT IN A TEXT BOX

To anchor the text layout within a text box, select the position where the text will start, click the **Vertical Alignment** down arrow, and click the position to which you want the text anchored. Your choices are: Top, Middle, Bottom, Top Centered, Middle Centered, and Bottom Centered.

Continued . . .

COPY A TEXT BOX

To copy a text box with its contents and drag it to another part of the slide:

1. Click the text within the text box.

2. Place the pointer on the border of the text box (not over the handles), where it becomes a four-headed arrow.

3. Drag the text box while pressing CTRL.

ROTATE A TEXT BOX

When you first insert a text box (or click it to select it), a rotate handle allows you to rotate the box in a circle.

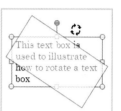

1. Place the pointer over the rotate handle.

2. Drag it in the direction it is to be rotated.

3. Click outside the text box to "set" the rotation.

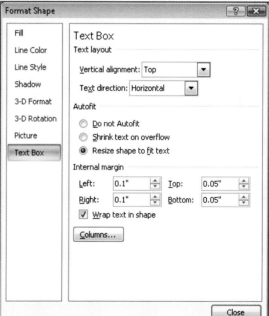

Figure 4-12: A text box can have its own margins and alignment. You can set defaults for AutoFit and automatic word wrap features and establish columns.

UICKSTEPS

SETTING MARGINS, WORD WRAP, AUTOFIT, AND COLUMNS *(Continued)*

SET UP COLUMNS WITHIN A TEXT BOX

To set up columns within a text box, click the **Columns** button. The Columns dialog box appears. Click the **Number** spinner and the **Spacing** spinner to set your column attributes, and click **OK**.

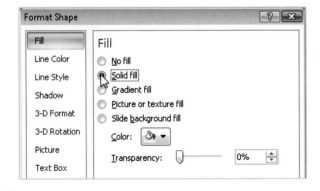

CAUTION

When you adjust the line spacing, the AutoFit feature, which is on by default, may cause the text to be resized to fit within the text box. See "Setting Margins, Word Wrap, AutoFit, and Columns" to change the default.

POSITION A TEXT BOX PRECISELY

To set the position of a text box precisely on a slide:

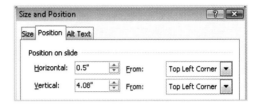

1. Click the text box to select it. A Drawing Tools Format tab will appear.

2. Click the **Format** tab, in the **Arrange** group, click **Rotate**.

3. On the Rotate menu, click **More Rotation Options**. The Size And Position dialog box will appear.

4. Click the **Position** tab.

5. Click the **Horizontal** or **Vertical** spinners to enter the exact measurements in inches of the text box. Click the drop-down list boxes to select the originating location of the text box between the upper-left corner and center.

6. Click **Close**.

CHANGE THE FILL COLOR IN A TEXT BOX

To change the background color of a text box, you use the Drawing Tools Format Shape dialog box.

1. Right-click the text box, and click **Format Shape** from the context menu. The Format Shape dialog box appears.

2. Click **Fill** and then select the type of fill you want to see. A group of options will appear, depending on your choice.

3. Click the **Color** or other drop-down list box to select a color. Set other attributes as you wish. Drag the dialog box to one side so that you can see the changes in the text box as you try out different shades or types of fill, as illustrated in Figure 4-13

4. When finished, click **Close**.

SET PARAGRAPH AND TAB SETTINGS

To change the default paragraph spacing and tab settings, you can use the Paragraph dialog box, as seen in Figure 4-14.

If none of the colors is exactly right, click the **Color** down arrow, and then click **More Colors** and click the **Standard** tab. Click a color unit to select it. In the preview box, you can see the new color compared to the current color. Click **OK** and then click **Close**.

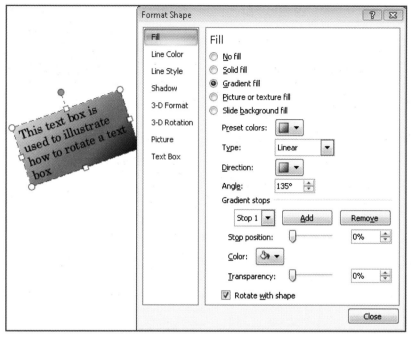

Figure 4-13: You can drag the dialog box (or sometimes the text box) to the side so that you can see the effects of settings as you work with the options.

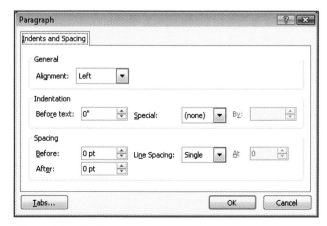

Figure 4-14: The Paragraph dialog box allows you to change paragraph and tab settings.

1. Click the paragraph text in a placeholder or text box to be changed. Click the **Home** tab, and click the **Paragraph Dialog Box Launcher** on the lower-right of the Paragraph group.

   | Paragraph |

   –Or–

   Right-click the paragraph text in a placeholder or text box to be changed, and click **Paragraph**. The Paragraph dialog box appears.

2. Set the settings as required:

   - Set the General positioning by clicking the **Alignment** down arrow, and then click **Left**, **Centered**, **Right**, **Justified**, or **Distributed** (which forces lines to be justified to the end of the line), depending on how you want the text aligned.

   - Set the indentation. Click the **Before Text** spinner to set the spacing before the text begins on a first line; click the **Special** down arrow to allow for hanging indents, an indented first line, or no indents.

USING LISTS

Lists are either numbered or bulleted. You can choose the shapes of bullets, change the style of numbering, and use SmartArt for your lists.

CHOOSE BULLET SHAPES

1. Select the text to be bulleted.

2. Right-click the text and point to **Bullets**. The context menu opens.

   –Or–

   On the Home tab, click the **Bullets** down arrow. A context menu will open.

3. Use the options presented, or, to display more options, click **Bullets And Numbering** at the bottom of the menu. The Bullets And Numbering dialog box appears, as shown in Figure 4-15.

4. To select the bullet appearance, click one of the seven options:

   - To change the size, adjust the **Size** spinner to the percentage of text you want the bullet to be.

   - To change the color, click the **Color** down arrow, and click a color.

   - To select or import a picture to use as a bullet shape, click **Picture** and select one of the menu images, or click **Import** to find your own. Then click **OK**.

   - To select a character from a variety of symbol fonts, click **Customize**. Make your selection, and then click **OK**.

5. Click **OK** to close the dialog box.

Continued . . .

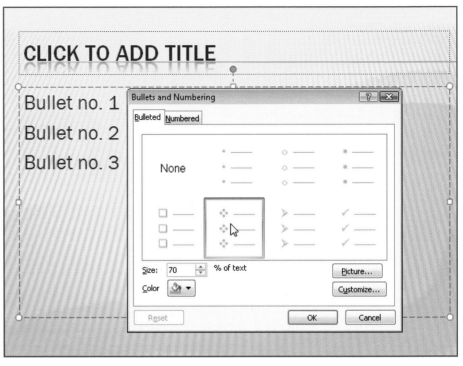

Figure 4-15: The Bullets And Numbering dialog box offers ways to change the appearance, size, and color of bullets or numbers in a list.

- Set the spacing. Click the **Before** spinner to set spacing before the line starts (in points); click the **Line Spacing** down arrow, and click **Single**, **Double**, **1.5**, **Exactly** (where you set the exact spacing in points in the At box), or **Multiple** (where you enter the number of lines to space in the At box.).

- Click the **Tabs** button to set tabs precisely in the Tabs dialog box. Click **OK**.

3. Click **OK**.

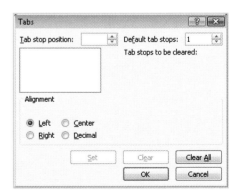

UICKSTEPS

USING LISTS *(Continued)*

CHANGE NUMBERING STYLES

1. Select the text to be numbered.

2. Right-click the text and point to **Numbering**. A context menu opens.

   –Or–

   On the Home tab, click the **Numbering** down arrow. A context menu will open.

3. Use the options presented, or, to display more options, click **Bullets And Numbering**. The Bullets And Numbering dialog box will appear.

   - To change the size, adjust the **Size** spinner to the percentage of the text size you want the numbering to be.

   - To change the color, click the **Color** down arrow, and click a color.

   - To set a beginning number or letter, change **Start At**.

4. Click **OK**.

USE SMART ART FOR LISTS

To make your lists artistic and professional-looking, you can choose some of the SmartArt options offered by PowerPoint 2007. These dramatically change the look and feel of lists. See Chapters 6 through 8 for additional discussions about SmartArt.

1. Select the list.

2. On the Home tab, click the **Convert To SmartArt Graphic** down arrow in the Paragraph group.

   –Or–

Continued . . .

CHANGE CAPITALIZATION

To set your capitalization standard or to correct text typed in the wrong case:

1. Select the text on which you want to change the case.

2. Click the **Home** tab, and click the **Change Case** button in the Font group.

3. Select one of the following options:

   - **Sentence case** capitalizes the first word in a sentence.

   - **lowercase** makes all text lowercase.

   - **UPPERCASE** makes all text uppercase.

   - **Capitalize Each Word** capitalizes all words.

   - **tOGGLE cASE** switches between uppercase and lowercase letters, for instance, when you have accidentally typed text in the wrong case.

Use the Font Dialog Box

To set multiple font and character attributes at once or to set the standard for a slide, it is easier to use the Font dialog box than individual buttons. (See "Changing Font Attributes" QuickSteps earlier in this chapter.)

More SmartArt Graphics...

1. Select the text to be changed.

2. Click the **Home** tab, and click the **Font Dialog Box Launcher** in the lower-right area of the Font group. The Font dialog box will appear, as shown in Figure 4-16.

3. Click the **Latin Text Font** down arrow, and select the type of theme text (Heading or Body) or font name. This establishes what will be changed in the selected text.

4. Choose the options you want, and click **OK**.

UICKSTEPS

USING LISTS (Continued)

Right-click the list or place on the slide where you want special effects applied, and point to **Convert To SmartArt**. A gallery of styles is displayed.

3. Click an option, and you will see the SmartArt effect on the slide plus a text box enabling you to enter the text into the list, as displayed in Figure 4-17. Type your text into the **Type Your Text Here** text box, and it will appear in the SmartArt object.

4. To redisplay the text box, click the SmartArt text. Click in the text box to type text and add to the SmartArt graphic.

5. To change shapes, right-click the SmartArt icon, and point to **Change Shape**. A gallery of shapes will display. Click the one you want.

6. When you are finished, close the Type Your Text Here box by clicking **X** in the upper-right corner.

NOTE

All the cut-and-paste techniques can also be used to copy information. Just select **Copy** instead of Cut from the context or ribbon menus, or press **CTRL+C**. To copy using the drag-and-drop technique, right-drag the text (drag using the right mouse button depressed), and click **Copy Here**.

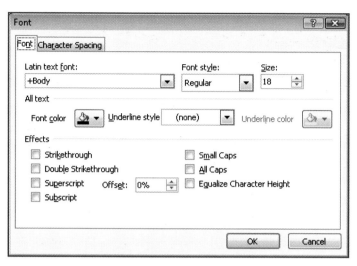

Figure 4-16: Using the Font dialog box, you can change all occurrences of certain fonts within selected text.

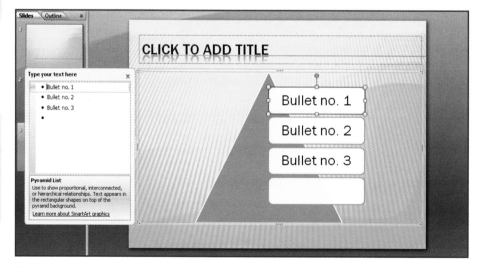

Figure 4-17: SmartArt effects can make your lists dramatic and professional-looking.

EDITING WITH THE KEYBOARD

Working with text in PowerPoint is similar to working with text in Microsoft Word. This section presents familiar ways to move the pointer and to select, delete, and insert text.

MOVE THE POINTER WITHIN YOUR TEXT

- To move to the beginning of the line, press **HOME**.
- To move to the end of a line, press **END**.
- To skip to the next word, press **CTRL+RIGHT ARROW**.
- To skip to the previous word, press **CTRL+LEFT ARROW**.

SELECT TEXT

- To select all text contained within a text box, press **CTRL+A**.
- To select a word, double-click it.
- To select a paragraph, click within the paragraph three times.
- To select all text from where your cursor is to the end of the line, press **SHIFT+END**.
- To select all text from where your cursor is to the beginning of the line, press **SHIFT+HOME**.
- To select multiple lines, press **SHIFT+UP ARROW** or **DOWN ARROW**.
- To select one character at a time, press **SHIFT+LEFT ARROW** or **RIGHT ARROW**.

DELETE TEXT

- To delete the character to the right, press **DELETE**.
- To delete the character to the left, press **BACKSPACE**.
- To delete other text as needed, select text using the keyboard, highlighting it, and press **DELETE**.

Align Text

You have several ways to align text: horizontally on a line, vertically on a page, or distributed horizontally or vertically. This section describes how to use these aligning techniques.

ALIGN TEXT ON A LINE

You align text by centering (placing text in the center of the horizontal margins), left-justifying, right-justifying, or justifying it (where the left and right edges are equal). All four options are available on the Home tab Paragraph group.

1. Select the text to be aligned, and click the **Home** tab.

2. From the Paragraph group, choose one of these options:

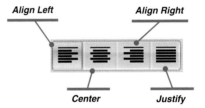

ALIGN TEXT IN A PLACEHOLDER

To align text with the top, middle, or bottom of a text box or placeholder, click the **Align Text** button (Home tab, Paragraph group), and click your choices from the menu. Click **More Options** to precisely specify measurements.

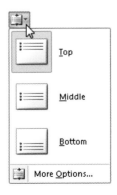

QUICKSTEPS

MOVING OR COPYING TEXT

There are at least four ways you can move text. You can use the cut-and-paste technique, the ribbon, right-click from a context menu, or use the drag-and-drop technique.

CUT AND PASTE TEXT WITH THE KEYBOARD

1. Select the text to be moved, and press **CTRL+X** to cut the text.

2. Click the pointer to place the insertion point, and press **CTRL+V** to paste the text in the new location.

CUT AND PASTE WITH THE RIBBON

1. Select the text to be moved.

2. Click the **Home** tab, and click **Cut** in the Clipboard group.

3. Click where you want the text inserted, and click **Paste** in the Clipboard group.

CUT AND PASTE WITH A CONTEXT MENU

1. Select the text to be moved.

2. Right-click and click **Cut**.

3. Right-click the new location, and click **Paste**.

Continued . . .

TIP

If you want to copy more than one text selection, double-click the **Format Painter** to turn it on. You can copy multiple text selections, one after the other. To turn it off, click **Format Painter** again or press **ESC**.

ALIGN TEXT TO THE SLIDE

You can align a placeholder or text box horizontally or vertically on a slide—that is, the spacing on the top and bottom will be equal or the spacing from the left and right edges of the slide will be distributed evenly.

1. Click the placeholder or text box to select it.

2. On the Drawing Tools **Format** tab, click the **Align** button in the Arrange group. A menu will appear.

3. Click one of these options:

   ● Click **Distribute Horizontally** to align the object horizontally to the slide.

   ● Click **Distribute Vertically** to align the object vertically on the slide.

Copy Formatting with Format Painter

To copy all formatting attributes from one placeholder to another, you use Format Painter. With it, you can copy fonts, font size and style, line and paragraph spacing, color, alignment, bullet selection, and character effects.

1. Select the text containing the formatting attributes to be copied.

2. On the Home tab, click **Format Painter** in the Clipboard group.

3. Find the destination text to contain the copied attributes, and drag the paintbrush pointer over the text to be changed.

MOVING OR COPYING TEXT (Continued)

USE THE DRAG-AND-DROP TECHNIQUE

To use the drag-and-drop technique to move text within
the same text box, to other text boxes, or to other slides
(when moving to other slides, you can only use the
Outline tab):

1. Select the text to be moved.

2. Using the pointer, drag the text to the new location. An insertion point shows you where the text
   is about to be moved.

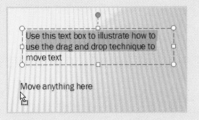

3. Release the pointer when the insertion point is in
   the correct location.

Use AutoCorrect

AutoCorrect is a feature that helps you type information correctly. For example,
it corrects simple typing errors and makes certain assumptions about what you
want to type. You can turn it off or change its rules.

TURN AUTOCORRECT OPTIONS ON OR OFF

The AutoCorrect feature assumes that you will want certain corrections always
to be made while you type. Among these corrections are: change two initial
capital letters to the first one only, capitalize the first letter of each sentence,
capitalize the first letter of table cells and names of days, correct accidental
use of the **CAPS LOCK** key, and replace misspelled words with the results it
assumes you want. (See "Change AutoCorrect Spelling Corrections" to retain
the correction of misspelled words but to change the correction made.) To turn
off the automatic spelling corrections that PowerPoint makes:

1. Click the **Office Button**, and click **PowerPoint Options**.

2. Click **Proofing**, and the dialog box shown in Figure 4-18 will appear.

3. Find the option you want to turn off or on, and click the relevant check box. If a check
   mark is in the box, the option is enabled. If it is not, the option is turned off.

USE AUTOFIT

AutoFit is used to make text fit within a text box or AutoShape. It often resizes
text to make it fit. You can turn it on or off.

1. Click the **Office Button**, click **PowerPoint Options**, and then click **Proofing**.

2. Under AutoCorrect Options, click **AutoCorrect Options**. The AutoCorrect dialog box
   appears.

3. Click the **AutoFormat As You Type** tab.

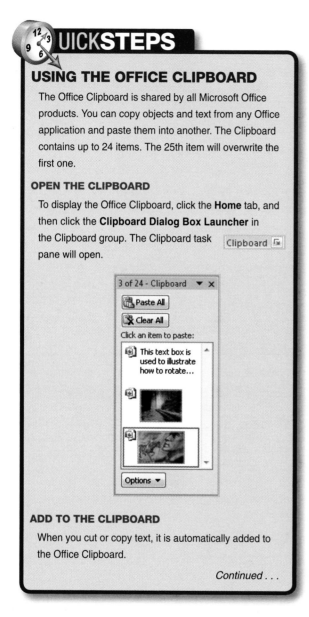

QUICKSTEPS

USING THE OFFICE CLIPBOARD

The Office Clipboard is shared by all Microsoft Office products. You can copy objects and text from any Office application and paste them into another. The Clipboard contains up to 24 items. The 25th item will overwrite the first one.

OPEN THE CLIPBOARD

To display the Office Clipboard, click the **Home** tab, and then click the **Clipboard Dialog Box Launcher** in the Clipboard group. The Clipboard task pane will open.

ADD TO THE CLIPBOARD

When you cut or copy text, it is automatically added to the Office Clipboard.

Continued . . .

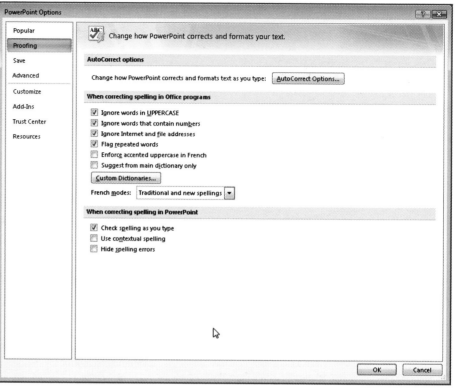

Figure 4-18: The AutoCorrect dialog box is where you change the automatic corrections made to text and spelling.

4. Under the Apply As You Type section, choose these options:

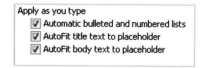

- To remove the AutoFit feature for titles, clear the **AutoFit Title Text To Placeholder** check box.

- To remove the AutoFit feature for body text, clear the **AutoFit Body Text To Placeholder** check box.

5. Click **OK** twice.

QUICKSTEPS

USING THE OFFICE CLIPBOARD
(Continued)

COPY THE CLIPBOARD TO A PLACEHOLDER

To paste one item:

1. Click to place the insertion point in the text box or placeholder where you want the item on the Office Clipboard inserted.

2. Click the item on the Clipboard to be inserted.

   –Or–

1. With the Clipboard item selected but no insertion point placed, right-click where you want the item.

2. Select **Paste** from the context menu.

To paste all items:

1. Click to place the insertion point in the text box or placeholder where you want the items on the Office Clipboard inserted.

2. Click **Paste All** on the Clipboard.

DELETE ITEMS ON THE CLIPBOARD

1. To delete all items, click **Clear All** on the Clipboard task pane.

2. To delete a single item, click the arrow next to the item, and click **Delete**.

Continued . . .

CHANGE AUTOCORRECT SPELLING CORRECTIONS

PowerPoint may automatically correct spellings that are not really incorrect. You can add a new spelling correction, replace a current spelling correction with a new one, or replace the result that is now used. You do this by replacing one word with another in the AutoCorrect dialog box. When you first open the dialog box, both the Replace and With boxes are blank. In this case, you simply add what you want. To replace an entry, you first delete an entry—one that is not a mistake you typically make—and then you replace it with a typing error you commonly make. To replace a current spelling result, you type over the current result with the correction you want.

1. Click the **Office Button**, and click the **PowerPoint Options** button. Then click **Proofing**.

2. Click the **AutoCorrect Options** button, and the AutoCorrect dialog box appears. If it is not already selected, click the **AutoCorrect** tab. Figure 4-19 shows this dialog box:

- To add new entries when both the Replace and With boxes are blank, fill in the **Replace** and **With** boxes, and click **Add**.

- To replace entries in the Replace and With boxes, click the text in either box, and replace it with your new entries. Click **Add**. The "old" text will be not be deleted; it is still in the list. You must use the DELETE button to actually get rid of an entry in the list.

- To delete and replace an entry, click the entry to be replaced, and press DELETE. Then type the new spelling option. Click **Add**.

Replace:	With:	
wouldn;t	wouldn't	
woudln't	wouldn't	▲
would of been	would have been	
would of had	would have had	
wouldbe	would be	
wouldn;t	wouldn't	▼

Replace   Delete

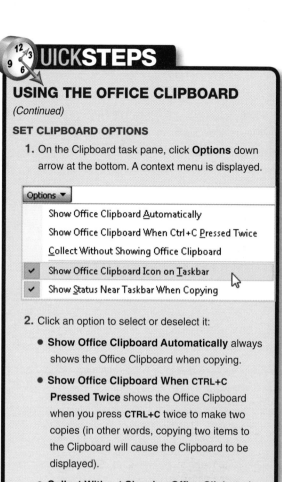

QUICKSTEPS

USING THE OFFICE CLIPBOARD
(Continued)

SET CLIPBOARD OPTIONS

1. On the Clipboard task pane, click **Options** down arrow at the bottom. A context menu is displayed.

Options ▼

    Show Office Clipboard <u>A</u>utomatically

    Show Office Clipboard When Ctrl+C <u>P</u>ressed Twice

    <u>C</u>ollect Without Showing Office Clipboard

✓ Show Office Clipboard Icon on <u>T</u>askbar

✓ Show <u>S</u>tatus Near Taskbar When Copying

2. Click an option to select or deselect it:

- **Show Office Clipboard Automatically** always shows the Office Clipboard when copying.

- **Show Office Clipboard When CTRL+C Pressed Twice** shows the Office Clipboard when you press **CTRL+C** twice to make two copies (in other words, copying two items to the Clipboard will cause the Clipboard to be displayed).

- **Collect Without Showing Office Clipboard** copies items to the Clipboard without displaying it.

- **Show Office Clipboard Icon On Taskbar** displays the icon 📋 when the Clipboard is being used.

- **Show Status Near Taskbar When Copying** displays a message about the items being added to the Clipboard as copies are made.

Figure 4-19: The AutoCorrect dialog box is where you control which spelling errors are automatically corrected and insert your own corrections.

Use the Spelling Checker

One form of the spelling checker automatically flags words that it cannot find in the dictionary as potential misspellings. It identifies these words with a red underline. However, even when the automatic function is turned off, you can still use the spelling checker by manually opening it.

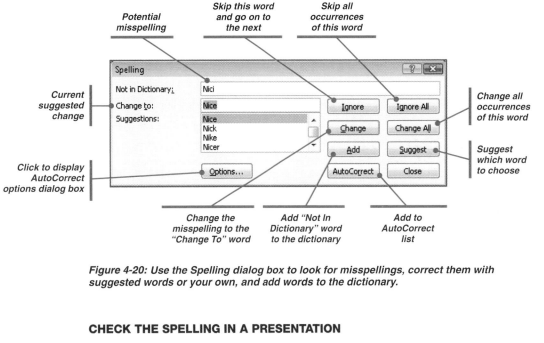

Current suggested change

Click to display AutoCorrect options dialog box

Potential misspelling

Skip this word and go on to the next

Skip all occurrences of this word

Change all occurrences of this word

Suggest which word to choose

Change the misspelling to the "Change To" word

Add "Not In Dictionary" word to the dictionary

Add to AutoCorrect list

Figure 4-20: Use the Spelling dialog box to look for misspellings, correct them with suggested words or your own, and add words to the dictionary.

CHECK THE SPELLING IN A PRESENTATION

The spelling checker goes through all text in all placeholders on a slide looking for words that are not in the spelling dictionary. When it finds one, it displays the Spelling dialog box, seen in Figure 4-20.

1. Click in the presentation where the spelling checker should begin.

2. To display the spelling checker, press **F7**. The Spelling dialog box will appear when the spelling checker finds a word that is not in the dictionary.

3. Choose any of these options to use the spelling checker:

   - If the word is incorrect, look at the Suggestions list, and click the one you want to use. It will appear in the Change To box. Click **Change** to change the one occurrence of the word, or click **Change All** to change all occurrences of that same word.

   - If the identified word is correct but not in the dictionary, you can add the word to a custom dictionary by clicking **Add**, or you can skip the word by clicking **Ignore** or **Ignore All** (to skip all occurrences of the same word). The spelling checker will continue to the next misspelled word.

- Click **AutoCorrect** to add the word to the AutoCorrect list of automatic spelling changes that will be made as you type. Immediately the word will be placed in the AutoCorrect list.

- Click **Suggest** if you are unsure of the correct spelling and want PowerPoint to suggest the most likely spelling.

- Click **Options** to open the AutoCorrect Options dialog box.

3. Click **Close** to end the search for spelling errors. When the spelling checker is finished, a message will be displayed to that effect. Click **OK**.

The Exceptions button in the AutoCorrect dialog box is used to provide exceptions to the capitalization rules. Clicking the button provides an opportunity to add to a list of either initially capitalized exceptions or exceptions about when to capitalize a word, such as after an abbreviation.

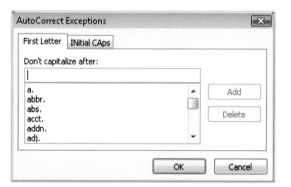

To quickly use the spelling checker, right-click the misspelled word. A context menu will display several options for correct spellings. Click the correct word if it is on the list. You can also click **Ignore All** to ignore all usages of the misspelling or click **Add To Dictionary**. You can display the Spelling dialog box by clicking **Spelling**.

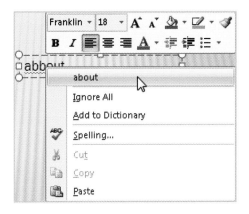

SET SPELLING DEFAULTS

Set these options to determine how the spelling checker works.

1. Click the **Office Button**, click **PowerPoint Options**, and click **Proofing**. The AutoCorrect Options dialog box appears, shown in Figure 4-21.

2. Select or deselect these options to best meet your needs. The defaults already have check marks in the check boxes. Click to remove them. Click to select any that have no check mark.

3. Click **OK** to accept your changes.

Figure 4-21: The AutoCorrect Options dialog box sets the defaults for the changes PowerPoint will make to your text as you type.

Chapter 5
Creating Tables in Slides

This chapter addresses how to create tables in slides. This includes how to insert tables into slides, enter text into tables, select text, adjust columns and rows, and add or delete more columns and rows. It discusses how to format and align text held within tables, how to add borders, and how to work with cells, including how to shade, merge and split them, and rotate text within the cells. You will also learn to enter formulas.

Create Tables

Creating tables is easily handled in PowerPoint. You select the Table command in the Tables group on the Insert tab and choose an option, specifying the number of rows and columns you want, and then fill in the data. That's just about all there is to it. Of course, thinking about what data will be included is a decision that PowerPoint can't do much to help you with. But once you have answered those basic questions, PowerPoint offers a wide variety of choices about how to present that data clearly and professionally.

QUICK**FACTS**

UNDERSTANDING TABLE BASICS

A PowerPoint table, similar to a worksheet in Microsoft Excel, is a matrix, or grid, with *column headings* across the top and *row headings* down the side. The first row of a typical table is used for column *headers*. Column headers represent categories of similar data. The rows beneath a column header contain data further categorized by a row header along the leftmost column or listed below the column header. In a table, columns are sometimes referred to as *fields*, and each row represents a unique *record* of data. Each intersection of a row and column is called a *cell* and contains a unique bit of information. A cell is considered to be *active* when it is clicked or otherwise selected as the place in which to place new data.

Insert a Table

There are four ways to create a table on a slide. You can insert one from layout templates, directly insert a table onto a slide, draw a table, or insert one from Microsoft Word or Excel. Figure 5-1 shows an example of a typical table.

INSERT A TABLE FROM A LAYOUT

A common way to create a table is to use one from the various templates that Microsoft provides. With this approach, you insert a table into a placeholder.

1. Click the slide immediately before the one on which the table is to be inserted.

2. On the Home tab, in the Slides group click the **New Slide** down arrow to insert a new slide into the presentation. The slide layout menu will be displayed, as shown in Figure 5-2.

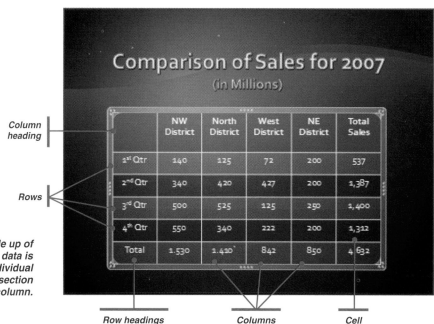

Figure 5-1: A table is made up of columns and rows, and data is contained in each individual cell—the unique intersection between a row and a column.

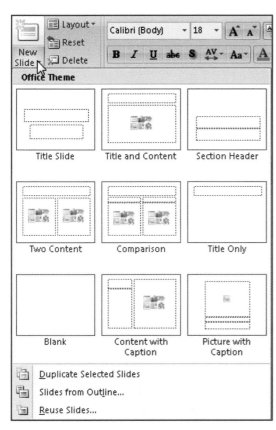

Figure 5-2: *When you insert a new slide, you can select a layout that allows you to define the contents you expect on a slide, such as a table or other object.*

NOTE

When a table is inserted, PowerPoint adds two new contextual tabs, Design and Layout, to the Table Tools group.

3. Find a layout with a content icon (such as the Title and Content layout), select it, and click the **Table** icon .

4. In the Insert Table dialog box, fill in the number of columns and rows, and click **OK.** The table will be inserted onto your slide, as shown in Figure 5-3.

INSERT A TABLE FROM SCRATCH

In this case, you simply insert a table onto the slide.

1. Click the slide where you want the table inserted.

2. Click the **Insert** tab, and in the Tables group click **Table**.

3. Drag the pointer until the number of squares selected represents the number of columns and rows you want, as shown in Figure 5-4. The table will be immediately placed on your slide. Point to a table border, and drag it to where you want it on the slide.

–Or–

4. On the Table menu, click **Insert Table**, fill in the number of columns and rows, and click **OK.**

DRAW A TABLE

To draw a table, you use the table drawing pen in Normal view to draw the boundaries and interior design of the table. (See "Work with Borders" for more information on drawing a table.)

1. If you need a blank slide, click the **Home** tab, and then in the Slides group click the **New Slide** down arrow. Select the **Blank** or **Title Only** slide layout. If you want to draw the table on an existing slide, click the slide to select it.

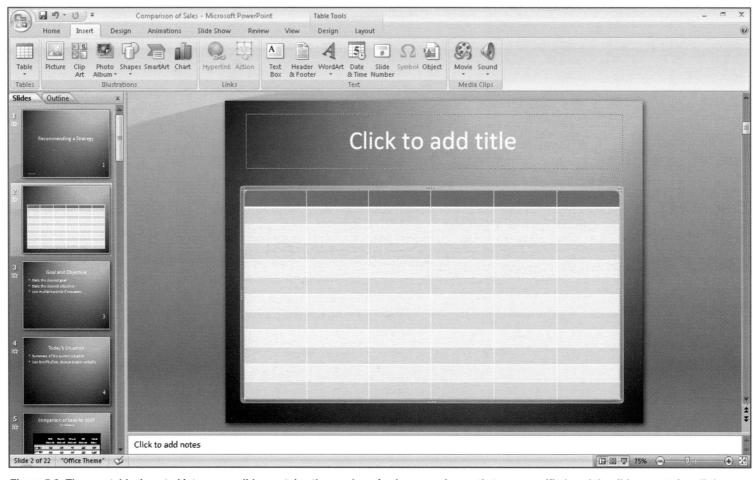

Figure 5-3: *The new table, inserted into a new slide, contains the number of columns and rows that you specified, and the ribbon contains all the tools you need.*

2. To help you draw more precisely, display gridlines: On the Home tab, in the Drawing group click the **Arrange** button to see a menu of options. Under Position Objects, click **Align**, and on the context button, click **View Gridlines** to display a grid of lines on your slide. (See Chapter 6 for additional information on using gridlines.)

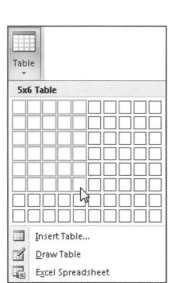

Figure 5-4: *You can create a table by dragging over the squares in the menu for the number of rows and columns you want in the table.*

TIP

To draw diagonal lines, start the line from an intersection or corner of two lines.

TIP

When the table is selected, the Table Tools Design and Layout tabs are displayed on the ribbon. When the table is deselected, the Design and Layout tabs are closed.

3. On the Insert tab, in the Tables group click **Table**, and on the context menu, click the **Draw Table** option. Your pointer will turn into a drawing tool in the shape of a pencil.

4. Drag to create the outline of the table:

- Drag the pointer diagonally across the slide to define the outside border of the table. When you release the pointer, a selected placeholder box will be in place.

- Begin to draw the table you want. Draw vertical and horizontal lines. When you start a line, it will be extended in the direction you want until it reaches a border or another horizontal or vertical line.

- To turn the drawing tool on and off, click the **Draw Table** button in the Draw Borders group on the Design tab. (Depending on which commands you use, you may need to click the **Insert** tab, click **Table**, and then click **Draw Table** to restore the drawing tool.)

- To erase a line, click the **Eraser** button on the selected table Design tab. The pointer will morph into an eraser, which you can use to click the line you want to remove.

- To insert color into the columns and rows you have drawn, select the cells to be colored, and click the **Shading** down arrow in the Table Styles group. Click the color you want.

- To add a bevel, shadow, or reflection effect to the table, highlight the cells to be altered, and click **Effects** in the Table Styles group. Click the effect you want, and then choose the variation you want.

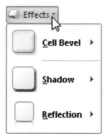

- To add text, click a cell to select it, and then type your text.

Figure 5-5 shows an example of a table drawn in PowerPoint.

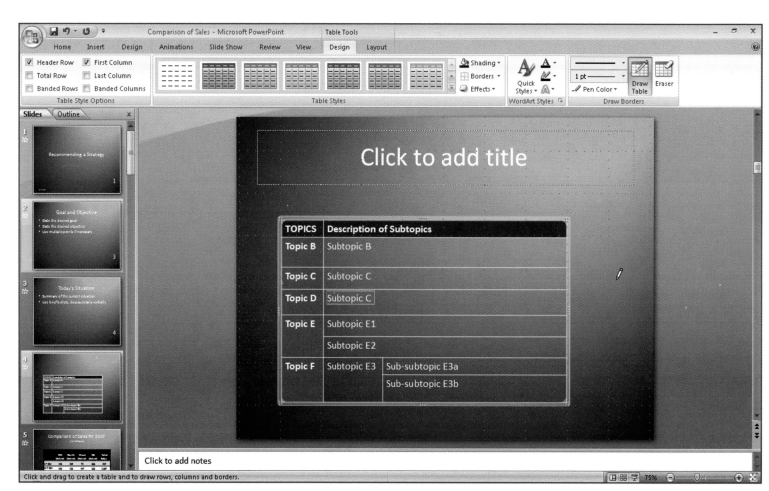

Figure 5-5: *A table drawn in PowerPoint can have irregular column and row sizes placed in creative ways.*

COPY A TABLE FROM WORD

You can create a table in Microsoft Word and copy it using the Clipboard onto a PowerPoint slide.

1. In Word, create your table.

2. Select it by dragging across all the cells of the table.

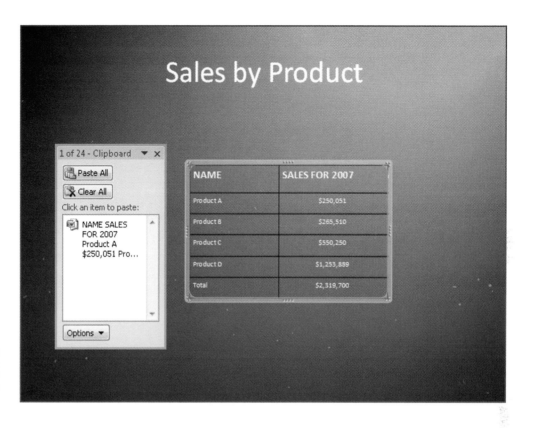

Figure 5-6: Since the Clipboard is shared between Microsoft Office programs, it is easy to create a table in Excel or Word and then copy it into PowerPoint.

3. Click the **Home** tab, and click **Copy**. The table will be placed on the Clipboard.

4. In PowerPoint, find the slide where you're going to insert the Word table.

5. Click the **Home** tab, and click the **Clipboard** icon. Then click the appropriate item from the Clipboard task pane. The table will be inserted onto the slide, as shown in Figure 5-6.

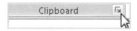

USE EXCEL TO CREATE A POWERPOINT TABLE

You can insert an empty Microsoft Excel spreadsheet within Powerpoint and still use Excel's commands and functions to enter data and create a table.

This enables you to retain the calculating functions found in Excel. A PowerPoint table cannot calculate; it can only be displayed. To use Excel to create a table within PowerPoint:

1. In PowerPoint, create or select the slide that is to contain your Excel spreadsheet. On the Home tab, click **New Slide** in the Slides group, and click the **Title Only** or **Blank** layout, or select a different layout from the slide layout menu.

2. Click the **Insert** tab, and in the Tables group click **Table**. From the menu, click **Excel Spreadsheet**.

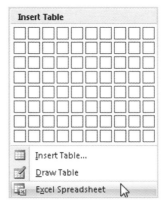

3. An Excel spreadsheet will be inserted. Click the border and drag the spreadsheet where you want it on the slide. You can resize it by dragging the sizing handles. Then click in the cells and type your data. You will be able to use Excel commands while working with the spreadsheet.

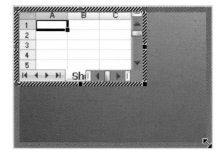

4. When your table is ready, click outside the Excel table. The Excel commands will close, and PowerPoint will open.

TIP

For more information on using Excel commands within PowerPoint, see Chapter 6 for information on working with charts or graphs, or refer to *Microsoft Excel 2007 QuickSteps*, published by McGraw-Hill/Osborne.

TIP

See Chapter 6 to learn how to simply copy data to the Clipboard from an Excel worksheet and paste it onto a slide in PowerPoint.

QUICKSTEPS

ALIGNING TEXT

Text is aligned in the upper-left corner of a cell by default. You can align text vertically and horizontally within a cell.

ALIGN TEXT HORIZONTALLY

First, click in a cell, or select a row, column, or the whole table by dragging over it or clicking the edge or border of the table. The tools for aligning text can be found in the Layout tab or on the mini-toolbar that appears when you move the pointer over the selected text a bit.

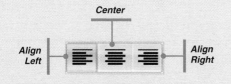

- Click **Center** to center-align text.

Center	Center	Center

- Click **Align Left** to left-align text.

Left	Left	Left

- Click **Align Right** to right-align text.

Right	Right	Right

ALIGN TEXT VERTICALLY

Select the cell, row, column, or whole table by dragging over it or clicking the edge or border of the table.

Continued . . .

Work with Tables

When working with tables, you can enter and format text, add color, and add table effects.

Enter Text

To enter text into a table cell, you have several navigational tips to keep in mind:

- To add data to a table, click a cell and type. If you type to the end of the cell, your text will wrap to the next line, making the cell taller.

- Press **TAB** to move the insertion point to the next cell on the right in the same row.

- When you are at the last cell in a row, pressing **TAB** will move the insertion point to the first cell of the next row. If you are in the last cell in a table, pressing **TAB** will insert a new row and place the insertion point in the first cell of that row.

- Press **DOWN ARROW** or **UP ARROW** to move the insertion point up or down one row in the same column.

- Press **ENTER** to insert another line within a cell—that is, to make the cell taller by one line.

Format Text

To format text, that is, to change fonts and font style, font size, font color, and character effects (such as **Bold,** <u>Underline</u>, and *Italics*), you can either use the Font group on the Home tab or the formatting toolbar that appears when you select text. (Detailed information on using text formatting is described in Chapter 4.)

USE THE FONT GROUP

1. Select the text in the cells that you want to format by highlighting them.
2. Click the **Home** tab, and click the one of the buttons in the Font group.

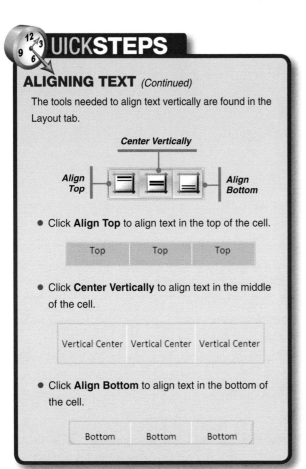

QUICKSTEPS

ALIGNING TEXT (Continued)

The tools needed to align text vertically are found in the Layout tab.

Center Vertically

Align Top — Align Bottom

- Click **Align Top** to align text in the top of the cell.

Top	Top	Top

- Click **Center Vertically** to align text in the middle of the cell.

Vertical Center	Vertical Center	Vertical Center

- Click **Align Bottom** to align text in the bottom of the cell.

Bottom	Bottom	Bottom

TIP

To insert a tab in a table cell, press **CTRL+TAB.**

TIP

If the formatting toolbar doesn't appear when you select the text, double-click it and move your pointer over the vague image of the toolbar.

USE THE FORMATTING TOOLBAR

1. Select the text in the cells by highlighting them.

2. When the toolbar appears over the selected cells, move your pointer over the selected cells to make the toolbar available.

3. Click the button you want on the formatting toolbar.

Set Cell Margins

You can change the margins within a cell. The default margin setting is "Normal" and is a margin of .05 inches at the top and bottom of the cell and .1 inches on either side. You can choose No Margins, Narrow, or Wide margins.

1. Click the table so that it is selected. The Table Tools Design and Layout tabs should be showing.

2. Select the cell or cells for which the margins will be changed.

3. Click the **Layout tab**, and click **Cell Margins** in the Alignment group, as shown in Figure 5-7.

4. Click the margin you want.

Delete a Table

To delete a table and its contents:

1. Click the border or edge of the table to select it.

2. Press **DELETE**.

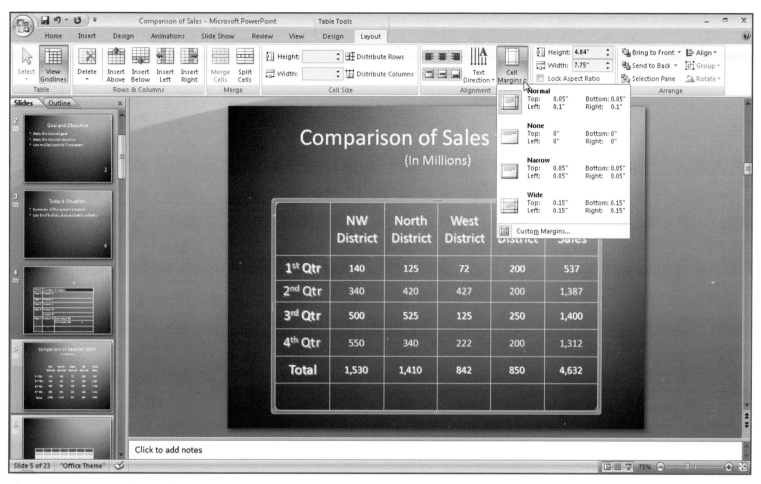

Figure 5-7: You can set the margins for the cell from the Layout tab and the Alignment group.

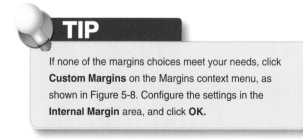

TIP

If none of the margins choices meet your needs, click **Custom Margins** on the Margins context menu, as shown in Figure 5-8. Configure the settings in the **Internal Margin** area, and click **OK**.

Figure 5-8: You can set the internal margins of cells using the Cell Text Layout dialog box.

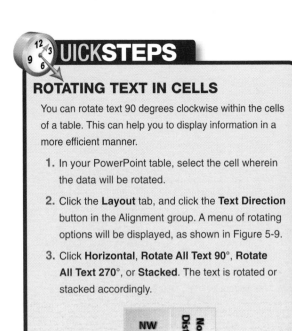

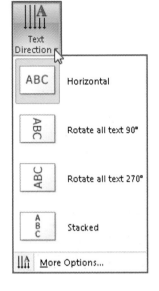

*Figure 5-9: **Using the Text Direction command, you can rotate text in several ways to position it exactly within a table.***

Use the Table Design Tab

The table Design tab is an important tool when working with tables. You display it by clicking the table you're working on. The tab provides tools to manipulate and format the table. Table 5-1 shows the functions of the tab.

Use Table Style Options

When designing your table, you can quickly specify some special formatting. This is particularly useful when you have column or row headings, total columns or rows, or want the table to be banded so that the columns or rows can be more easily read.

Highlight your table and place check marks in the pertinent check boxes on the Table Tools Design tab in the Table Style Options group to enable the features. (See Table 5-1 for explanations for each of the check boxes.)

GROUP NAME	TOOL NAME	DESCRIPTION	SEE THIS SECTION FOR MORE INFORMATION
Tables Style Options			
☑ Header Row	Header Row	Identifies that special formatting exists for the header row.	"Use Quick Style Options"
☐ Total Row	Total Row	Identifies a total row on the bottom of the table that is holding totals.	"Use Quick Style Options"
☑ Banded Rows	Banded Rows	Indicates that rows are banded to distinguish between odd and even rows.	"Use Quick Style Options"
☐ First Column	First Column	Indicates that the first column is to contain special formatting.	"Use Quick Style Options"
☐ Last Column	Last Column	Indicates that the last column of the table is to have special formatting.	"Use Quick Style Options"
☐ Banded Columns	Banded Columns	Indicates that columns are banded to distinguish between odd and even columns.	"Use Quick Style Options"
Table Styles			
Table Styles	Table Styles	Displays a menu of color and design styles for tables.	"Enhance Tables with Preset Styles"
Shading ▾	Shading	Applies the current color or displays a menu of fill colors. You can fill a table or selected cells with a selected color. You can also fill with gradient colors, patterns, textures, or a picture.	"Use Special Effects in the Table Background"
Borders ▾	Borders	Determines which lines in the table will be displayed.	"Use Special Effects in the Table Background"
Effects ▾	Effects	Allows for beveling, shadowing, and reflections to be used for special effects in tables.	"Use Special Effects in the Table Background"
Draw Borders			"Work with Borders"
Draw Table	Draw Table	Use to draw a table with irregular columns and row sizes.	"Insert a Table"

Table 5-1: Tools on the Table Design Tab

GROUP NAME	TOOL NAME	DESCRIPTION	SEE THIS SECTION FOR MORE INFORMATION
Eraser	Eraser	Erases lines as you click them.	
	Pen Style	Displays a menu of border styles.	"Work with Borders"
1 pt	Pen Weight	Displays a menu of border sizes in points.	"Work with Borders"
Pen Color	Pen Color	Converts lines to a selected color when you click them.	"Work with Borders"

Table 5-1: Tools on the Table Design Tab (Continued)

Enhance Tables with Preset Styles

PowerPoint 2007 contains preset styles for quickly giving tables color and other design styles. Figure 5-10 shows the styles available to you. These can then be modified with further special effects. (See "Use Special Effects in the Table Background.") The original style comes from the presentation's theme.

1. Click the table border to select it and display the Table Tools Design tab. (Or right-click the table and click **Select Table.)**

2. Click the **More** button on the Table Styles group. The menu of preset styles will open.

3. Move your pointer over the choices, and you will see the results of each on the table beneath the menu. (You may have to move the table to the side to see the results.) When you see a choice you'd like to try, click it. The table will be formatted with that style. You can easily change it again.

TIP

To remove all formatting of table styles and begin again, click the **Clear Table** button on the bottom of the menu.

NOTE

Chapter 4 describes how to use WordArt for text. In a table, you find WordArt features on the Table Tools Design tab in the WordArt Styles group.

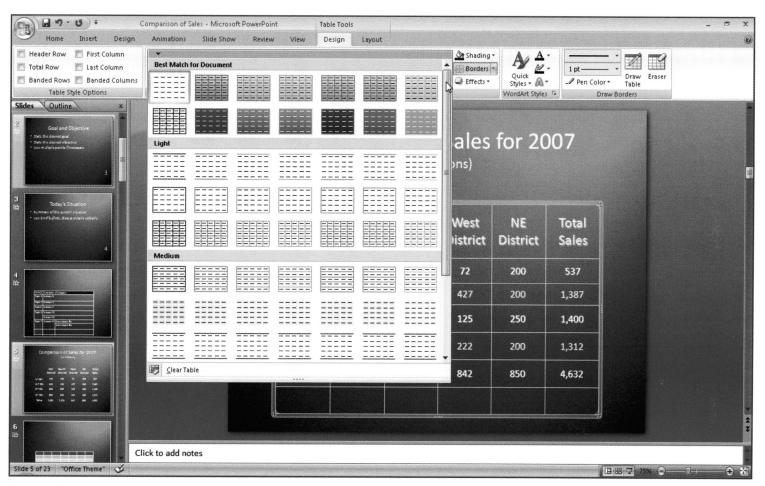

Figure 5-10: Preset table styles are available to format the table with a professional-looking and colorful design, which you can then modify.

Use Special Effects in the Table Background

You can use some special effects, such as gradient colors, and texture, in the table background.

1. Select the cells you want to have the special effect; click the border or edge of the table to select the whole table.

Comparison of Sales for 2007
(In Millions)

	NW District	North District	West District	NE District	Total Sales
1st Qtr	140	125	72	200	537
2nd Qtr	340	420	427	200	1,387
3rd Qtr	500	525	125	250	1,400
4th Qtr	550	340	222	200	1,312
Total	1,530	1,410	842	850	4,632

*Figure 5-11: **Shaded columns and rows enable readers to find the totals more easily.***

2. On the Table Tools Design tab, click the **Shading** down arrow. A menu is displayed.

3. Click an option, such as **Gradient** or **Texture**. A submenu is displayed.

4. Click your choice and the gradient effect or texture will be applied to your table.

SHADE CELLS, COLUMNS, ROWS, OR A TABLE

You can create automatic banding using PowerPoint's preset table styles, or you can do it on your own. Shading cells, columns, or rows makes them more easily read. If you shade the background of the whole table, you can add color and a refining touch. Background shading can also be used to distinguish the table from the slide itself. Figure 5-11 shows an example of a table with shaded columns and rows that make it more readable.

1. Select the row, column, or cell to be shaded. To select the whole table, click the border or edge of the table, or highlight all cells in the table.

2. On the table Design tab, click the **Shading** down arrow, and click the shade of color to be applied to the selected area of the table. The selected area will be filled accordingly. You can point at various shades before selecting one to see the effect they will have on the table—you may have to move the table to see it clearly when the menu is displayed.

USE A PICTURE IN YOUR TABLE

You can add pictures to your table. The picture will be entered into a cell. If need be, you can enlarge the picture by merging cells.

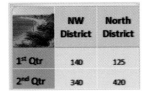

	NW District	North District
1st Qtr	140	125
2nd Qtr	340	420

1. Select the cell to contain the picture.

2. On the Table Tools Design tab, click the **Shading** down arrow, and click **Picture** from the menu.

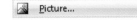

3. The Insert Picture dialog box will appear. Find the path to the picture you want, click the picture and click **Insert**. The picture will be inserted into the cell.

MERGE CELLS TO ENLARGE A PICTURE

You can either select multiple cells that will hold the picture at the beginning of the process or right before you merge the cells.

1. Select the cell or cells that will contain the picture.

2. On the Table Tools Design tab, click the **Shading** down arrow, and click **Picture** from the menu.

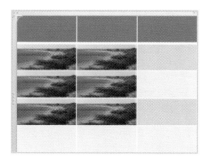

3. The Insert Picture dialog box will appear. Find the path to the picture you want, click the picture, and click **Insert**. The picture will be inserted into the cell, or, if multiple cells were selected, each cell will contain a copy of the picture.

4. To combine the pictures into a single large one, select the cells you want to contain the larger picture.

5. Click the Table Tools **Layout** tab, and click **Merge Cells** in the Merge group. The cells will be merged into one cell containing the picture.

DISPLAY OR HIDE INSIDE AND OUTSIDE BORDER LINES

To change the appearance of the borders (or cells) by controlling which inside or outside border lines appear:

1. Click the edge or border of the table to select it, or highlight the cells to select them. The Table Tools Design tab is displayed.

2. Click the **Borders** button to see a menu of border selections, as shown in Figure 5-12.

3. Click the border option you want. If you selected the table, the whole table will conform to the new border selection. If you selected one or more cells, only the cells' outlines will change.

Work with Borders

You can vary the style (solid versus dotted line, for example), weight or thickness, and color of table borders.

CHANGE BORDER STYLE

To change the style or appearance of a border:

1. Click the border or edge of the table to select it. The Table Tools Design tab is displayed.

2. On the Table Tools Design tab, click the **Pen Style** button in the Draw Borders group.

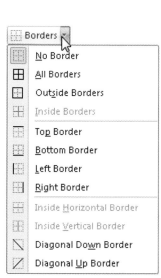

*Figure 5-12: **Borders of a cell or entire table can be set with the Borders button on the Design tab.***

3. Select the style of line you want. The pointer will morph into a pencil.

140	125
340	420
500	525

4. With the pencil icon, click or draw along the borders you want to have the new style.

CHANGE BORDER WEIGHT

To change the thickness or weight of a border:

1. Click the border or edge of the table to select it. The Table Tools Design tab is displayed.

2. On the Design tab, click the **Pen Weight** button in the Draw Borders group.

3. Select the weight of line you want. The pointer will morph into a pencil.

4. With the pencil icon, click or draw along the borders you want to have the new weight.

1 pt ——— ▼
¼ pt ———
½ pt ———
¾ pt ———
1 pt ———
1½ pt ———
2¼ pt ———
3 pt ———
4½ pt ▬▬
6 pt ▬▬

CHANGE BORDER COLOR

To change the color of a border:

1. Click the border or edge of the table to select it. The Design tab is displayed.

2. On the table Design tab, click the **Pen Color** down arrow in the Draw Borders group. A dialog box appears, shown in Figure 5-13.

3. Select the line color you want. The pointer will morph into a pencil.

4. With the pencil icon, click or draw along the borders or lines on which you want to change the color.

Use the Table Layout Tab

Tables are managed and manipulated using the Layout tab. It contains commands to select, insert, and delete rows and columns; merge and split them; manipulate cell size; and align text within cells. Table 5-2 shows the commands on the Layout tab.

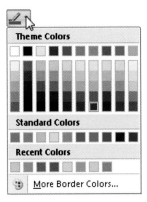

Figure 5-13: The Pen Colors dialog box presents a palette of color options for the borders and lines of your table.

GROUP NAME	TOOL NAME	DESCRIPTION	SEE THIS SECTION FOR MORE INFORMATION
Table			
Select	Select	Allows you to select a table, column, or row	"Selecting Table Components"
View Gridlines	View Gridlines	Displays or hides gridlines on the table	"Show or Hide Gridlines"
Rows and Columns			
Delete	Delete	Deletes selected rows or columns	"Deleting Columns and Rows"
Insert Above	Insert Above	Inserts a row above the selected row	"Insert Columns and Rows"
Insert Below	Insert Below	Inserts a row below the selected row	"Insert Columns and Rows"
Insert Left	Insert Left	Inserts a column to the left of the selected column	"Insert Columns and Rows"
Insert Right	Insert Right	Inserts a column to the right of the selected column	"Insert Columns and Rows"
Merge			
Merge Cells	Merge Cells	Merges selected cells into one cell	"Merging or Splitting Cells"
Split Cells	Split Cells	Splits selected cells into rows and columns	"Merging or Splitting Cells"

Table 5-2: Tools on the Table Layout Tab

GROUP NAME	TOOL NAME	DESCRIPTION	SEE THIS SECTION FOR MORE INFORMATION
Cell Size			
0.58"	Height	Type the height of the cell	"Change the Size of Columns and Rows"
1.29"	Width	Type the width of the cell	"Change the Size of Columns and Rows"
	Distribute Rows	Make the height of the selected rows equal	"Change the Size of Columns and Rows"
	Distribute Columns	Make the width of the selected columns equal	"Change the Size of Columns and Rows"
Alignment			
	Align Horizontally	Left-align, center, or right-align within a cell	"Aligning Text"
	Align Vertically	Top-align, center vertically, or bottom-align within a cell	"Aligning Text"
Text Direction	Text Direction	Rotate or stack text within a cell	"Rotating Text in Cells"
Cell Margins	Cell Margins	Set cell margins	"Set Cell Margins"
Table Size			
Height: 4.88"	Height	Type the height of a table	
Width: 7.75"	Width	Type the width of a table	
Lock Aspect Ratio	Lock Aspect Ratio	To insure proportional changes as height and width changes are made	

Table 5-2: Tools on the Table Layout Tab (Continued)

GROUP NAME	TOOL NAME	DESCRIPTION	SEE THIS SECTION FOR MORE INFORMATION
Arrange			
Bring to Front	Bring to Front	Brings the selected object to the front	
Send to Back	Send to Back	Puts selected object at the back	
Selection Pane	Selection Pane	Displays a task pane to work with objects more easily	
	Align	Displays all column and row alignment options	
	Group	Options for grouping or ungrouping selected objects	
	Rotate	Rotates objects	

*Table 5-2: **Tools on the Table Layout Tab (Continued)***

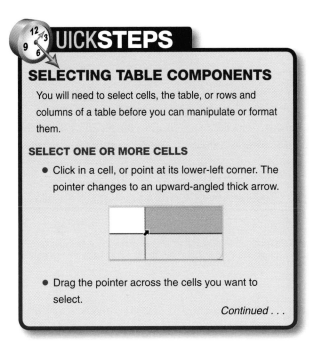

QUICKSTEPS

SELECTING TABLE COMPONENTS

You will need to select cells, the table, or rows and columns of a table before you can manipulate or format them.

SELECT ONE OR MORE CELLS

- Click in a cell, or point at its lower-left corner. The pointer changes to an upward-angled thick arrow.

- Drag the pointer across the cells you want to select.

Continued . . .

Show or Hide Gridlines

To show or hide gridlines so that you can see the cells more clearly or to position objects more precisely:

1. Click the border or edge of the table to select it
2. Click the **Layout** tab:

   - Click **View Gridlines** to toggle the gridlines on and off.

   - Move the pointer over the table to see the gridlines or to see them disappear.

Insert Columns and Rows

You may find that you need to add rows or columns to your table.

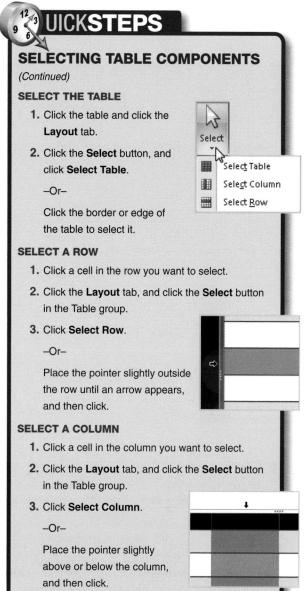

QUICKSTEPS

SELECTING TABLE COMPONENTS

(Continued)

SELECT THE TABLE

1. Click the table and click the **Layout** tab.

2. Click the **Select** button, and click **Select Table**.

   –Or–

   Click the border or edge of the table to select it.

SELECT A ROW

1. Click a cell in the row you want to select.

2. Click the **Layout** tab, and click the **Select** button in the Table group.

3. Click **Select Row**.

   –Or–

   Place the pointer slightly outside the row until an arrow appears, and then click.

SELECT A COLUMN

1. Click a cell in the column you want to select.

2. Click the **Layout** tab, and click the **Select** button in the Table group.

3. Click **Select Column**.

   –Or–

   Place the pointer slightly above or below the column, and then click.

To insert a row:

1. Click in the row above or below where the new row is to be inserted.

2. Click the **Layout** tab, and click **Insert Above** or **Insert Below** in the Rows & Columns group.

   –Or–

1. Click in the row above or below where the new row is to be inserted.

2. Right-click the table and click **Insert**. A context menu will be displayed. Click **Insert Rows Above** or **Insert Rows Below**. The row will be inserted above or below the selected row.

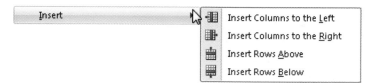

To insert a column:

1. Click in the column to the left or right of where the new column is to be inserted.

2. Click the **Layout** menu, and click **Insert Left** or **Insert Right** on the Rows & Columns group.

   –Or–

1. Click in the column to the right or left of where you want the new column inserted.

2. Right-click the table and click **Insert**. From the context menu, click **Insert Columns To The Left** or **Insert Columns To The Right**. The column will be inserted to the right or left of the selected one.

Change the Size of Columns and Rows

You can change the width of columns and the height of rows manually by dragging the border of the column or row, you can type the specific height or width, or you can let PowerPoint do it automatically.

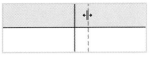

UICKSTEPS

DELETING ROWS AND COLUMNS

You can easily delete rows or columns on your table.

1. Click in the row or column, or highlight multiple rows or columns to be deleted by dragging over them.

2. Click the **Layout** tab, and click the **Delete** button:

   - To delete selected columns, click **Delete Columns**.

   - To delete selected rows, click **Delete Rows**.

   –Or–

   Highlight the group of rows or columns to be deleted, and then right-click (or if deleting a single row or column, right-click the row or column to be deleted). Then select **Delete Rows** or **Delete Columns** from the context menu.

NOTE

To set a specific height and width for selected cells, select the cells, click the **Layout** tab, and click the **Table Row Height** or **Table Column Width** spinners in the Cell Size group.

CHANGE COLUMN WIDTH

To adjust the size of the column, first click inside the table to select it:

- Place your pointer on the right border or edge of a column so that it morphs into a two-headed arrow. Drag the border right or left to increase or decrease the size, respectively.

  –Or–

- Click the **Layout** tab, and then click **Distribute Columns** in the Cell Size group. This makes the columns the same width and adjusts the contents to fit.

  –Or–

- Place your pointer on the right border of a column so that it morphs into a two-headed arrow. Double-click the column border to have PowerPoint adjust it to match the width of the longest content within the column.

  –Or–

- Highlight the columns you want resized. Click the **Layout** tab, and type the **Table Column Width** (or use the spinner) in the Cell Size group.

CHANGE ROW HEIGHT

To adjust the size of rows, first click outside the table to deselect any cells:

- Place your pointer on the lower border of a row so that it morphs into a two-headed arrow. Drag the border up or down to decrease or increase the size, respectively.

  –Or–

- Click the table. Click the **Layout** tab, and then click **Distribute Rows** on the Cell Size group. This makes the rows the same height and adjusts the contents to fit.

Enter Formulas

To create formulas to display on slides and in tables, you use the Equation Editor. This is a separate application that interfaces closely with PowerPoint. The formulas are only for display. They do not calculate anything.

1. Click the **Insert** tab, and select **Object** in the Text group.

2. In the Insert Object dialog box, shown in Figure 5-14, click **Microsoft Equation 3.0**, and click **OK**. The Equation Editor will open, as shown in Figure 5-15.

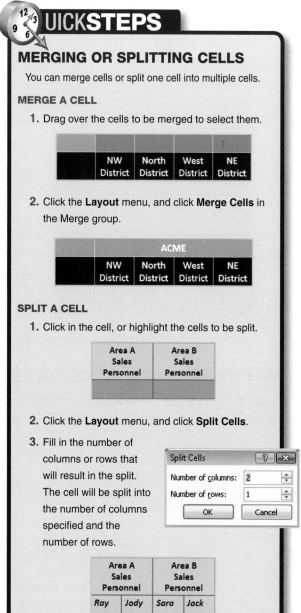

QUICKSTEPS

MERGING OR SPLITTING CELLS

You can merge cells or split one cell into multiple cells.

MERGE A CELL

1. Drag over the cells to be merged to select them.

NW District	North District	West District	NE District

2. Click the **Layout** menu, and click **Merge Cells** in the Merge group.

ACME			
NW District	North District	West District	NE District

SPLIT A CELL

1. Click in the cell, or highlight the cells to be split.

Area A Sales Personnel	Area B Sales Personnel

2. Click the **Layout** menu, and click **Split Cells**.

3. Fill in the number of columns or rows that will result in the split. The cell will be split into the number of columns specified and the number of rows.

Split Cells

Number of columns: 2
Number of rows: 1

OK   Cancel

Area A Sales Personnel	Area B Sales Personnel
Ray	Jody	Sara	Jack

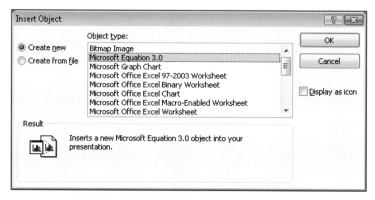

Figure 5-14: *The Insert Object dialog box allows you to open the Equation Editor so that you can enter formulas and equations.*

3. From the bottom row of the toolbars, click a template. From the top toolbar, click the symbols you need, and type the text you need to complete the equation or formula.

4. When you are finished with the equation, double-click the equation to select it. Then press **CTRL+C** to copy it. Click the **File** menu, and click **Exit And Return To** *filename*, or click **Close**. The equation will appear in your table. If you do not see it, you can also click in the cell where you want the equation, and press **CTRL+V** to paste it.

5. If the equation is not exactly where you want it, drag the box to the cell where you want it, and drag the borders to resize it.

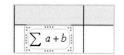

To edit the equation once it is in PowerPoint, just double-click it. The Equation Editor will open. You can nest templates by clicking a template and then clicking another template within the first one.

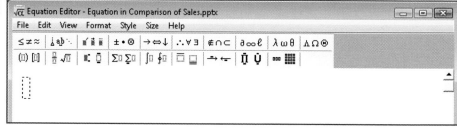

Figure 5-15: *The Equation Editor is used to display equations and formulas in PowerPoint.*

Chapter 6
Using and Organizing Clips

This chapter looks at how you can add some pizzazz to your presentation by using *objects*, such as clip art, to make your presentations more interesting. By adding colorful elements to your presentations, you keep your viewer's attention, balancing the narrative parts with visual effects. You will see how to work with clip art and the Clip Organizer to manage your libraries of clip art.

Work with Clip Art

PowerPoint is installed with many "clips." Clips can be media files, such as sound, graphics, videos, and animation. In this section, we look at *clip art*, which is comprised of photos, drawings, and bitmaps. You will see how to find clip art on your own computer and online, then how to insert it, position it, and modify it to get the results you want. You will see how to place clip art using a grid and ruler lines to help you position it more precisely. You will see how to change the image color, resize it, crop photos to refine the image, and delete clip

Figure 6-1: *The Clip Art task pane allows you to search for and organize clip art.*

art when necessary. You will also learn how to improve an image by increasing or decreasing contrast and brightness, and about the Clip Organizer, which enables you to find clips easily.

Find and Insert Clip Art

With your presentation open, you find clip art using the Clip Art task pane.

1. Click the **Insert** tab. Click **Clip Art** in the Illustrations group. The Clip Art task pane will open, as shown in Figure 6-1.

2. In the **Search For** text box, type keywords for the subject you are looking for (for example, **meetings, family, cars,** or **holidays**).

3. Click the **Search In** down arrow. A check mark is the default, indicating the selected search category is to be searched. You'll need to click the check marks to remove them from those search categories you do not want. You can refine the searches within the Everywhere, My Collections, Office Collections, or Web Collections categories by clicking to remove check marks where you do not want to search.

4. Under **Results Should Be**, open the drop-down list box, and verify that appropriate check boxes are selected. If a check box is selected, that media type will be searched for. (By default, all choices are selected.) Click **Go** to start the search.

5. The search results will be displayed as thumbnails in the preview pane, as shown in Figure 6-1. Scroll through the list. Click the thumbnail of the picture you want to insert. (Alternatively, you can right-click the thumbnail, and click **Insert**.)

Change the Color of Clip Art

You can change the color of clip art to be a different color, grayscale, sepia, washout, or dark and light variations on a color. You can make a color transparent. To change the color of clip art in a presentation:

1. Click the clip art whose color you want to change. That will make the Picture Tools upper-level tabs available to you. Click the **Format** tab, if it is not already displayed.

2. Click the **Recolor** button. A menu of color choices will be shown, as you can see in Figure 6-2:

   - As you point to a color, you can see how it would change the selected clip art. Under Color Mode you can see grayscale, sepia, and washout options. Under Dark Variations and Light Variations you can vary the intensity of a color.

   - Click **More Variations** to see additional color choices.

   - Click **Set Transparent Color** to turn the pointer into a pencil-and-arrow icon, which you can use to click the color you want made transparent. For example, clicking the color of the auto in Figure 6-2 turns the color transparent.

3. Click a color to select it.

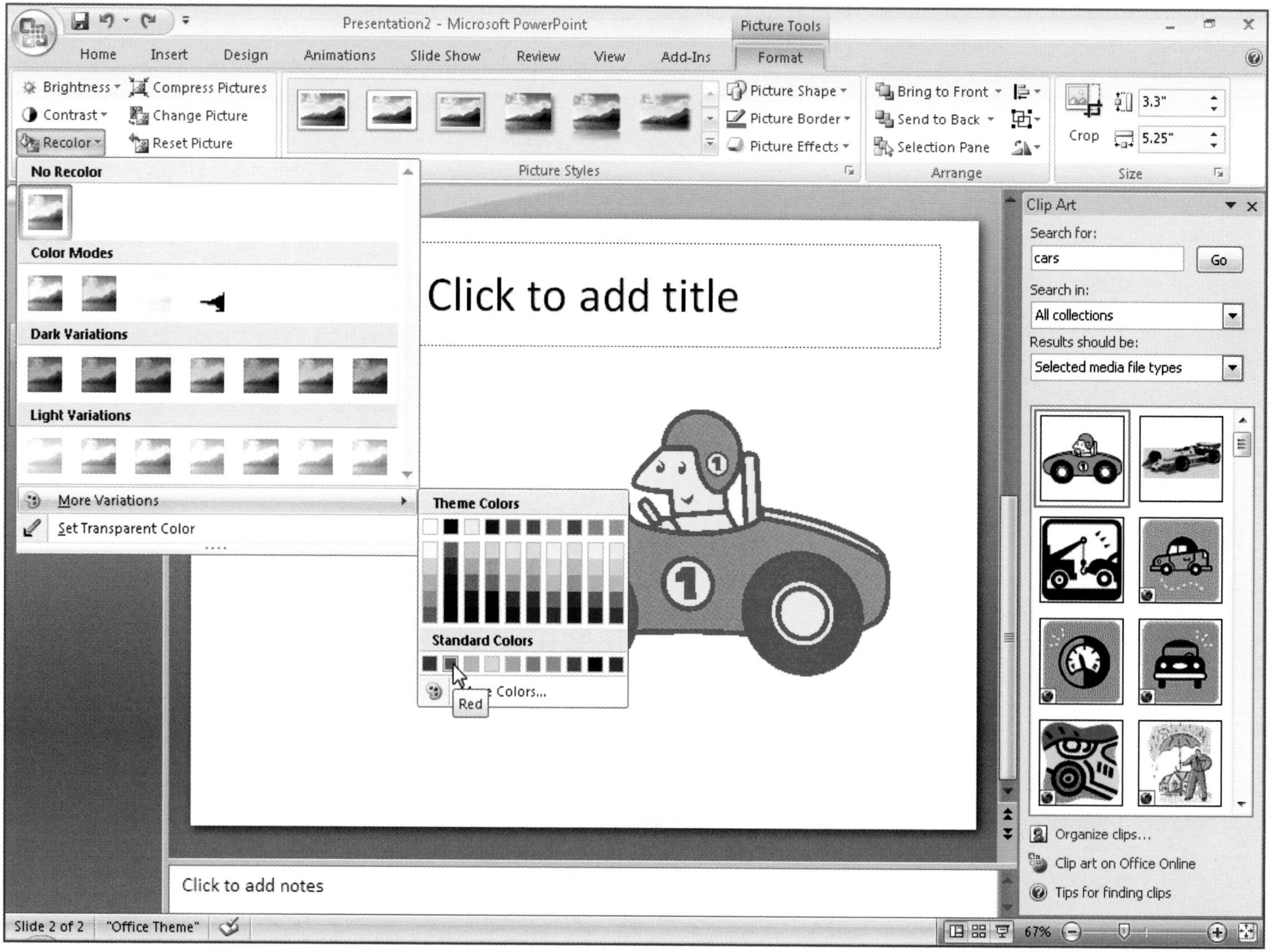

Figure 6-2: *The Recolor button allows you to display and then change the color of clip art.*

WORKING WITH OBJECTS

An object is something added to a slide that can be selected, such as clip art, photos, a graph or chart, a table, a drawing, or text.

SELECT OBJECTS

Click an object to select it. You will know it is selected when the sizing handles and rotating handle are visible.

–Or–

Press **TAB**. If several objects are on the screen, press **TAB** until the one you want is selected.

MOVE OBJECTS

1. Select the object by clicking it.

2. Place the pointer on the selected object (but not on the sizing handles). The pointer will morph into a four-headed arrow.

3. Drag the object to its new location.

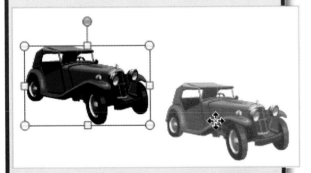

Continued . . .

Insert a Picture

Insert a picture using the Insert tab, as you did with clip art.

Picture

1. Click the **Insert** tab, and then click the **Picture** button in the Illustrations group. The Insert Picture dialog box will appear.

2. Click the picture you want, and click **Insert**. The picture will be inserted on your slide.

Crop Objects

Cropping clip art or a picture allows you to zero in on the essential elements. You can cut the irrelevant part of the picture and retain the part you want to focus on.

1. Click the picture to be cropped to select it so that you can see the sizing handles on all four edges. The Picture Tools upper-level tab is now available as well.

2. Click the **Format** tab, and then click the **Crop** button in the Size group. Cropping marks will appear where the sizing handles are, and the pointer will morph between a four-headed arrow (when the pointer is within the picture) and a cropping tool, depending on where it is pointing. To use the cropping tool:

Crop

- Place the four-headed arrow on top of the cropping handles. It will turn into a cropping tool (an "elbow" or "T" shape, depending on the cropping handle it is on top of) when it is accurately placed.

Before pointer is placed correctly over crop handles

After pointer is correctly placed

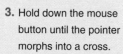

QUICKSTEPS

WORKING WITH OBJECTS (Continued)

RESIZE OBJECTS

1. Select the object by clicking it.

2. Place the pointer on any of the sizing handles so that the pointer arrow morphs into a two-headed arrow.

3. Hold down the mouse button until the pointer morphs into a cross.

4. Drag the border of the object inward or outward to the size you want. Press **SHIFT** to size it proportionally.

DELETE OBJECTS

Select the object by clicking it, and then press **DELETE**.

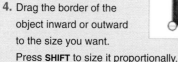

Figure 6-3: **Cropping a picture lets you narrow the focus to exactly what you want to see.**

TIP

As the picture is reduced in size by cropping, you might alternate between resizing the picture and cropping it to gain a better idea of what else to crop. To do that, you need to click outside the picture to change from cropping to sizing, click the picture, drag the sizing handles, click the **Crop** tool, drag the cropping handles, and so on.

- To cut an unwanted portion from one side of the picture, place the crop tool on a cropping handle, and drag it inward (vertically or horizontally) until the picture is reduced to what you want to see.

- If you want to cut unwanted portions equally from both sides of the picture (vertically or horizontally), press **CTRL** while dragging the crop tool. You can also press **SHIFT** to crop proportionally. Figure 6-3 shows an example of a picture being cropped.

3. When you have finished cropping your picture, click **ESC** to clear the cropping tool mode, and save your presentation. (Or click **Crop** again to turn it off.)

Manage Clips with the Clip Organizer

Clip Organizer is an application that works with other Microsoft Office applications and is used to organize your clips into a list of readily searchable

QUICKSTEPS

CHANGING CONTRAST AND BRIGHTNESS

See Figure 6-4 for examples of contrast and brightness.

CHANGE CONTRAST

1. If the Format tab is not selected, double-click the picture.

2. Click the **Contrast** button ▮ Contrast ▾ , and point to the menu options to see the effects on the picture.

3. Click the percentage that you want. Positive percentages increase the contrast; negative percentages decrease it.

CHANGE BRIGHTNESS

1. If the Format tab is not selected, double-click the picture.

2. Click the **Brightness** button ☼ Brightness ▾ , and point to the menu options to see the effects on the picture.

3. Click the percentage that you want. Positive percentages increase the brightness; negative percentages decrease it.

CHANGE BRIGHTNESS AND CONTRAST PRECISELY

1. If the Picture Tools Format tab is not showing, click the picture to be altered.

2. To display the Format Picture dialog box, where brightness and contrast can be applied, click either the **Brightness** or **Contrast** button to open the menu.

Continued . . .

▮ Contrast
◑ +40 %
◑ +30 %
◑ +20 %
◑ +10 %
◐ 0 % (Normal)
◑ -10 %
◑ -20 %
◑ -30 %
◑ -40 %
🎨 Picture Corrections Options...

Before applying contrast or brightness

After contrast is increased by 30%

After brightness is increased by 10%

Figure 6-4: **Examples of before and after increasing both contrast and brightness.**

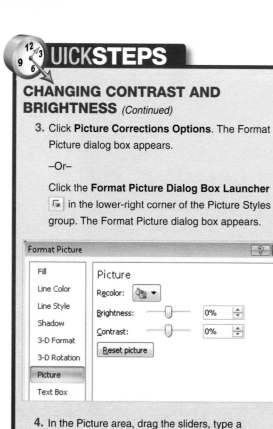

QUICKSTEPS

CHANGING CONTRAST AND BRIGHTNESS *(Continued)*

3. Click **Picture Corrections Options**. The Format Picture dialog box appears.

   –Or–

   Click the **Format Picture Dialog Box Launcher** ⌐ in the lower-right corner of the Picture Styles group. The Format Picture dialog box appears.

4. In the Picture area, drag the sliders, type a percentage, or click the respective spinners to apply the contrast and brightness. Click **Close** when you're done.

NOTE

You can display the Clip Organizer without being in a Microsoft application. Click **Start**, point to **All Programs**, select **Microsoft Office**, select **Microsoft Office Tools**, and click **Microsoft Clip Organizer**. Although some of the functions may not work or may work differently, you can still use it to find your most used clips.

collections. (Another way to see this: a list of folders currently containing your clips is organized into collections of shortcuts.) The collection names are taken from the folder name containing the clip art. The clips and folders are not physically moved to the collection list; rather, a shortcut to the clips is created and organized within the list, which can be searched. The clips include any art, audio, movies, or animation files.

DISPLAY THE CLIP ORGANIZER

1. Display the Clip Organizer by clicking the **Insert** tab and selecting **Clip Art**. The Clip Art task pane is displayed.

2. Click **Organize Clips** at the bottom of the task pane. The Microsoft Clip Organizer window opens, as shown in Figure 6-5.

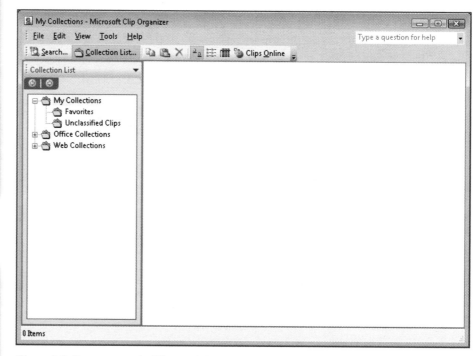

Figure 6-5: *You can use the Microsoft Clip Organizer to automatically organize your clips into a catalog or to organize only those folders you specify.*

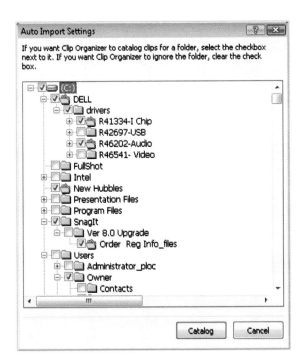

ADD CLIPS TO EXISTING FOLDERS

In Figure 6-5, you can see that there are three categories set up for you: My Collections, Office Collections, and Web Collections. Beneath My Collections, you have Favorites and Unclassified Clips for loosely organizing clips. If you have clips you want in these general categories, you can place them into a folder.

1. Open the Microsoft Clip Organizer window as described in "Display the Clip Organizer."

2. Click the **File** menu, click **Add Clips To Organizer**, and then click **On My Own**. The Add Clips To Organizer dialog box appears.

3. Click the clips you want. To select contiguous clips, press **SHIFT**, or to select non-contiguous clips, press **CTRL** while you click the clips. Then click **Add**

AUTOMATICALLY CATALOG CLIPS

To have the Clip Organizer automatically catalog your clips (which may take several minutes):

1. Click the **File** menu, click **Add Clips To Organizer**, and click **Automatically**. An Add Clips To Organizer dialog box will appear.

2. Click **OK** to start the process. It may take several minutes to complete. When it is done, it will display the completed catalog for you.

   –Or–

1. If you want to only catalog specific folders, click the **Options** button on the Add Clips To Organizer dialog box for the Auto Import Settings dialog box. A disk scan will be performed that will take a few minutes. Then you will be able to select the folders you want included.

2. Then remove the check marks next to those folders you do not want to be included in the catalog.

3. Click **Catalog** to start the process.

ADD FOLDERS TO THE CLIP ORGANIZER

You can also add other folders to the initial set to organize and establish pointers to other important clip folders.

1. Open the Microsoft Clip Organizer window as described in "Display the Clip Organizer."

DELETING A CLIP FROM THE CLIP ORGANIZER

To delete a clip from the catalog:

1. On the Clip Organizer dialog box, select the clip you want to delete.

2. Click the down arrow, and select one these options:

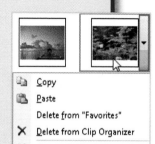

- **Delete From** *collection name* deletes the clip only from that catalog collection.

- **Delete From Clip Organizer** deletes the clip from the whole catalog.

---

2. Click the **File** menu, and click **New Collection**. The New Collection dialog box appears.

3. Type a name in the **Name** text box, and click the folder in which the new collection will be placed.

4. Click **OK**.

Search for Clip Art on the Web

To search the Internet for clip art, display the Clip Art task pane. Then:

1. Click the **Insert** tab, and click **Clip Art** in the Illustrations group.

2. On the Clip Art task pane, click **Clip Art On Office Online**. Your browser will open the Microsoft Online Clip Art site. Continue searching for the art you want.

3. Use Search to display categories of clip art. Type a keyword for the clip you want, and click the **Search** down arrow to limit the search to a specific category.

4. When you find a clip that you want to keep, click one of these options:

- Click the leftmost icon beneath the thumbnail image to add the image to the selection basket. Use this when you are collecting a number of images.

NOTE

The clip is not deleted from your computer. It is only removed from the collection reference, or its shortcut is removed from Clip Organizer. To delete the clip completely, you must delete it as you would any other file.

NOTE

You may be asked to download an add-on/ActiveX control before you can access the page.

RENAMING A COLLECTION

Although you cannot rename the default collections, such as Favorites and Unclassified Clips, you can change the names of your own collections. To change the name of a collection of clips:

1. In the Microsoft Clip Organizer window, in the Collection List task pane, select the collection to be renamed.

2. Right-click the collection to be renamed, and click **Rename** *collection name* from the context menu.

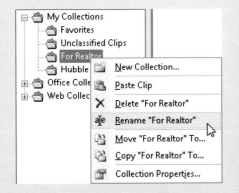

3. Type over the collection name in the Collection List. Press **ENTER**.

You can disable Snap To for one specific action by pressing **ALT** while you drag an object.

- Click the middle icon to look at an enlarged image and to see information under which it may be found, such as file name, media type, dimensions, resolution, file size, and keywords.

- Click the rightmost icon to copy the image to your Clipboard, where you can then paste it into a slide.

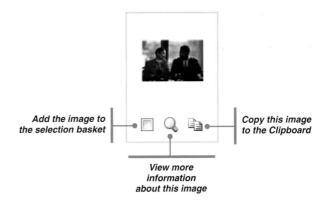

Add the image to the selection basket | **Copy this image to the Clipboard**

View more information about this image

5. Follow the prompts to complete the download of the selection basket and to close the browser window when you are finished.

Display a Grid and Guides

Grids and guides can help you align objects precisely.

1. Right-click the slide. Select **Grid And Guides** from the context menu. The Grid And Guides dialog box appears.

ADDING KEYWORDS OR CAPTIONS TO CLIPS

To add a keyword or a caption to the clips, use the Microsoft Clip Organizer.

1. To open the Microsoft Clip Organizer, click the **Insert** tab, and then click **Clip Art**. In the Clip Art task pane, click **Organize Clips**. The window will open.

2. Click the **Collection List** button to display the Collection List task pane. Select the clip to which you want to add keywords.

   📁 Collection List...

3. Right-click the clip and select **Edit Keywords** from the context menu. The Keywords dialog box appears. In the dialog box, the clip is displayed in the Preview pane; an example is seen in Figure 6-6.

   Edit Keywords...

ADD KEYWORDS

1. Under Keyword, type the keyword you want to associate with the clip. It will be added to the list of keywords that are already in the catalog.

2. Click **Add** to add the keyword to the list of keywords for the clip.

3. Click **Apply** when you are finished.

4. Click **OK** when you want to close the Keyword dialog box.

DELETE KEYWORDS

1. To delete a keyword, select it under Keyword, and click **Delete**.   Continued . . .

2. Select one or more of the following options by clicking the relevant check box:

   - **Snap Objects To Grid** aligns objects to a gridline.
   - **Snap Objects To Other Objects** aligns objects to adjacent objects.
   - The **Spacing** list box offers options to specify exact grid spacing.
   - **Display Grid On Screen** displays the grid on the screen.
   - **Display Drawing Guides On Screen** displays the guide settings on the computer screen.
   - **Set As Default** makes your current grid and guides settings the default settings.

3. Click **OK** to close the Grid And Guides dialog box.

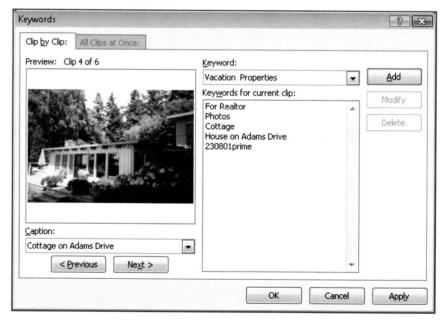

Figure 6-6: *Entering keywords and captions for your clips enables you to track and find them more easily.*

ADDING KEYWORDS OR CAPTIONS TO CLIPS *(Continued)*

2. Click **Apply** to make the change final. Click **OK** to close the dialog box.

MODIFY A KEYWORD

1. Select the keyword to be modified.

2. Under Keyword, type the keyword as you would like it to be. Click **Modify**.

3. Click **Apply** to make the change final. Click **OK** to close the dialog box.

ADD A CAPTION TO A CLIP

1. Under Caption, type the caption you want to assign to the clip.

2. Click **Apply** to make the change. Click **OK** to close the dialog box.

REVIEW OTHER CLIPS FOR KEYWORDS OR CAPTIONS

1. Click **Previous** to view the previous clip.

2. Click **Next** to view the next one.

NOTE

An object, as mentioned in the "Working with Objects" QuickSteps, is clip art, photos, a graph or chart, a table, a drawing, or text, and so on. OLE (Objects Linked or Embedded) objects, such as a spreadsheet, are either linked or embedded from another application, such as Microsoft Excel, and work in a slightly different way, as you'll see later in this chapter.

To move guidelines, click a line and drag it to where you want it. As you drag the line, a small box with a number in it changes to mark where you are from the starting point.

Use Format Painter

Use the Format Painter to copy attributes from one object to another. All attributes will be copied, such as color, border formatting, and text formatting. If the object is not ungrouped (see Chapter 8 for a discussion on grouping/ungrouping), the entire image will receive the copied attributes. In addition, if the object is a photo, the formatting won't be copied.

1. Select the object containing the attributes to be copied, whether it is a picture, clip art, AutoShape, or WordArt.

2. On the Home tab, click the **Format Painter** button in the Clipboard group.

3. Click the object where you want the formatting to be copied.

Use SmartArt Graphics

PowerPoint provides predefined graphics for inserting many flexible and professional-looking diagrams and connecting symbols. Figure 6-7 shows the categories, such as the "Cycle" category of SmartArt graphics that are available. Each category contains a description of the selected graphic and several variations.

Choose SmartArt Categories

Some of the SmartArt categories you can choose from include:

- **List**: Shows a list format. Items in the list may contain more text than other categories, and do not necessarily show relationships or processes, although they can. An example would be an artistic bulleted list.

If you have imported clip art, you may need to convert it to a Microsoft Office drawing object before it can be separated into the individual drawing shapes. To do this, click the clip art, click the **Home** tab, and click the **Arrange** button in the Drawing group. Click **Ungroup**. You will be asked if you want to convert your imported object to a Microsoft Office drawing object, click **Yes**. Then click the **Arrange** button again, and click **Ungroup**. This time, the image will be ungrouped.

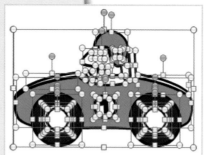

- **Process**: Shows a step-by-step relationship, such as a process moving from one task or situation to the next to accomplish a goal. Variations show processes emerging from a center, for example.

- **Cycle**: Shows a circular relationship, where items are on the same level, or priority. Variations can show overlapping processes or relationships to a central core.

- **Hierarchy**: Shows a hierarchical relationship with levels, for example, higher levels with lower ones reporting up, as in a traditional corporate organization.

- **Relationship**: Shows a variety of related items, some very complex—from A+B=C to a Venn diagram, and more.

- **Matrix**: Shows a relationship of parts to a whole, such as four quadrants to a whole.

- **Pyramid**: Shows a pyramid-shaped relationship, where a larger base supports an increasingly smaller tip (or the reverse, where the top is larger).

To choose between them, you must be clear on what you are trying to show, what structure best displays the data, and how much data there is to display (some of the graphics do not hold a lot of text).

Insert a Diagram

To insert a SmartArt graphic:

1. Click the **Insert** tab, and click **SmartArt**. The Choose A SmartArt Graphic dialog box appears (see Figure 6-7).

2. Click the category on the left, and then select a graphic on the right. When you click a graphic, a display of it is previewed on the right along with a description.

3. When you find the graphic you want, select it and click **OK** to close the dialog box and insert the graphic. The SmartArt Tools tabs, Design and Format, are now available on the ribbon.

4. In the Type Your Text Here text box, click a bullet and type your text. As you type, the text will be recorded in the appropriate shape.

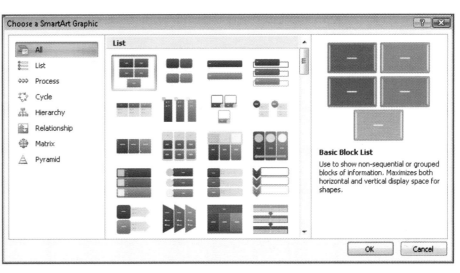

Figure 6-7: SmartArt graphics offer you many choices for adding professional-looking and complex "working" graphics to your presentation.

Change SmartArt Designs

When you click a SmartArt object, the SmartArt Tools Design and Format tabs are made available. The SmartArt Tools Design tab contains several ways to change your SmartArt:

- Click the **Add Shape** down arrow in the Create Graphic group to add another shape to the graphic. It may be another text box, circle, layer, bullet, or whatever shape makes up the design. Click the placement option you want.
- Click **Add Bullet** in the Create Graphic group to add another label or bullet to the text box. The bullet is initially added as a sub-bullet to an existing shape.
- Click **Right To Left** to orient the shape in the opposite direction.
- Click **Layouts** to work with organization chart branch layouts, if you have selected that type of chart from the Hierarchy category.
- Click the **Promote** and **Demote** buttons in the Create Graphic group to move the selected circle, level, text box, or whatever the shape is, to a higher or lower level.
- Click **Text Pane** to add or alter the text on the graphic, as is being done in Figure 6-8.

NOTE

The SmartArt Tools Format tab contains many familiar tools to change the graphic, such as Shape Fill, Shape Outline, and Shape Effects. However, the Shapes group is a bit unique. It allows you to make *selected* graphic elements larger, smaller, or to change shape. If your graphic is 3-D, you can edit it in 2-D in order to resize or move it.

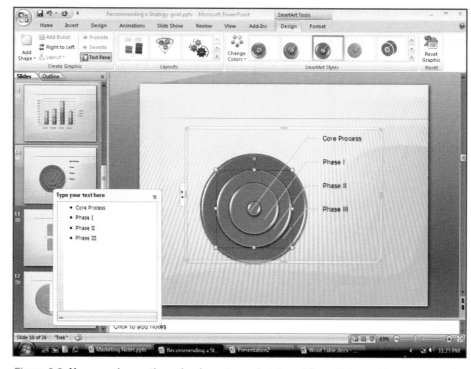

Figure 6-8: *You can change the color, layouts, and styles of SmartArt graphics; you can also add or remove graphic elements to make them fit your needs.*

- Click the Layouts group **More** down arrow to display a menu of layout options for the graphic. Point to the options to see the effects on your graphic.

- Click **Change Colors** in the Quick Styles group to change the colors of the design. Note that when you insert another of the same type, it reverts to the default theme colors.

- Click a **SmartArt** thumbnail in the SmartArt Styles group to change the style of the graphic, as was done in Figure 6-8.

- Click **Reset Graphic** to return the graphic to its original state.

Chapter 7

Using Charts in a Presentation

You add graphs and charts to make your presentations more interesting and informative. With these tools, you can add visual information to your presentation, making it more easily absorbed and understood. You reach more viewers with complete information, as it is easier to absorb pictures than numbers or words.

In this chapter you will see how to insert and format charts in your presentation. You will insert charts from scratch or import them from Microsoft Excel. You will learn how to perfect them by entering your own data, selecting your own type of chart, and formatting chart components—such as titles, data series, x- and y-axes, plot area, text, and axis numbers.

Work with Graphs and Charts

You can create a chart or graph from scratch within PowerPoint or import one from Excel. In this book, graphs and charts are the same thing. When you first create a chart or graph in PowerPoint (and if you have Microsoft Excel 2007 installed), you'll see a model chart displayed on the selected slide and the data creating it contained in a separate Excel window. If the data or chart comes from Excel 2007, that application is opened and its ribbon and toolbars are available in a separate window, integrated with the PowerPoint ribbon and toolbars, to modify its own component. You can embed the chart, wherein the data is totally contained within PowerPoint, copy or paste the Excel chart as an image (it cannot be edited), or you can link the chart back to an Excel worksheet, wherein it is able to be updated when the original worksheet is modified.

Insert Charts

When you first insert a chart, PowerPoint inserts a sample chart with a separate window containing an Excel worksheet. You replace the data in the worksheet with your own data, and it is reflected in the PowerPoint chart. You can also replace the chart with one of a different type, that is, a pie or radial graph for a bar chart. You'll have plenty of room. A chart can contain up to 255 data series. A *data series* is a group of related data points that are plotted on a chart. Each data series can have up to 4,000 data points.

INSERT A CHART FROM WITHIN POWERPOINT

When you insert a chart using PowerPoint's tools, you are embedding a chart; that is, the data defining the chart is wholly contained within PowerPoint even though you use Excel to define the data. To insert a graph within PowerPoint:

1. Click the slide that is to contain the chart or graph. Find a layout that contains the layout format and enough space for the chart you want.

2. If the layout contains a chart icon, click the **Insert Chart** icon 📊. Otherwise, click the **Insert** tab, and then click **Chart**.

3. An Insert Chart dialog box will appear. Choose the type of chart you want, and click **OK**. A sample chart will be inserted in the Slide pane and a separate window containing a worksheet in Excel 2007 will open, as shown in Figure 7-1.

NOTE

In this book, charts and graphs refer to the same component.

NOTE

If you do not have Microsoft Excel 2007 installed, or if you are using a chart or graph created in a previous version of PowerPoint, Microsoft Graph will be the application used to create charts. When you work with Microsoft Graph, a separate window opens with the toolbars and commands of that application.

NOTE

Here is some chart terminology: **x-axis** is the horizontal axis that normally contains the categories or types of data in a chart; **y-axis** is the vertical axis that normally contains the value or quantities of a chart; **z-axis** is the depth axis that is present in a three-dimensional (3-D) chart.

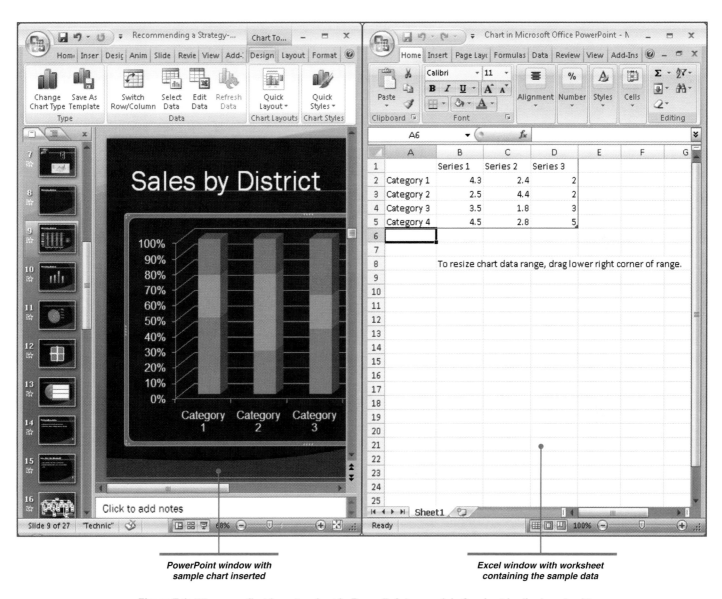

*PowerPoint window with
sample chart inserted*

*Excel window with worksheet
containing the sample data*

*Figure 7-1: When you first insert a chart in PowerPoint, a model of a chart is displayed, with
a separate Excel window containing the data for it.*

4. Modify the chart and worksheet as needed. (See "Enter Chart Data".)

5. Save the Excel worksheet and then the PowerPoint presentation.

COPY AND PASTE A CHART FROM EXCEL USING SMARTTAG

Excel is primarily a data collection and analysis program; PowerPoint presents data and other information. You can use Microsoft Office 2007 to achieve the best of both worlds by using Excel to retain and manipulate the data and then copying the charts to PowerPoint for use in presentations. You have several options as to the relationship between the data in Excel and the charts in PowerPoint.

1. In Excel, right-click a blank area of the chart, and click **Copy** (or use one of several alternative copying techniques, such as dragging over the chart cells).

2. Open PowerPoint 2007. Find the slide you want, right-click where you want the Excel chart inserted, and click **Paste**. The chart appears as it did in Excel.

3. Click the **Paste Options Smart-Tag** in the lower-right corner of the chart, as shown in Figure 7-2. There are two sets of options, the first set determines the relationship with Excel:

- **Chart (Linked To Excel Data)** copies the chart and maintains a link with the source workbook, so changes made to the data are updated in the PowerPoint chart as well (assuming the link isn't broken by removing the workbook or deleting the data). Updates are made automatically when both source and destination documents are opened, unless default settings have been changed.

*Figure 7-2: **Charts are easily copied from Excel to PowerPoint, where you can link to the data or transfer the entire workbook into the destination file.***

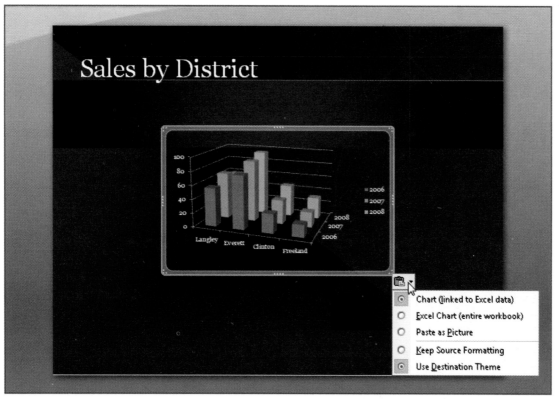

QUICKSTEPS

VIEWING AND CHANGING EXCEL SOURCE DATA

You can easily navigate between the data contained in an Excel worksheet and the chart in PowerPoint.

EDIT THE CHART DATA

To display the Excel worksheet containing the data for a chart so you can edit it:

1. Click the chart to display the Chart Tools ribbon.

2. On the Chart Tools Design tab, click **Edit Data** in the Data group. The Excel window will open, displaying the chart data.

EDIT THE DATA SOURCE ATTRIBUTES

To change the attributes of the data itself:

1. Click the chart to display the Chart Tools ribbon.

2. On the Chart Tools Design tab, click **Select Data** in the Data group. The chart data is displayed and the Select Data Source dialog box will appear, as shown in Figure 7-3:

- **Excel Chart (Entire Workbook)** embeds the chart and workbook data into the destination file so that both the chart and data can be changed independently of the source workbook.

- **Paste As Picture** inserts the chart as a standalone picture. No changes to the component are allowed by the destination program, and no data updates are provided by Excel.

4. The second set of options on the SmartTag menu control how the copied chart appears in the destination program:

- **Keep Source Formatting** copies the chart as it appears in Excel.

- **Use Destination Theme** resets the chart's styling to match the current theme in PowerPoint, providing a more unified look.

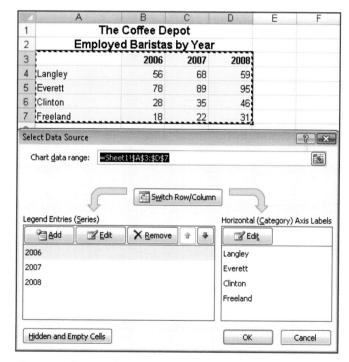

Figure 7-3: Use the Select Data Source dialog box to change attributes of the source data, such as its range, labels, row-and-column orientation, and how empty and hidden cells will be plotted.

QUICKSTEPS

VIEWING AND CHANGING EXCEL SOURCE DATA *(Continued)*

- To change the data range included in the chart, either select a new range or type over the range in the **Chart Data Range** text box. (To manipulate the worksheet more easily, click the **Collapse** button 📄 to minimize the dialog box; click it again to maximize it.)

- To switch the x and y-axis, click the **Switch Row/Column** button. The data previously plotted horizontally in rows will now be plotted vertically in columns.

- To work with the data series entries, click **Add** to add a new series (a new legend entry), click **Edit** to edit the current data series, or click **Remove** to delete a data series.

- To rearrange the legend entries, click the **Move Up** or **Move Down** arrows.

- To edit the range of cells included in the category axis labels, click **Edit**.

- To establish how empty cells will be plotted, and whether the data contained in hidden rows and columns will be plotted as well, click **Hidden and Empty Cell Settings**.

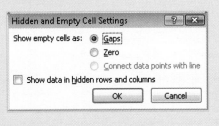

3. Click **OK**.

Enter Chart Data

When inserting a new chart, you will need to replace the sample data in the chart with your own data. Be sure to replace all the data and delete the contents of any leftover cells; otherwise, any remaining data will be used to generate the chart.

1. If the Microsoft Excel 2007 window is not open, click the chart to display the Chart Tools ribbon. Click the **Design** tab, and click the **Edit Data** button in the Data group. Figure 7-4 shows the sample datasheet automatically inserted.

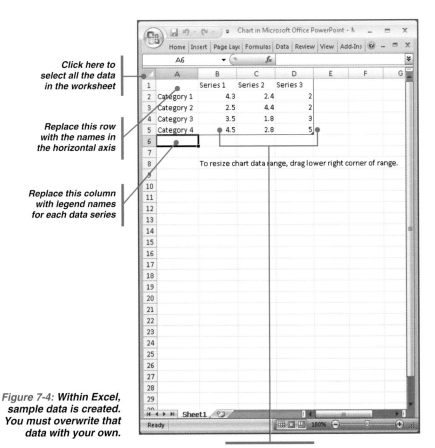

Figure 7-4: Within Excel, sample data is created. You must overwrite that data with your own.

2. To clear the current contents, click the **Select All** button on the upper-left corner of the datasheet, and then press DELETE.

3. Enter your legend titles on the leftmost column. Enter the titles of your *horizontal axis* on the top row by clicking in a cell and typing. As you make your changes, you will see the chart instantly change.

4. Enter the data series points; that is, the series of data pertaining to one row or column on the datasheet.

Select the Type of Chart

When you insert a chart or graph, you are asked what type of chart you want to create. You can select the type of chart you want to create from several options, depending on your data and how you want it displayed.

1. Click the chart to display the Chart Tools ribbon. On the Design tab, click the **Change Chart Type** button in the Type group.

   –Or–

   Right-click in a background area of the chart, and choose **Change Chart Type**. (If you don't see that option in the context menu, right-click in a different spot on the chart.) The Change Chart Type dialog box displays a menu of chart type options, as shown in Figure 7-5.

2. Click a chart type on the left of the menu. You will see the variations available for that type.

3. Choose the variation you want by clicking it. Then click **OK**.

Show or Hide Leader Lines on a Pie Chart

Leader lines connect the chart to data labels, which identify the data being viewed. (See the following "Personnel Profile" illustration.)

1. Click the pie chart to display the Chart Tools ribbon. Right-click the "pie" elements on the chart and click **Add Data Labels**. Click the data labels and drag them where you want them.

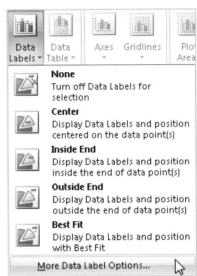

Figure 7-5: *You can choose among many different chart types and variations among each type.*

2. Click the **Layout** tab, and click **Data Labels** in the Labels group. A context menu is displayed.

3. Click **More Data Label Options**. The Format Data Labels dialog box will appear.

4. Click the **Show Leader Lines** check box.

5. Click **Close**. The chart will be displayed with leader lines, as shown here.

CAUTION

If the data labels are placed too close to the chart, the leader lines will not appear. Move your data labels away from the chart, allowing enough space for leader lines to make a difference.

NOTE

To display the Format Data Labels, you can also right-click the chart and click **Format Data Labels**.

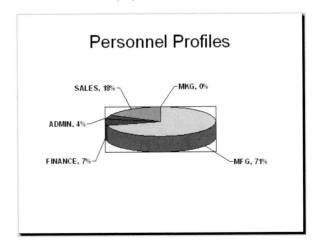

Format Charts

Formatting is used to change color, contents, text font and size, chart lines, and plot area. The formatting options vary depending on the type of chart. This chapter primarily discusses formatting for bar charts. Other chart types are similar, but not exactly the same as what is discussed here.

Most formatting is available:

- From the Chart Tools Format tab

  –Or–

- By choosing the More *element* Options menu option, listed in the menus of the layout commands in the Labels, Axes, and Background groups found on the Chart Tools Layout tab (for example, click Chart Title in the Labels group and select More Title Options).

USE FORMAT DIALOG BOXES

When you right-click an element, the context menu will contain a Format *element* option. This displays the same dialog box as when you choose More *element* Options on the menus of commands on the Chart Tools Layout and Format tabs. Since, for the most part, the options for a type of element are similar, they are described here. In other words, you have the same options for modifying lines—whether they are on the plot area, gridlines, or legend—as you do for text—whether the text is in the legend, the labels, the title, or the axes. See Table 7-1 as a reference. When the options are unique to the element, they are described in the appropriate "Format *element*" section that follows.

To use the common formatting options:

1. To display the Format *elements* dialog box, right-click the element and choose the **Format *element*** option:

   - Click **element Options** (if available) to set unique element options. (For example, for chart legends, Legend Options positions the element on the chart and specifies whether the legend can overlay the chart.

TIP

The element displayed in the Chart Elements button on the Chart Tools Format tab changes as you select an element on the chart. For example, when you select a column, the option will be Series *name*; when you select an axis, the option will be *named* Axis; when you select the legend, the option will be Legend.

NOTE

The options on the Format *elements* dialog box will vary, depending on the type of chart. For instance, a pie chart will have different options than a bar chart. In addition, the attributes within an option will be different. For example, the Fill attributes for a pie chart are different from those for a bar chart.

QUICKSTEPS

SELECTING CHART ELEMENTS

Depending on the type of changes to be made, there are several ways to select the chart element you want. Either:

- Click the element. In some cases, you may have to click more than once to get a single element out of a group. For instance, click the first time to select all elements of a type, such as the data series (columns in a bar chart, for instance). Click a second time to select only a single element (such as a single column).

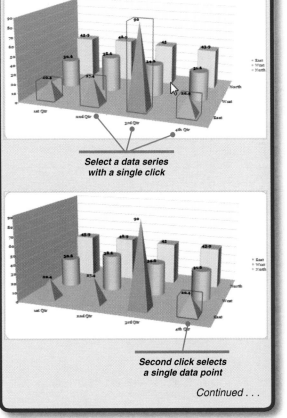

Select a data series with a single click

Second click selects a single data point

Continued . . .

FORMATTING OPTIONS	DESCRIPTION	APPLY TO
Fill	Provides options for gradient, picture, or texture fill, as well as color choices, degrees of transparency, and gradient options	Axis, chart area, data labels/series, legend, plot area, titles, walls/floors
Line	Offers solid or gradient lines, as well as color choices, degrees of transparency, and gradient options	Axis, chart area, data labels/series, error bars, gridlines, legend, plot area, titles, trendlines, walls/floors
Line Style	Provides options for width, dashed, and compound (multiple) lines, as well as styles for line ends and line joins	Axis, chart area, data labels/series, error bars, gridlines, legend, plot area, titles, trendlines, walls/floors
Shadow	Provides preset shadow styles and controls for color, transparency, size, blur, angle, and distance	Axis, chart area, data labels/series, legend, plot area, titles, trendlines, walls/floors
3-D Format	Adds 3-D effect to shapes; provides top, bottom, material, and lighting presets and controls for depth contours and color	Axis, chart area, data labels/series, legend, plot area, titles, walls/floors
3-D Rotation	Provides angular rotation and perspective adjustments, as well as positioning and scaling controls	Walls/floors
Number	Provides the same number formats as the Format Cells Number tab, such as currency, accounting, date, and time	Axis, data labels
Alignment	Vertically aligns, rotates, and stacks text	Axis, data labels, titles, legends

Table 7-1: Formatting Options for Chart Elements

–Or–

- Click the **Chart Tools Layout** tab, and, from the ribbon commands, click the element you want. You will be shown a menu of layout choices.

–Or–

- Click the **Chart Tools Format** tab, and, from the Current Selection group, click the **Chart Elements** down arrow. From the menu of elements, click the one you want. (When you use this approach, you then select the changes you want by clicking **Format Selection** from the Current Selection group for the Format *element* dialog box for formatting choices.)

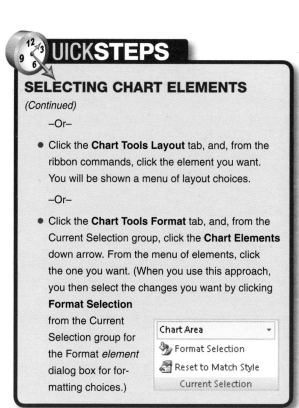

- Click **Number** to define what kinds of numbers are being formatted—for instance, currency, dates or times, percentages, fractions, etc. Also, you can establish whether the number is linked to a source worksheet.

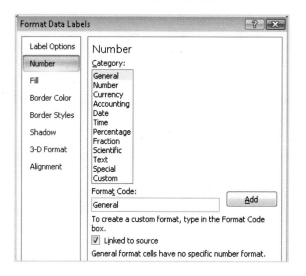

- Click **Fill** to add a color background to the element. Choose No Fill, Solid Fill, Gradient Fill, and Picture or Texture Fill. Each option displays unique content in the dialog box.

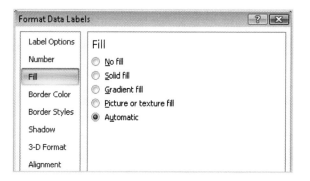

- Click **Border Color** to format the border of the element. Choose No Line, Solid Line, and Gradient Line (and Rounded Corners for Chart Area), or the default Automatic.

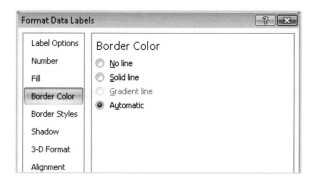

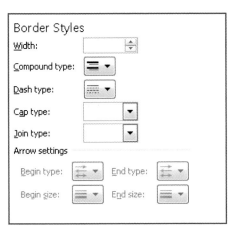

Border Styles

Width:

Compound type:

Dash type:

Cap type:

Join type:

Arrow settings

Begin type: End type:

Begin size: End size:

*Figure 7-6: **Use the Border Styles formatting dialog box to change attributes relating to line style.***

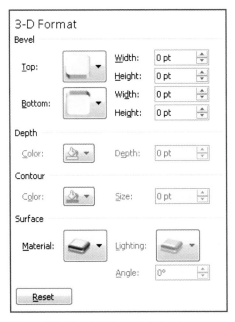

3-D Format

Bevel

Top: Width: 0 pt
        Height: 0 pt

Bottom: Width: 0 pt
        Height: 0 pt

Depth

Color: Depth: 0 pt

Contour

Color: Size: 0 pt

Surface

Material: Lighting:

            Angle: 0°

Reset

*Figure 7-7: **The 3-D Format dialog box controls the degree of "3-D look" to a chart.***

- Click **Border Styles** to change the width, **Compound Type** for a single or double line, **Dash Type** for the type of dashed line, **Cap Type** for the shape of the line, **Join Type** for how lines are joined to other lines, and **Arrow Settings** to set the beginning and end style and size of the arrows. Figure 7-6 shows this dialog box.

- Click **Shadow** to apply a shadow effect to a chart element. You can select a preset style of shadow; set the shadow color, darkness, or transparency; set the size of the shadow; set the blur or distinctness of the shadow; and determine the angle and distance from the border.

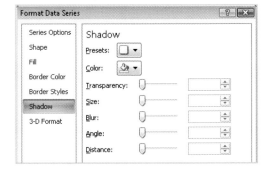

- Click **3-D Format** (see Figure 7-7) to format the element with a bevel effect. You can change the shape of the bevel, its depth and color, the contours and color, and surface material and lighting.

- Click **3-D Rotation** (see Figure 7-8) to establish the rotation of the chart, whether the text is rotated or flat, the object's position from the ground of the chart, and the chart scale for a chart wall or floor (its depth and height as a percentage of the base or whether it is automatically scaled).

- Click **Alignment** (or sometimes **Text Box)** to change the text layout (its vertical alignment and text direction), whether AutoFit should be applied to the text (the text box is resized for the text or the text is downsized for the text box), and what the internal margins are within the text box.

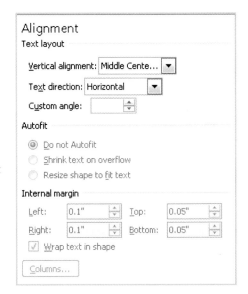

2. Click **OK** to close the Format *elements* dialog box.

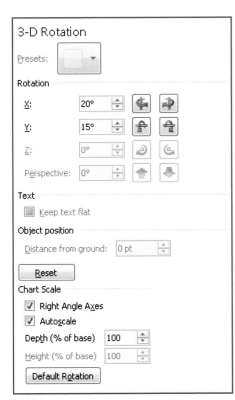

Figure 7-8: *The 3-D Rotation dialog box controls the rotation of walls and floors and related text, and sets the chart scale.*

FORMAT LEGENDS

1. Click the **Chart Tools Layout** tab, and click **Legend**. A menu will open, as shown in Figure 7-9.

2. Click one of the options to hide the legend or position it on the chart.

–Or–

Click the **More Legend Options** to open the Format Legend dialog box. Under Legend Options, you can establish where on the chart the legend will be placed and whether it will be permitted to overlay the chart itself. See "Use Format Dialog Boxes" for detailed information on other formatting options.

ALTER A CHART TITLE

To change the title of a chart:

Right-click the title and select **Format Chart Title**. The Format Chart Title dialog box appears. See "Use Format Dialog Boxes" for detailed information on other formatting options. Click **OK** to close the Format Chart Title dialog box.

–Or–

Click the chart to display the Chart Tools tabs, click the **Layout** tab, and click **Chart Title** in the Labels group. From the menu, click one of these options:

- Click **None** to hide the chart title.
- Click **Centered Overlay Title** to center the title on the chart and to overlay contents, if needed.
- Click **Above Chart** to display the title at the top of the chart and to avoid overlaying the contents by reducing the size of the chart.

Click **More Title Options** to open the Format Chart Title dialog box. See "Use Format Dialog Boxes" for detailed information on other formatting options. Click **OK** to close the Format Chart Title dialog box.

–Or–

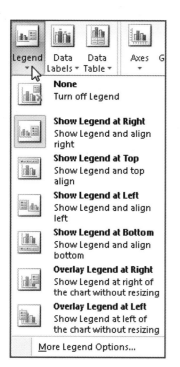

Figure 7-9: *You can modify the legend of a chart by changing its position on the chart or by formatting its lines and text.*

To just change the title contents and the text attributes, highlight the title to select it, type over the title, click the **Home** tab, and use the tools in the Font group. However, if you are changing a linked chart, you'll have to make any revisions to the source data in the Excel worksheet.

FORMAT A DATA SERIES

To format a data series:

1. Click the chart to display the Chart Tools tabs. Click the **Format** tab.

2. Click **Chart Elements** in the Current Selection group to see a list of elements on the chart. Click the data series you want to change. The element will be selected, as you can verify on the chart.

3. Click **Format Selection** in the Current Selection group. The Format Data Series dialog box appears.

4. Select from these options:

   ● In **Series Options**, drag the **Gap Depth** slider to set the distance the data series is from the front of the chart (only available for 3-D charts).

   ● In **Series Options**, drag the **Gap Width** slider to set the width of the gap between data series, as you can see in Figure 7-10.

5. See "Use Format Dialog Boxes" for detailed information on other formatting options.

FORMAT DATA LABELS

To format the data labels:

1. Click the chart to display the Chart Tools tabs. Click the **Layout** tab.

2. Click **Data Labels** in the Labels group to display a menu of options.

   ● Click **None** to hide or turn off data labels. They cannot be selected when this option is selected.

   ● Click **Show** to show or turn on the data labels so that they can be selected.

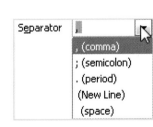

Figure 7-10: *The Format Data Series dialog box contains options to position the data series from the front of the 3-D chart and to set the width of the gap between data series.*

Gap Depth establishes how far back the data series rests on the chart

Gap Width sets the width of the data series

Label Options

Label Contains

- ☐ Series Name
- ☐ Category Name
- ☑ Value

[Reset Label Text]

- ☐ Include legend key in label

Separator [▌] [▼]

Separator [▌] [▲]

, (comma)
; (semicolon)
. (period)
(New Line)
(space)

3. Click **More Data Labels Options** for additional formatting options. In the Label Options category, select from among the following:

- **Series Name** indicates that the label will contain the name of the data series.

- **Category Name** includes the category in the label.

- **Value** includes the value in the label. Value is the default label content.

- **Reset Label Text** restores the default of Value only.

- **Include Legend Key In Label** places the key (identifying color, for example) in the label.

- **Separator** indicates how multiple elements in the label will be separated. A comma is the default.

4. See "Use Format Dialog Boxes" for detailed information on other formatting options.

5. Click **Close** to close the dialog box.

FORMAT AN AXIS

To format an axis for a bar chart and define the maximum, minimum, and incremental values, set tick marks, positioning, and more:

1. Click the chart to display the Chart Tools tabs. Click the **Layout** tab.

2. Click **Axes** in the Axes group to display a menu of options. Select **Primary Horizontal Axis** (the x-axis), **Primary Vertical Axis** (the y-axis), and, when available, **Depth Axis** (the z-axis). With the Primary Horizontal Axis option of a column chart, you have the following choices:

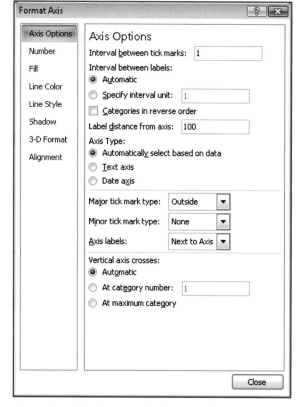

- Click **None** to hide or turn off the axis.

- Click **Show Left To Right Axis** to display vertical labels on left edge of chart and start the category axis on the left.

- Click **Show Axis Without Labeling** to suppress the labels and tick marks.

- Click **Show Right To Left Axis** to display vertical labels on the right edge of chart and start the category axis on the right.

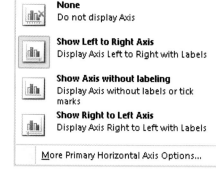

3. If you click **More Primary Horizontal Axis Options**, you'll see a dialog box of additional formatting options. (Step 4 explains the More Primary Vertical Axis Options menu.) These options are shown in Figure 7-11. In the Axis Options category, you have the following options:

- **Interval Between Tick Marks** sets the number of units between tick marks.

- **Interval Between Labels** can be set in two ways. Select **Automatic** to have PowerPoint determine the interval between labels, click **Specify Interval Unit**, and then type a number if you want to refine the interval.

- **Categories In Reverse Order** displays the x-axis categories in reverse, from right to left.

- **Label Distance From Axis** sets how many units are between the label and the axis.

Figure 7-11: ***The Format Axis dialog box is used to define the attributes of a selected axis. This example shows the options for the horizontal axis (the category axis) of a column type chart.***

- **Axis Type** determines whether the axis is numeric, dates, or text. Select between **Automatically Select Based On Data**, **Text Axis**, and **Date Axis.**

- **Major Tick Mark Type** and **Minor Tick Mark Type** determine whether the tick marks are inside the axis, outside the axis, or positioned across it.

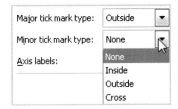

- **Axis Labels** indicates where the labels are in relation to the axis: Next to Axis places them adjacent to the axis; High places them on the top of the chart; Low places them beneath the axis; None causes no labels to be displayed.

- **Vertical Axis Crosses** establishes where the y-axes will intersect with the x-axis. Normally, they cross at the left or right end of the horizontal axis. You can have them cross somewhere within the middle of the plot area, based on the choices offered. Select **Automatic** to let PowerPoint determine the crossover; select **At Category Number** to manually set the crossover; or select **At Maximum Category** to establish the point on the y-axis where the largest value will cross the x-axis

4. If you click **More Primary Vertical Axis Options** at the bottom of the Primary Vertical Axis menu, you'll see a different dialog box of additional formatting options, shown in Figure 7-12. You have the following choices:

- **Minimum** changes the lowest value automatically; or you can type a fixed value in the text box.

- **Maximum** changes the highest value automatically; or you can type a fixed value in the text box.

- **Major Unit** shows the largest increments displayed automatically; or you can type a value in the text box.

- **Minor Unit** shows the smallest increments displayed automatically; or you can type a value in the text box.

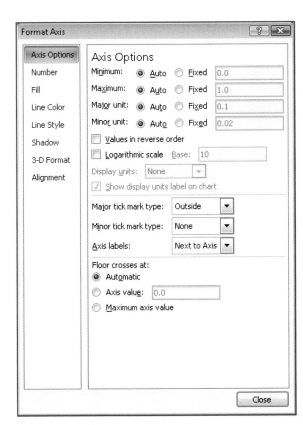

Figure 7-12: **The Vertical Axis Format Axis dialog box defines the attributes of the y-axis.**

- **Values In Reverse Order** displays the largest value at the bottom of the axis and the smallest at the top.

- **Logarithmic Scale** displays the values in a logarithmic relationship, rather than in an arithmetic one.

- **Display Units** shows a menu of units that can be displayed. If you select a quantity, you can select Show Display Units Label On Chart.

- **Major Tick Mark Type** and **Minor Tick Mark Type** determine whether the tick marks are inside the axis, outside the axis, or positioned across it.

- **Axis Labels** indicates where the labels are in relation to the axis. Next To Axis places them adjacent to the axis; High places them on the top of the chart; Low places them beneath the axis; None causes no labels to be displayed.

- **Floor Crosses At** establishes the point or value on the vertical axis where the horizontal axis will cross it. Select **Automatic** to have PowerPoint to determine this; select **Axis Value** to set the value yourself; or select **Maximum Axis Value** to establish the point on the horizontal axis where the largest value will cross the vertical axis.

3. Click **Close** to close the dialog box.

FORMAT THE PLOT AREA

The chart area encompasses the total chart area, whereas the plot area is a subset of the total chart area. The plot area is the background upon which the chart rests. It can be formatted with color and fill effects, and its border can be formatted to take on a different style, thickness, or color.

1. Click the chart to display the Chart Tools tabs. Click the **Format** tab.

2. Click **Chart Elements** in the Current Selection group, and click **Plot Area**. Then click **Format Selection** in the Current Selection group. The Format Plot Area dialog box appears.

3. See "Use Format Dialog Boxes" for detailed information on the formatting options.

4. Click **OK** to close the dialog box.

FORMAT TEXT

You can format text in a chart by changing its font, font style, font size, and color. If you are changing data in a linked file, you must make the changes in the source worksheet, in Excel, for instance. However, text in a label is changed in PowerPoint.

1. Select the chart element that contains the text to be formatted.
2. Click the **Home** tab, and use any of the tools in the Font group.

FORMAT GRIDLINES

To make gridlines less obvious or more apparent (usually in order to help viewers visually):

1. Click the chart to display the Chart Tools tabs.
2. Click the **Layout** tab, and click **Gridlines** in the Axes group. A menu is displayed.
3. Choose among these options:

   ● **Primary Horizontal Gridlines** displays or hides major and minor horizontal (or x-axis) gridlines.

   ● **Primary Vertical Gridlines** displays or hides the major and minor vertical (or y-axis) gridlines.

   ● **Depth Gridlines (3-D Only)** shows or hides the major depth and minor depth (or z-axis) gridlines.

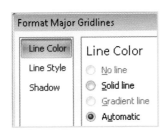

4. For any of the gridlines, click **More *type* Gridlines Options** to display the Format Gridlines dialog box, where you can change the line and line styles. (See "Format Dialog Boxes" for detailed information on the options.)
5. Click **Close** when you have made your choices.

How to...

- *Transition Between Slides*
- *Animate Objects and Slides*
- *Understanding Animation Effects*
- *Use Special Effects for Placeholders*
- *Work with WordArt*
- *Draw a Shape*
- *Working with Curves*
- *Type Text Within a Shape*
- *Combine Shapes by Grouping*
- *Create a Mirror Image*
- *Positioning Shapes*
- *Format Shapes*
- *Aligning Shapes*
- *Use Zoom*

Chapter 8
Using Special Effects and Drawing in PowerPoint

This chapter works with two interesting and creative aspects of PowerPoint: its special-effects capabilities and its drawing features. Special effects make your slides more interesting, allowing transitioning between slides, animating objects or slides, and creating engaging backgrounds. With the drawing features, you can create shapes or use predefined shapes to design your own diagrams, charts, clip art, and other objects to enhance your presentations.

Work with Special Effects

Special effects add that touch of "professionalism" that dresses up your presentation. For example, transitions between slides are easy to implement and add interest when moving from one slide to the next. Animation also makes a presentation come alive by adding action to your slides. Finally, you can add gradient colors, textures, patterns, or pictures to your slide backgrounds.

Transition Between Slides

Transitions are used to lead from one slide to the next. For example, you can have one slide dissolve and another emerge, have slides slip in from the side, or have them emerge from the center. There are many more possibilities—all easy to implement. You can also add sounds, vary the speed of transitions, and vary the effect on each slide. Or, you can make all transitions the same. Figure 8-1 shows the transition commands available in the Animations tab:

1. First, display the slides in Slide Sorter view by clicking **Slide Sorter** view ⊞ . This will make it easier to see the slides to which you will apply the transitions.

2. Select one or more slides that will have the transition effect. To select adjacent slides, hold down **SHIFT** while you click the first and last slides in the range. To select noncontiguous slides, hold down **CTRL** while you click the desired slides.

3. Click the **Animations** tab on the ribbon, and then click the **More** button in the Transition To This Slide group. The menu shown in Figure 8-2 will be displayed.

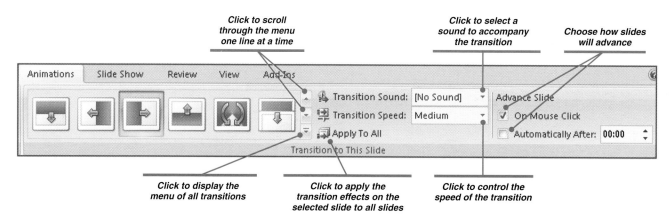

Click to scroll through the menu one line at a time

Click to select a sound to accompany the transition

Choose how slides will advance

Click to display the menu of all transitions

Click to apply the transition effects on the selected slide to all slides

Click to control the speed of the transition

Figure 8-1: **The Transition To This Slide group on the Animations tab displays commands for slides transition .**

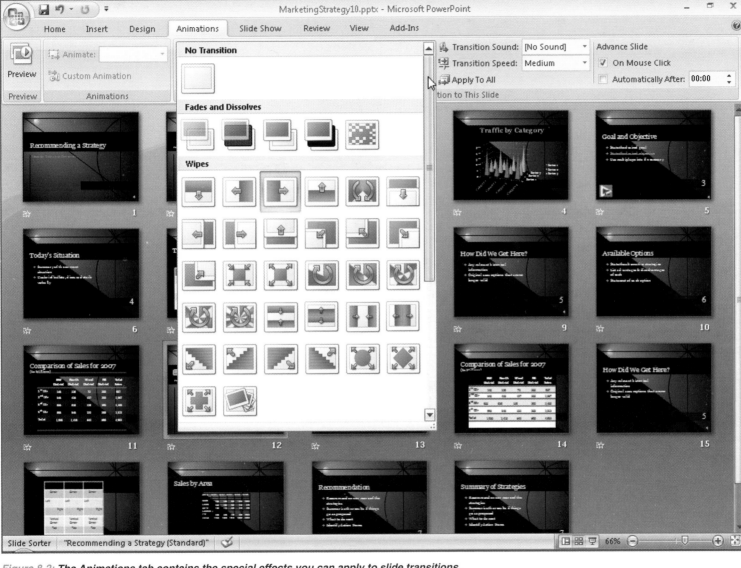

Figure 8-2: *The Animations tab contains the special effects you can apply to slide transitions.*

4. Select from these options:

- Scroll through the list of transitions, as shown in Figure 8-2, and click a transition for the slides selected in step 2.

- In the Transition To This Slide area, click the **Transition Sound** down arrow, and choose a sound to accompany the transition. "No Sound" is the default. (If you click "Other Sound" you can install a sound file of your own.)

- Click the **Transition Speed** down arrow, and choose **Slow**, **Medium**, or **Fast**.

- Click **On Mouse Click** if you want to advance to the next slide by clicking the mouse.

- Click **Automatically After** and fill in the time if you want the slides to automatically advance after a certain period of time.

- Click **Apply To All** to assign the transition effects and sound to the whole presentation. Otherwise, the effects will be applied only to selected slides.

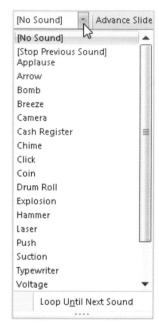

5. Click the **Preview** button in the Preview group to see the effects for one slide.

6. Click **Slide Show** 🖵 to view the slide show with transition effects.

Animate Objects and Slides

Transitions apply when one slide is advanced to another. Animation, on the other hand, is applied to objects on a slide. You can animate text, graphics, charts, and other objects. You can apply animation to all the text, bullets, and graphics on a slide as a whole or to selected objects, such as one line of text. (To apply animation selectively, see "Add Custom Animation.")

APPLY ANIMATION TO SLIDES

1. Display the slide in Normal view so that you can easily see what needs to be animated. Select the placeholder containing the objects or text on the slide that you want to animate as a whole.

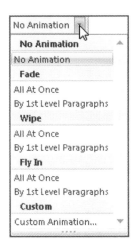

Figure 8-3: *You can animate objects or text as a whole on a slide simultaneously. This figure shows the menu for text, which can be animated as a whole or by paragraphs.*

2. On the Animations tab, click the **Animate** down arrow in the Animations group. A menu is displayed, an example of which is shown in Figure 8-3. The menu options will vary with the type of placeholder (text is different from a chart, for instance).

3. If you have selected text, choose from among these options:

   - **No Animation** removes all animation effects from the selection.
   - **Fade** causes the selected object to fade in.
   - **Wipe** causes the selected object to appear bit by bit, from bottom of the object to the top.
   - **Fly In** causes the selected object to fly into position from the bottom of the slide.
   - **Custom Animation** applies separate animation to the objects on a slide.

4. Select from these additional options when working with text:

   - Click **All At Once** to apply the selected animation to the entire text placeholder. For example, all lines in the selected text will fade in at one time.
   - For text, click **By 1st Level Paragraphs** to apply the selected animation to the first-level paragraphs one at a time.

5. Click **Preview** to see the animations played on the selected slide.

6. Click **Slide Show** to play the presentation.

ADD CUSTOM ANIMATION

Use the Custom Animation feature to apply animation to selected objects on a slide.

1. Display the slide in Normal view ▣.

2. Select the object or text to be animated. For instance, if you want all text in a text box to be animated the same way, click in the text box. If you want to have different effects or timing, select each section of text (such as one bulleted item) or object individually by clicking it or highlighting it.

3. On the Animations tab, click **Custom Animation** in the Animations group. The Custom Animation task pane will open. Figure 8-4 shows the task pane before an animation effect has been applied.

4. To add an effect, click the **Add Effect** down arrow, and click a choice. You can choose to use animation for an entrance or exit or for emphasis. Select the motion path that determines which direction the motion will take. Each of these displays a popup menu with several animation choices. You may see a fifth choice, Object Actions, if you select an object (such as a chart).

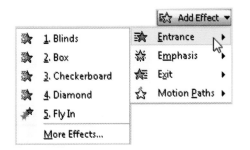

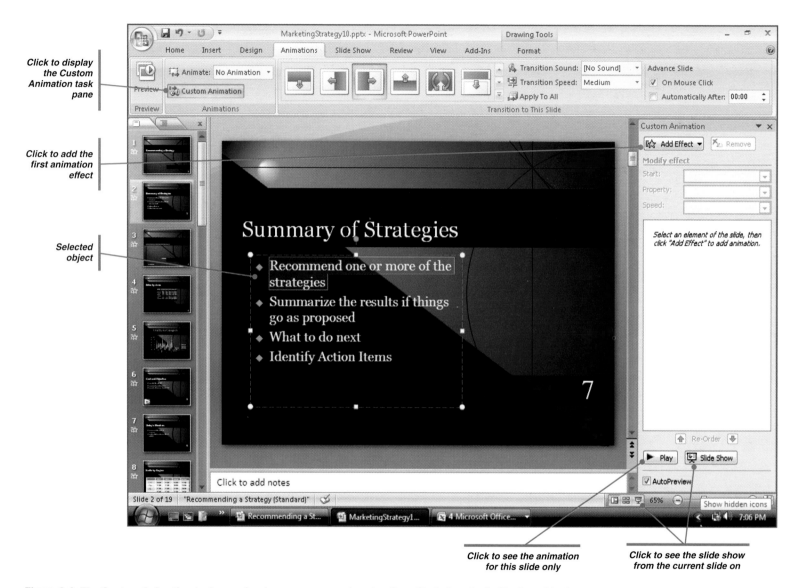

Figure 8-4: *The Custom Animation task pane is where you can apply animation effects to selected text or objects.*

5. To change or delete an animation, first select the effect to be changed from the task pane effects list, shown in Figure 8-5. (You can also click the tag number of the effect on the slide.) Then select from these options:

- Click **Change** to switch to another effect.

- Click **Remove** to delete an animation.

- Under Modify, click the **Start** down arrow, and select when to start the animation.

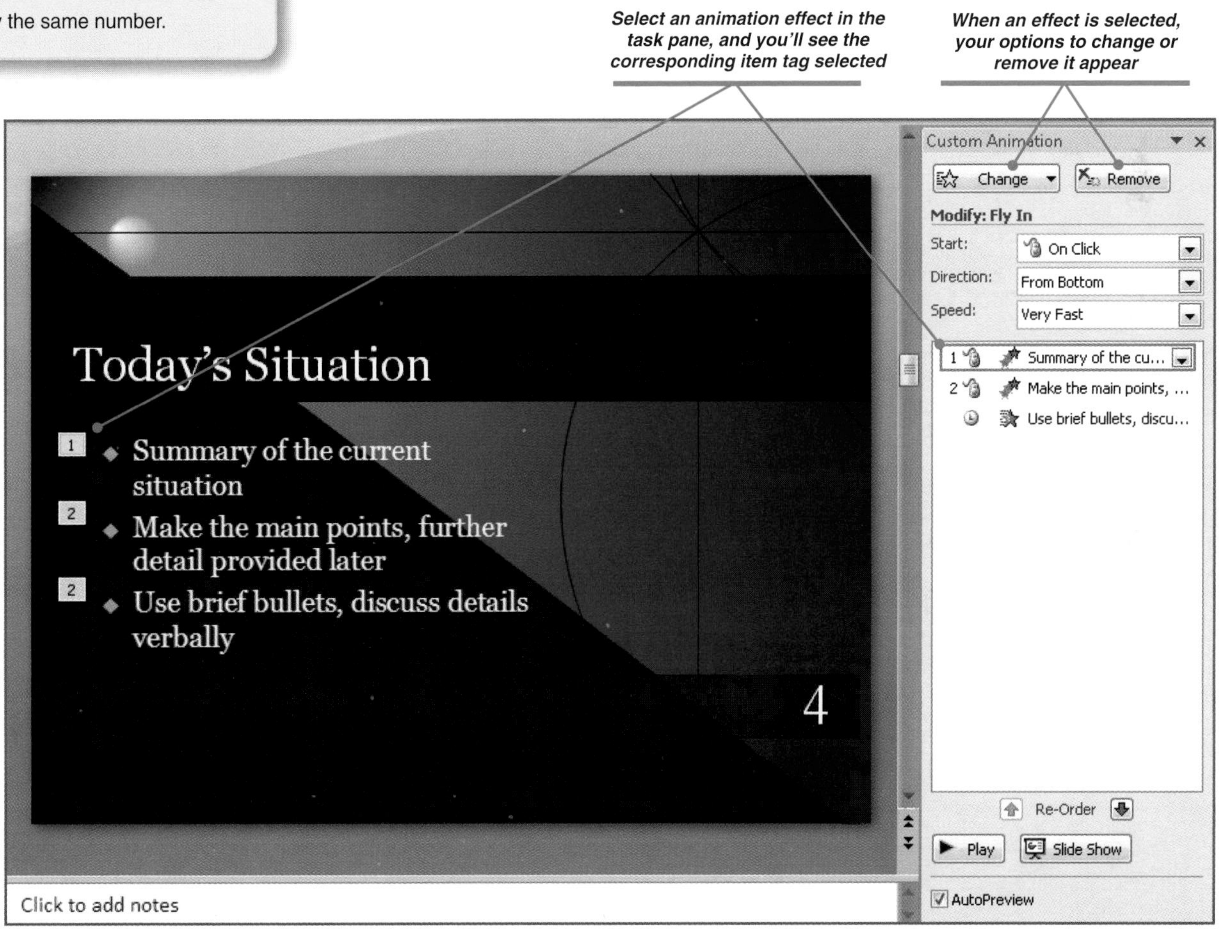

Select an animation effect in the task pane, and you'll see the corresponding item tag selected

When an effect is selected, your options to change or remove it appear

Figure 8-5: *Having selected the effect on the task pane, you can identify the associated item on the slide by its tag number.*

TIP

If you place the pointer over an effect in the task pane, you will see a tooltip describing the effect. The effects are listed and numbered in the sequence in which they will occur, and the corresponding slide items contain tags with the same numbers. So you can look at the tags on the slide and identify which effect controls each item.

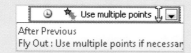

TIP

On the Animations tab, the Custom Animation button in the Animations group is a toggle. Clicking it turns the Custom Animation task pane on and off.

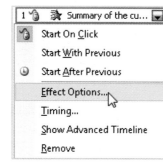

NOTE

You will not see any animations based on "On Click" until you view the presentation with the Slide Show view. Clicking Play does not show them.

- Depending on the effects chosen, the additional options under Modify might differ. You may find Font, Path, Direction, or Size. Select what makes sense.

- The third option under Modify will probably be Speed or Duration. The options on the menu may differ as well. Again, click the option that makes sense for the effect you have chosen.

6. Click **Play** to see the effect played out for the current slide. Click **Slide Show** to see the presentation from this slide on.

ANIMATE BULLETED TEXT

You can animate a bulleted list so that it displays one bullet at a time, allowing you to finish speaking about one item before moving to the next. Using this procedure, each bullet will be displayed on a click of the mouse button in the sequence you choose. The bulleted text will be displayed in a different color when you have moved on to the next bullet.

1. If the Custom Automation task pane is not displayed, click **Custom Animation** in the Animations group of the Animations tab.

2. Display the slide in Normal view.

3. Select the text in the first bullet to be animated.

4. From the task pane, click **Add Effect** and choose an Entrance style.

5. Click any other options under Modify as needed; for instance:

   - Click the **Start** down arrow, and click **On Click**.

   - Click the **Direction** down arrow (if the effect you've chosen displays it), and choose how the animation will appear or move on the slide.

6. Click the down arrow by the selected effect on the task pane, and choose **Effect Options**.

7. Click the **Effect** tab, and click the **After Animation** down arrow. A popup menu is displayed.

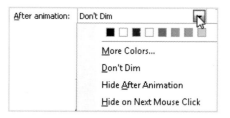

UNDERSTANDING ANIMATION EFFECTS

As you add animation effects, you see them displayed in the Custom Animation task pane in a scrollable list. The icons describe the effects: a mouse is for "on click" timing; a clock, for "after previous"; a yellow star, for "emphasis"; a green star, for "entrance"; a red star, for "exit"; a white star, for "motion path"; and cogs, for "object actions." A selected effect contains a down arrow for accessing other options on a popup menu.

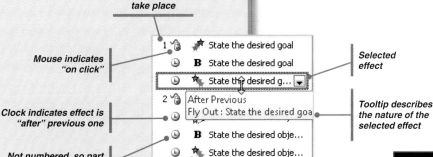

First effect to take place

Mouse indicates "on click"

Clock indicates effect is "after" previous one

Not numbered, so part of the second effect

Red star for "exit"

Indicates change in font size

Green star for "entrance"

Selected effect

Tooltip describes the nature of the selected effect

8. Click a color that is less dominant than the beginning text color. Click **OK**.

9. Repeat steps 3–8 for each bulleted item. Be sure to choose **On Click** in step 5.

10. When you are finished, click **Slide Show** to see how it works. Click the screen or slide image , and then click for each new bullet and for the next slide to be displayed. Figure 8-6 shows an example.

USE EFFECT OPTIONS FOR ANIMATIONS

For any animation, you can specify a number of effects and timing considerations using the Effect Options dialog box.

1. Click the effect down arrow in the task pane for the effect you want to work on, and click **Effect Options.**

2. **Click the Effect** tab (an example for a Fly In Entrance effect is shown in Figure 8-7), and select among the options for that effect. In this case:

- Click the **Direction** down arrow, and choose how the animation will travel across the slide.

Figure 8-6: **The fourth bullet is currently being discussed and will turn the same color as the other three bullets when the presenter clicks the mouse.**

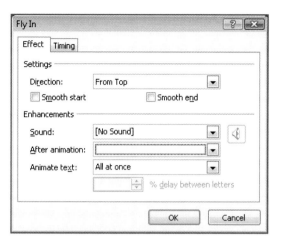

Figure 8-7: *Use the Effect Options dialog box to fine-tune the effect of your animation.*

- Click the **Sound** down arrow, and choose the sound to accompany the effect.

- Click the **After Animation** down arrow, and choose a color or effect that will distinguish an effect after it has been discussed.
- Click the **Animate Text** down arrow to choose how the line of text will be animated.

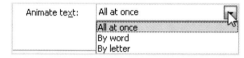

3. Click **OK** to close the Effect tab.

Use Special Effects for Placeholders

You can use special effects—such as gradient colors, texture, and patterns—in slide object or placeholder backgrounds.

FILL PLACEHOLDER BACKGROUNDS

1. Select the placeholder or shape you want to fill with a color or effect. (See "Draw a Shape" later in this chapter for information about shapes.) The Drawing Tools Format tab is displayed.

2. On the Format tab, click the **Shape Fill** button in the Shape Styles group:

   - To apply color to a shape or placeholder background, point to the colors in the menu until you find one you want, and then click it.

   - To remove fill from a shape or placeholder, click **No Fill**.

   - To have access to additional colors, click **More Fill Colors**. The Colors dialog box will appear. You can choose between the Standard and Custom tabs:

     - Click the **Custom** tab if you want to work with RGB (Red, Green, and Blue) or HSL (Hue, Saturation, and Luminosity) settings. This dialog box can be seen in Figure 8-8. Click the color palette to set the approximate color, or drag the **Colors** slider to get a more exact shade. Drag the **Transparency** slider to make the fill more transparent. Click **OK** when you're done.

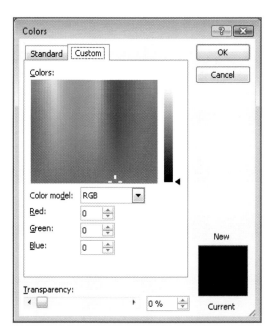

Figure 8-8: *The Colors dialog box, accessed by clicking the Custom tab, allows you to precisely work with color through RGB- and HSL-specific settings.*

–Or–

- Click the **Standard** tab to access a standard set of colors, as seen in Figure 8-9. Click a unit of color, and see the difference in the New preview box compared with the current color. Drag the Transparency slider to manage the transparency of the fill. Click **OK** when you're done.

CREATE A GRADIENT BACKGROUND FOR YOUR SLIDES

A gradient background lets you fill a placeholder or shape with a blend of colors. Figure 8-10 shows the Gradient menu, which you use to employ this special effect.

1. Select the placeholder or shape to contain the gradient effect. The Drawing Tools Format tab is displayed.

2. Click the **Format** tab, and click **Shape Fill**. Then click **Gradient** to see the menu shown in Figure 8-10.

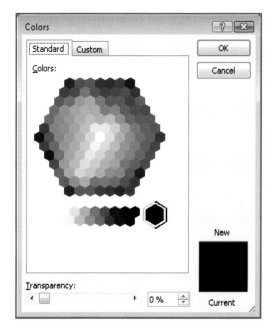

Figure 8-9: *Use the Standard tab to find more "Web-friendly" color selections.*

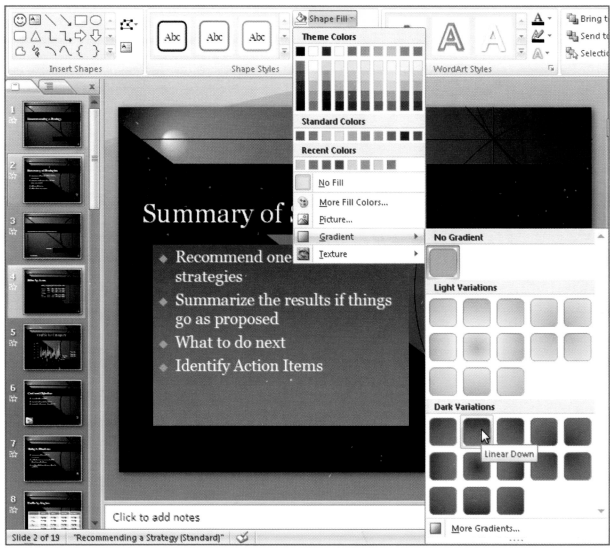

Figure 8-10: *You can point to the variations of gradient patterns on the Gradient menu and see the effects in the selected placeholder or shape.*

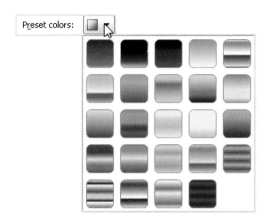

3. To select a gradient pattern on the menu, point to it and see the preview results on the shape or placeholder. When you find the one you want, just click it.

4. To have more control over the gradient possibilities, click **More Gradients** on the bottom of the gradient menu. The Format Shape dialog box appears. On the Fill category, click **Gradient Fill** and choose one of these options:

- Click the **Preset Colors** down arrow to select one of the gradient color schemes from the Preset Colors drop-down list box.

- Click the **Type** down arrow to display a menu of patterns for the gradient effect. Choose **Linear**, **Radial**, **Rectangular**, or **Path**.

- Click the **Direction** down arrow to set the way the pattern sweeps or moves.

- Click the **Angle** spinner to rotate the angle of the gradient fill within the shape.

- **Gradient Stops** sets a nonlinear distribution of the color within the pattern. The color will not be graduated from one color to another. Instead, it goes from the first color you specify to each of the colors in the stops. Each stop consists of a color; a stop position, which defines where each color stops and the next begins; and a transparency, which indicates how transparent the gradient pattern is. Set these three components, and click **Add**. To remove a stop, display the stop number, and then click **Remove**.

- Click the **Rotate With Shape** check box if you want the gradient fill to rotate within the shape's rotating context.

5. Click **Close** when you are through.

CREATE A TEXTURED BACKGROUND FOR YOUR PLACEHOLDER OR SHAPES

To create a slide with a textured background:

1. Click the placeholder or shape that you want to fill with texture. The Drawing Tools Format tab will be displayed.

2. Click **Shape Fill** and then, from the menu, click **Texture**. A popup menu will be displayed, as seen in Figure 8-11.

3. Point at the various textures until you find the one you want. You'll see the effects of the texture in the placeholder or shape as you point at them. When you find the one you want, click it.

> **TIP**
>
> To see how the gradient stops work, click a preset color pattern, and examine the stops for that effect.

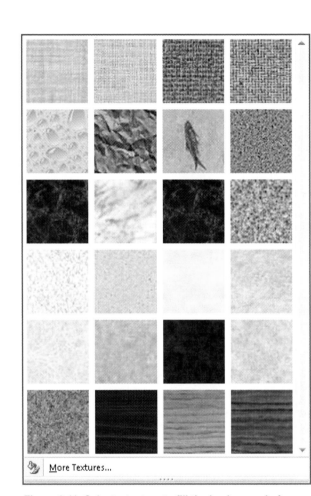

Figure 8-11: *Select a texture to fill the background of a placeholder or shape.*

USE A PICTURE AS THE BACKGROUND ON A SHAPE OR PLACEHOLDER

You can add a picture to your placeholder or shape as a background effect.

1. Select the shape or the placeholder that will contain the picture. The Drawing Tools Format tab will be displayed.

2. On the **Format** tab, click the **Shape Fill** down arrow in the Shape Styles group. A menu is displayed.

3. To place a picture in the placeholder or shape, click **Picture.** The Insert Picture dialog box appears. Fill in the path information to select the picture you want. Click **Insert**.

RESHAPE A PHOTO OR CLIP ART

You can take any photo or clip art object and reshape it using a specialized menu.

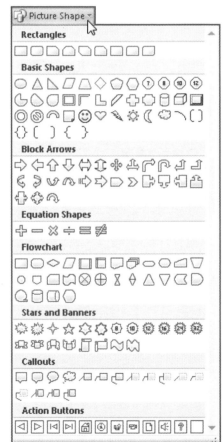

1. Insert a picture or clip art on to your slide by clicking the **Insert** tab and clicking **Picture** or **Clip Art**. Fill in the Insert Picture dialog box to select the picture. Click **Insert**. Or use the Clip Art task pane to find and insert an image on to your slide (see Chapter 7 for more information on using the Clip Art task pane).

2. If not selected, click your picture or clip art. The Picture Tools Format tab is displayed.

3. On the Format tab, click **Picture Shape**, and a menu will be displayed, as seen in Figure 8-12.

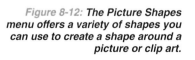

Figure 8-12: *The Picture Shapes menu offers a variety of shapes you can use to create a shape around a picture or clip art.*

4. Click a shape.

Shadow applied

ADDING SPECIAL EFFECTS TO A PICTURE

You can add special effects, such as a shadow, reflection, glow, soft edges, bevel or 3-D rotation effect, to a photo or clip art.

1. Select a photo or clip art object. The Picture Tools Format tab is displayed.

2. On the Format tab, click **Picture Effects** in the Picture Styles group.

Picture Effects ▾

3. Click an option, such as **Shadow** for a menu of choices. On the menu, click the effect you want. The special effect will be applied to the selected object.

Work with WordArt

You can add special effects to text by applying WordArt containing unique character styles; a text fill of varying colors, gradients, textures, and pictures; a text outline with varying colors, weights, and dashes; and text effects of shadows, reflections, glows, bevels, 3-D rotation, and "transform," which curves and distorts the character shapes.

WordArt Styles

APPLY A WORDART EFFECT

Special effects can be easily added to text using WordArt to give a graphic artist's professional touch.

1. Select the text to which you want to apply the WordArt. The Drawing Tools Format tab is displayed. Click the **Format** tab. Within the WordArt Styles group are the special effects commands.

2. Click the **WordArt More** button to display the WordArt gallery of text styles, shown in Figure 8-13.

3. Select a style you want. The WordArt style will be applied to the text.

FILL AND OUTLINE TEXT

You can add fill to text using color, pictures, gradient colors, and texture. In addition, you can outline text with a different color, a different weighted line, or a dashed line.

1. To apply fill or outline to text, first select the text. The text can be WordArt or regular text. The Drawing Tools Format tab is displayed with the commands you'll need.

2. To apply a fill, click the **Text Fill** down arrow in the WordArt Styles group of the Drawing Tools Format tab. A menu of choices is displayed, as shown in Figure 8-14. Select the color, find and select the picture, select the gradient, or select the texture. Your text will be displayed with the selected changes.

3. To apply an outline, click the **Text Outline** down arrow in the WordArt Styles group of the Drawing Tools Format tab. A menu similar to that shown in Figure 8-14 is displayed, except the options apply to lines instead of a fill. Select a color, weight of line, or a dash style from the submenu.

TIP

To change the text in a WordArt image, double-click the image so that the text is highlighted. Type the new text.

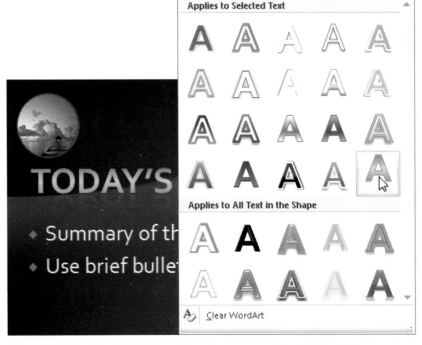

Figure 8-13: *The WordArt styles gallery displays a variety of styles that you can apply to text to give it a professional and artistic look.*

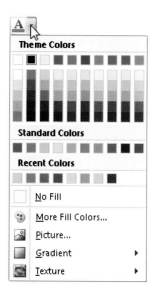

Figure 8-14: *Using the Text Fill option, you can change the color of WordArt or text with another color, a picture, gradient colors, or textures.*

The Text Effect option allows you to apply really interesting effects, such as shadows, reflections, glows, bevels, 3-D rotations, and transforming distortions of the character shapes.

1. Select the text to contain the special effect by highlighting it. The text can be WordArt or other text. The Drawing Tools Format tab is displayed.

2. Click **Text Effects** in the WordArt Styles group. A menu is displayed. Click the effect you want. A submenu will be displayed. Click the effect to be applied. Figure 8-15 shows examples of the various effects.

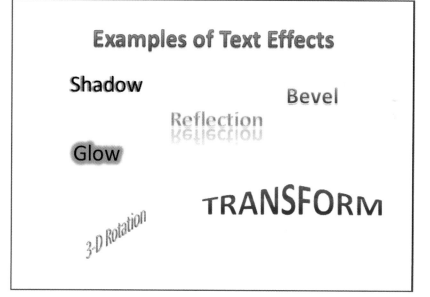

Figure 8-15: *Here are some examples of the interesting effects that the Text Effect command in the Drawing Tools Format tab can create.*

1 2 3 4 5 6 7 8 9 10

> **TIP**
>
> To create a perfect square or circle, press **SHIFT** while you drag the **Rectangle** or **Oval** tool. To make the rectangle or oval larger or smaller, select it by clicking it, and then drag the sizing handles that appear on the shape.

Draw Shapes in PowerPoint

The drawing feature in PowerPoint enables you to create line drawings and art with simple-to-use tools. It presents "canned shapes" that you can use to draw lines, circles, rectangles, and other common shapes. It also contains predefined shapes for inserting a variety of arrows and other connecting symbols, flow-chart symbols, callouts, stars and banners, and other useful shapes. Figure 8-16 shows the drawing shapes available. You can edit these canned shapes, making them uniquely yours. Within the toolbox for shapes are the colors and special effects that add interest and a professional look to your shapes.

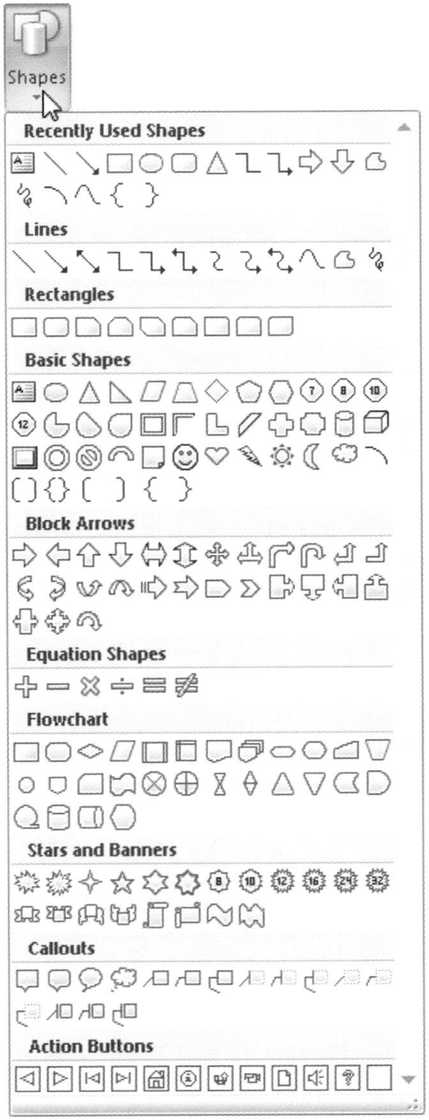

Figure 8-16: ***These are the "canned" shapes you can create in PowerPoint.***

Draw a Shape

You can draw a variety of shapes using the Shapes menu. The procedure that follows can be used as a model for drawing whatever shape you want.

1. Click the **Insert** tab, and click **Shapes** in the Illustrations group. A menu of shapes is displayed, as shown in Figure 8-16.

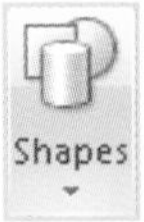

TIP

To change the size of a shape, select it and then drag the selection handles to increase or decrease it. Press **SHIFT** to change the size without changing the basic outline of the shape. You can select the shape and drag it into another position.

UICKSTEPS

WORKING WITH CURVES

Tools are available to draw curved shapes. They are found on the Insert tab, on the Shapes menu in the Illustrations group, under the Lines option, and in the Drawing Tools Format tab in the Insert Shapes group.

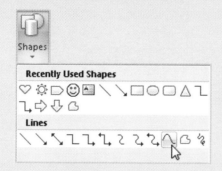

CREATE A CURVE

On the Drawing Tools Format tab, in the Insert Shapes group, click the **More** button for the Shapes menu. Then beneath the Lines option, click one of the following:

● **Curve** creates flowing shapes. Click the cross pointer to establish the curve's starting point. Move the pointer and click to continue creating other curvatures. Double-click to set the end point and complete the drawing.

–Or–

Continued . . .

2. Click the shape that you want to create. When you click the shape, your pointer will become a crosshair.

3. Place the crosshair pointer where you want the edge of the shape to begin. Drag the pointer diagonally across the slide, creating the shape. Release the pointer by releasing the mouse button.

Type Text Within a Shape

You type text into a shape by inserting a text box within it. You can both center and control the word-wrap within the shape by varying the size and shape of the text box. You might want to insert text within a shape for a label, for instance. To type text in a shape:

1. Click the shape to select it and then click the **Drawing Tools Format** tab.

–Or–

To create a shape, click the **Shapes** down arrow in the Illustrations group of the Insert tab, and click a shape from the Shapes menu. Then drag the pointer diagonally across the slide. The Drawing Tools Format tab will then become available. Click the **Format** tab.

2. Click the **Text Box** button in the Insert Shapes group. The pointer will become an insertion point, which you drag to form the text box. Drag the text box to conform to the size of your shape.

3. Type your text.

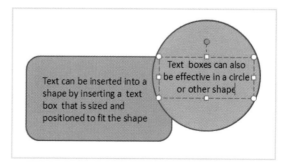

4. Drag the text box to position it within the shape and resize it as needed to fit the shape.

WORKING WITH CURVES *(Continued)*

1. **Freeform** 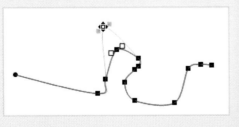 uses a combination of curve and scribble techniques. Click the cross pointer to establish curvature points, and/or drag the pencil pointer to create other designs. Double-click to set the end point and complete the drawing.

   –Or–

* **Scribble** creates pencil-like lines. Drag the pencil icon to create the shape you want. Release the mouse button to complete the drawing.

ADJUST A CURVE

1. Select the curve by clicking it. Click the **Drawing Tools Format** tab. Click **Edit Shape** in the Insert Shapes group.

2. Click the **Edit Points** option. Black rectangles (called *vertices*) appear at the top of the curvature points.

   > Change Shape ▶
   > Convert to Freeform
   > Edit Points
   > Reroute Connectors

3. Drag a vertex to reconfigure the curve's shape.

4. Change any other vertex, and click outside the curve when finished.

Continued . . .

Combine Shapes by Grouping

You can combine shapes for any number of reasons, but typically, you work with multiple shapes to build a more complex drawing. So you don't lose the positioning, sizing, and other characteristics of these components, you can group them. They are then treated as one object.

GROUP SHAPES

1. Select the shapes to be grouped by clicking the first shape and then holding **SHIFT** while selecting the other shapes.

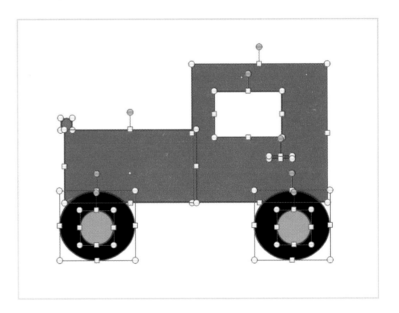

2. On the Drawing Tools Format tab, click the **Group** button on the Arrange group. A menu is displayed. Click **Group**. A single set of selection handles surrounds the perimeter of the combined shapes. Coloring, positioning, sizing, and other actions now affect the shapes as a group, instead of individually.

> ⊞ Group
> ⊞ Group
> 🗗 Regroup
> ⊞ Ungroup

8

QUICKSTEPS

WORKING WITH CURVES *(Continued)*

ROTATE A CURVE

1. Click a curve to select it. A green rotate handle will appear on the curve.

2. Place the pointer over the handle, and drag it to rotate the curve in the way you want.

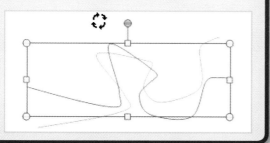

NOTE

If you cannot easily ungroup an image, it may be a bitmap, which can't be ungrouped and converted to an object. In this case, use an imaging program to edit the image before placing it back into your slide.

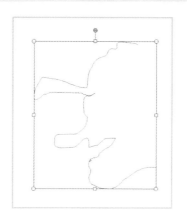

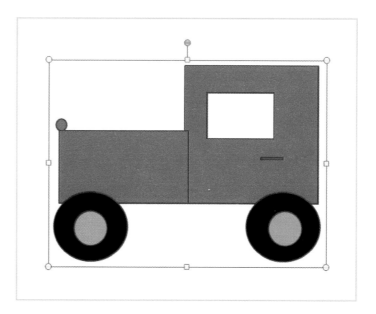

UNGROUP SHAPES

To separate a group into individual shapes again, select the group and, on the Drawing Tools Format tab, click the **Group** button on the Arrange group, and click **Ungroup**.

RECOMBINE A GROUP AFTER UNGROUPING

After making a modification to a shape that was part of a group, you don't have to reselect each component shape to reestablish the group. Select any shape that was in the group, click the **Drawing Tools Format** tab, and click the **Group** button on the Arrange group. Click **Regroup**.

Create a Mirror Image

You can create a mirror image of a shape using some of the Shape tools.

1. Select the shape (not a placeholder) you want to be half of the mirror image, right-click, and from the context menu, click **Copy Here**. A second copy of the image is placed on top of the original and is selected.

8

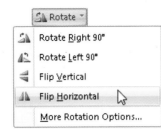

Rotate
- Rotate Right 90°
- Rotate Left 90°
- Flip Vertical
- Flip Horizontal
- More Rotation Options...

2. On the Drawing Tools Format tab, click the **Rotate** button, and click **Flip Horizontal** or **Flip Vertical**, depending on how you want the image to look.

3. Press **SHIFT** and select the original graphic. (You may need to separate the two images in order to select both of them.) Both graphics should be selected.

4. Click the **Align** button, and click an applicable alignment to make the graphics even. (In Figure 8-17, the Distribute Horizontally command was used.) ⌶ Align ▾

5. If you need to, select one shape, press and hold **CTRL**, and press the applicable arrow key to nudge the shape into a mirrored position.

Format Shapes

The Drawing Tools Format tab, available when a shape or object is selected, contains commands to format shapes by changing the color of the shape, defining its outline, and adding special effects.

TIP

If you cannot select the shape you want, send the shapes on top of the stack to the back until the one you want is on top.

TIP

You can see additional options by right-clicking a shape on its border and clicking **Format Shape**.

QUICKSTEPS

POSITIONING SHAPES

Shapes can be positioned by just dragging them, a technique with which you are probably familiar. However, PowerPoint also provides a number of other ways to help you adjust where a shape is in relation to other shapes and objects.

MOVE SHAPES INCREMENTALLY

Select the shape or group, and press the arrow key in the direction you want to move the shape in larger increments; hold down **CTRL** and press the arrow key to move the shape in smaller increments.

Continued . . .

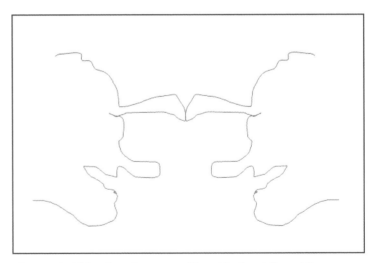

Figure 8-17: *This mirror image was flipped horizontally and then aligned using the Distribute Horizontally command to get facing witches.*

POSITIONING SHAPES (Continued)

REPOSITION THE ORDER OF STACKED SHAPES

You can stack graphics by simply dragging one on top of another. However, sometimes it is difficult to edit or format a shape within the stack. To reposition the order of the stack, display the Drawing Tools Format tab, and, in the Arrange group:

1. Click the **Bring To Front** down arrow, and choose to move the graphic to the top, or forward, in the stack.

2. Click the **Send To Back** down arrow, and choose to move the graphic to the bottom, or backward, in the stack.

USE THE SELECTION PANE TO ORDER THE STACK

1. On the Drawing Tools Format tab, click the **Selection Pane** button in the Arrange group. A Selection And Visibility pane will open, as shown in Figure 8-18.

2. Click **Show All** to show all the objects on the slide.

3. Click the **Bring Forward** and **Send Backward** arrows to re-order the objects.

4. Click the **Eyeball** icon to hide the object from the pane if it is not part of what you are trying to re-order.

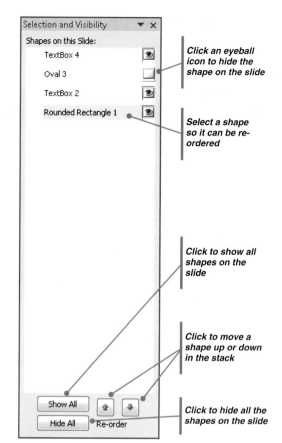

Figure 8-18: **The Selection And Visibility pane allows you to identify all the objects on a slide, even stacked objects, and to re-order them as needed.**

FILL AND OUTLINE SHAPES

You can add fill to shapes with color, pictures, gradient colors, and texture. In addition, you can outline a shape with a different color, a weighted line, or a dashed line.

1. To apply a fill or outline to shapes, first click the shape to select it. The Drawing Tools Format tab is displayed with the commands you'll need.

2. To apply a fill, click the **Shape Fill** button in the Shapes Styles group of the Drawing Tools Format tab. A menu of choices is displayed, as shown earlier in

ALIGNING SHAPES

Aligning shapes enables you to position shapes more precisely with the aid of an invisible grid and guides, as well as by aligning shapes horizontally or vertically in relationship to each other.

ALIGN SHAPES WITH GRIDS AND GUIDES

To align a shape to an invisible grid, select the shape, click the **Drawing Tools Format** tab, and click the **Align** button in the Arrange group. Click **Grid Settings**. The Grid And Guides dialog box appears:

- To align a shape to an invisible grid, select the **Snap Objects To Grid** check box.

- To align shapes to one another, select the **Snap Objects To Other Objects** check box. The shapes will be "attracted" to each other when they are moved close to each other. This is useful for stacking objects or for selecting and moving them as a unit.

- To display the grid or guides and establish grid and guide settings, set the appropriate settings in the **Grid Settings** and **Guide Settings** areas.

EVENLY SPACE SHAPES

Select the shapes (minimum of two), click the **Drawing Tools Format** tab, click the **Align** button on the Arrange group, and click **Distribute Horizontally** or **Distribute Vertically**.

Figure 8-14. Select the color, find and select the picture, select the gradient, or select the texture. Your shape will be displayed with the changes selected. An example is shown in Figure 8-19.

3. To apply an outline, click the **Shape Outline** button in the Shapes Styles group of the Drawing Tools Format tab. A menu similar to that shown earlier in Figure 8-14 is displayed, except the options apply to lines instead of fill. Select a color, weight of line, or a dash or arrow style from the submenu.

APPLY SHAPE EFFECTS

The Shape Effects option allows you to apply special effects, such as shadows, reflections, glows, soft edges, bevel, and 3-D rotations to shapes.

1. Select the shape to contain the special effect by clicking it. The Drawing Tools Format tab is available. If it is not displayed, click the **Format** tab.

Figure 8-19: **Using the Shape Fill button, you can create interesting effects by changing the color of shapes, adding a picture, gradient colors, or textures.**

CAUTION

Do not remove the outline around a shape unless you have first added a fill. Without the outline or a fill, the graphic is invisible except for the handles that display when it's selected.

TIP

To rotate or flip a shape, use the Rotate command in the Arrange group of the Drawing Tools Format tab. Click the **Rotate** button, and choose **Rotate Right 90°**, **Rotate Left 90°**, **Flip Vertical**, or **Flip Horizontal**. Rotating is turning a shape clockwise or counterclockwise by a specific amount. Flipping is turning it upside down, either vertically or horizontally.

TIP

If you click Rotate (Right or Left) 90° twice, you will turn the shape 180 degrees; three times, 270 degrees; four times, 360 degrees, or back to the original position. Similarly, if you flip a shape twice, it will return to its original position.

2. **Click Shape Effects** in the Shape Styles group. A menu is displayed. Click the effect you want. A submenu will be displayed. Click the effect to be applied.

REMOVE EFFECTS

- To **remove a fill**, select the shape, click the **Shape Fill** button in the Shape Styles group on the Drawing Tools Format tab, and click **No Fill**.

- To **remove the outline border** around a shape, select the shape, click the **Shape Outline** button in the Shape Styles group on the Drawing Tools Format tab, and click **No Outline**.

Use Zoom

Increasing and decreasing the size of an object may be essential to verifying that your work is accurate. In fact, you may find that you routinely move in and out of Zoom view as you review your slides.

1. Click the selected shape to be magnified.

2. Drag the slider on the **Zoom** bar in the lower-right area of the status bar. You can also click the minus (–) and plus (+) buttons to increase or decrease the magnification incrementally.

Chapter 9
Working with Multimedia and the Internet

Multimedia files and presentations on the Internet are two features that lend impact to your presentations. In this chapter you will see how to insert and play audio and video files and CD sound tracks in your presentation. You will see how to manage your sound files. You will then actually record sound files and package all linked files together with the presentation. Using the Internet, you will be able to see another way to make your presentation available to others who may not have PowerPoint. You will learn how to store the presentation as a Web page on a local computer or an intranet or to a site on the Internet.

Use Multimedia Files in Your Presentation

Music, sound, and video clips can be inserted on a slide or an object on a slide. The clips can come from files on your computer, Microsoft's Clip Organizer, the Internet, or from another network. You can record your own sounds and add them to the Clip Organizer or use tracks from a CD.

The sounds you insert can be made to start automatically when the slide is displayed or to start when you click the mouse.

Insert Sounds from the Clip Organizer

PowerPoint provides an inventory of sounds that you can use for your slides, or you can use files from Microsoft Online.

1. In Normal view, select the slide that will have the sound.

2. Click the **Insert** tab, and click the **Sound** down arrow in the Media Clips group. A menu will be displayed.

3. Click **Sound From Clip Organizer**. The Clip Art task pane is displayed, as shown in Figure 9-1. It contains a gallery of canned sounds. You may want more options.

4. Under **Search For** on the Clip Art task pane, type the subject, such as laugh, airplane, or fireworks, for which you want a sound.

Figure 9-1: *The Clip Art task pane contains canned sounds, and you can search for additional possibilities.*

5. In the Search In drop-down list box, click the sources you want to search. You may search for sounds in your own collections, from Office Online, or from Microsoft Online.

6. In the Results Should Be drop-down list box, **Sounds** should be selected (if it is not, select it). If you want only certain types of files (AIFF, MIDI, or WAV, for instance), display the Sounds list by clicking the plus sign (**+**) and clearing check boxes next to the files you do not want.

7. Click **Go**.

8. When the sound files are displayed in the preview of thumbnails, click the down arrow on the side of a thumbnail, and click **Preview/Properties** to hear the sound. The Preview/ Properties dialog box appears, and the sound is played.

9. If you want to hear it again, click the **Play** button, shown in Figure 9-2. Click **Close** when you are satisfied with the sound.

10. To insert the sound, on the Clip Art task pane, double-click the thumbnail of the sound file you want.

11. A message is displayed, asking how you want the sound to start in the slide show. Click **Automatically** to have the sound played whenever the slide is displayed. Click **When Clicked** to have the sound played when you click the mouse. The sound will be assigned to the selected slide.

12. A **Sound** icon will appear on the slide. Drag it to an "out-of-the-way" spot on the slide.

Insert a Sound from a File

On your computer or network, you may have your own sound files that are not part of a Clip Organizer collection. You can also insert them in your slides.

1. In Normal view, select the slide that you want to have the sound.

2. Click the **Insert** tab, click the **Sound** down arrow, and click **Sound From File**.

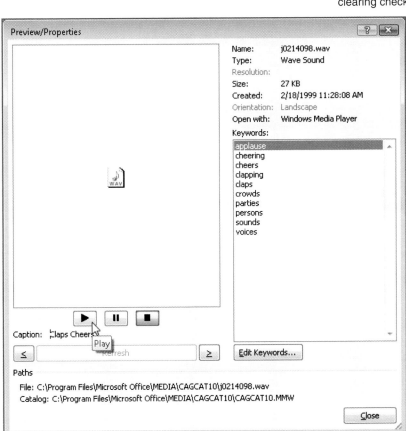

*Figure 9-2: **You can find and preview sounds before you choose the one that fits your needs.***

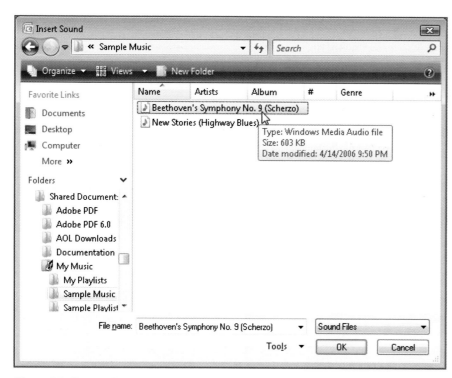

Figure 9-3: *You can insert sound files from your own computer or a computer on a network.*

3. The Insert Sound dialog box will appear, as shown in Figure 9-3.

4. Find and select your sound file, and click **OK**. A message is displayed, asking how you want the sound to start in the slide show. Click **Automatically** to have the sound played whenever the slide is displayed. Click **When Clicked** to have the sound played when you click the mouse. The sound will be assigned to the selected slide. Drag it to an inconspicuous spot on your slide.

Insert a CD Track

To insert one or more sound tracks from a CD on your slide.

1. Insert your CD into the CD drive. Close the dialog box that may appear.

2. Select the slide that will contain the CD sounds.

3. Click the **Insert** tab, click the **Sound** down arrow in the Media Clips group, and click **Play CD Audio Track**. The Insert CD Audio dialog box will appear, as shown in Figure 9-4.

Figure 9-4: *You can select specific tracks on a CD to insert on a slide.*

9

TIP

You may want to set the sound to play over a number of slides The CD will stop when the number of slides is over. Click the **Animations** tab, and click **Custom Animation** in the Animations group. The Custom Animation task pane is displayed. Click the CD media effect from the Effect list, click the down arrow, and click **Effect Options**. On the Play CD Audio dialog box, under Stop Playing Clip, click the **After __Slides** checkbox to insert a checkmark. Click the spinner to set the number of slides, and click **OK**.

Stop playing clip
- On click
- After current slide
- After: 1 slides

NOTE

If you are using a CD track for your slides, you must insert one for each slide, unless you specify that the CD track is to loop or that it is to continue to play through a number of slides. The time for the CD to begin to play or to advance to the next track, compared to the display of the slides, may be difficult to coordinate and cannot be done automatically.

TIP

You can apply sound to an animation. Select the animated object, click the **Animations** tab, and click **Custom Animation** in the Animations group. The Custom Animation task pane is displayed. On the Effects list, click the selected effect down arrow, and click **Effect Options** on the context menu. Under Enhancements on the Effect tab, click the **Sound** down arrow, and click a sound. Click **OK**. See Chapter 8 for more information about special effects and animation.

4. Select among these options:

- In the **Start At Track** box, click the spinner to set the beginning track number. In the **Time** field, set the number of seconds of delay before it should start to play.

- In the **End At** box, click the up and down arrows to set the number of the last track to play. In the **Time** field, set the number of seconds that this track is to play.

- Under Play Options, click the **Loop Until Stopped** check box if you want the CD sound track to repeat itself until you click the mouse. Set the sound volume by clicking the **Sound** icon and dragging the slider to the volume level you want.

- Under Display Options, click **Hide Sound Icon During Slide Show** if you want the CD icon to be hidden during the actual presentation.

- For your information, the total playing time is calculated so that you will know how long the slide will take to play.

5. Click **OK**. A message asking how you want to play the sound will display. Click **Automatically** to play the CD track automatically when the slide displays. Click **When Clicked** to play the CD track when you click the mouse. The CD icon will be inserted onto the slide. Drag it to an inconspicuous spot.

6. To start the slide show at the current slide and hear it with the CD track, click the **Slide Show** icon 🖳 (depending on your choice in step 5, you might have to click the mouse to hear the sound). To see the whole slide show from the beginning, select a slide and press **F5**.

Set Options for Sound Effects

Once a sound has been inserted onto a slide, you can change or refine how and when it plays.

1. Select the **Sound** icon for which you want to set options. Click the **Animations** tab, and, in the Animations group, click **Custom Animation**.

2. On the Custom Animation task pane, click the down arrow for the sound effect in the Effects list, and a context menu will open, as shown in Figure 9-5. (If the task pane is not displayed, click the **Animations** tab, and click **Custom Animation** in the Animations group. The Custom Animation task pane will display.)

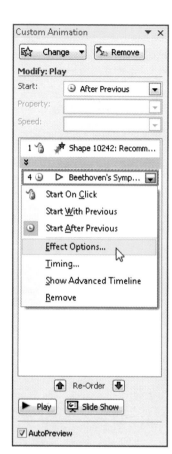

Figure 9-5: *The Custom Animation task pane allows you to select additional options for sound files.*

3. Click **Effect Options** to open the Play Sound dialog box. The options may vary, depending on the type of sound file you have selected.

4. On the Effect tab, shown in Figure 9-6:

- Under Start Playing Clip, click **From Beginning** to start playing the sound clip from the beginning.

- Click **From Last Position** to continue playing the sound clip from the previous location on the track.

- Click **From Time** and click the up and down arrows to set the number of seconds to advance into the sound clip before beginning to play.

- Under Stop Playing, click **On Click** to stop the sound when the slide is clicked.

- Click **After Current Slide** to stop playing when the next slide is displayed.

- Click **After** and click the up and down arrows to set the number of slides during which the sound continues to play before stopping.

- Under Enhancements, if the sound is connected to animation, click **After Animation** to indicate the action to take.

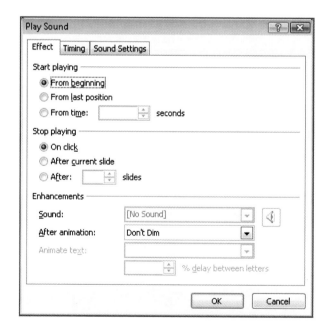

Figure 9-6: *The Play Sound dialog box is where you set specific performance, timing, and other sound attributes.*

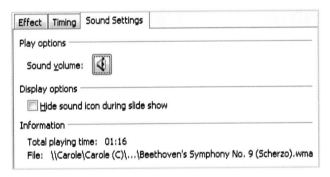

5. On the **Timing** tab:

- Click the **Start** down arrow, and select **On Click** (the sound starts when you click the **Sound** icon), **With Previous** (the sound starts at the same time as another effect), or **After Previous**.

- Set the **Delay** spinner with the number of seconds that are to pass after the slide is displayed but before the sound plays.

- Click the **Repeat** down arrow, and select the number of times the sound is to repeat.

- Click the **Rewind When Done Playing** check box to return the sound clip to the beginning when the clip has completed playing.

- Click the **Triggers** down arrow, and click **Animate As Part Of Click Sequence** if the sound is to be a part of another effect or group of effects.

  –Or–

  Click **Start Effect On Click Of** to connect the sound with the click of another effect. Click the down arrow to choose the other effect.

6. On the Sound Settings tab:

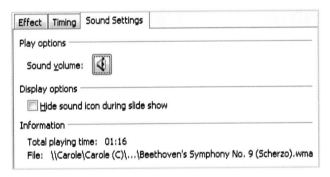

- Click **Sound Volume** to set the slider to the volume you want.

- Click the **Hide Sound Icon During Slide Show** check box to hide the **Sound** icon while the presentation is being played.

- Use the **Information** area to learn how long the sound clip plays and the path to the source file listed.

7. Click **OK** to close the Play Sound dialog box.

When you are inserting multiple sound clips on to a slide, the default is to play them in the order in which they are inserted. You can change this order in the Effect and Timing tabs of the Effect Options dialog box.

One potential problem with linked files is that if you move the presentation from its current location, you may lose linked sound files. So, it is important to keep the presentation and sound files together, in the same folder if possible. See "Package Presentation Files" later in the chapter.

Change the Size of Embedded Sound Files

PowerPoint *embeds* .wav sound files less than 100 kilobytes (KB) in size. That is, it makes the files part of the presentation structure. All other file types and .wav files larger than 100 KB are *linked*. That is, they are stored in their original location and loaded from there. To change the size of the file that will be embedded within PowerPoint:

1. Click the **Sound Tools Options** tab (displayed when the **Sound** icon is selected).

2. In the Sound Options group, in **Max Sound File Size (KB)**, click the spinner until you have, in kilobytes, the file size you want.

Record Sound Files

There are at least three reasons you might want to record a narrative for your slide show. First, recording prior to the presentation enables the slide show to run without your presence. You can produce a Web-based presentation or a kiosk trade show presentation this way. Secondly, recording during the presentation saves a record of your comments and the audience's response, if you choose. Finally, you might want to record short comments on just a few slides to note a change you'd like to make or to emphasize an important point. Before recording, however, you may need to set up and test your microphone equipment.

TEST YOUR MICROPHONE

To test your microphone's quality:

1. Click the **Slide Show** tab, and click **Record Narration**. The Record Narration dialog box appears, as seen in Figure 9-7.

2. To change the attributes of your sound, click **Change Quality**. The Sound Selection dialog box will appear:

   ● Click the **Format** down arrow to change it. You may have only one possibility: PCM (Pulse Code Modulation).

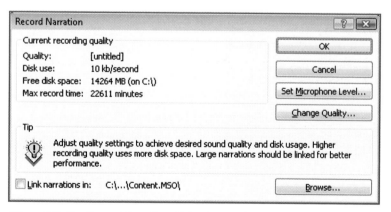

Figure 9-7: The Record Narration dialog box enables you to set the quality and level of your microphone.

- Click the **Attributes** down arrow to change the quality of the sound being captured by your microphone. (Note that quality and file size are directly related; the higher the quality, the larger the file.)

- To save the sound quality parameters selected, click the **Name** down arrow, and click a name, or type a name and click **Save As**. Enter the appropriate data, and click **OK**.

3. Click **Set Microphone Level** to test your microphone. The Microphone Check dialog box will appear.

- Talk into the microphone, and see the sound meter reflect your voice. There is a message on the dialog box that you can read into the microphone.

- Click **OK**.

4. Click **OK** to close the Record Narration dialog box.

5. If a slide other than the first one is selected, you will see a dialog box that asks if you want to start recording on the current slide or the first slide. Otherwise, if the first slide is selected, the slide show will begin with the first slide showing.

6. If you end the show, or if it ends naturally, you will see a message informing you that the timings, or the record of how long each slide took, will be saved with the narrations. Click **Save** to save the timings and the narrations. Click **Don't Save** to discard the timings.

RECORD SHORT COMMENTS

To record a short comment on a single slide:

1. Select the slide that will have the comments.

2. Click the **Insert** tab, click the **Sound** down arrow, and click **Record Sound**. The Record Sound dialog box appears.

Microphone Check

This will make sure the microphone is working and that the microphone's volume is appropriate. Please read the following text into your microphone:

"I am using the microphone setup wizard. It is checking to see whether my microphone is plugged in and working properly."

OK   Cancel

TIP

The narrative timings are used to time your slide display automatically without your needing to click to advance the slides. They can be turned off and on as you wish. (Click the **Slide Show** tab, and click **Use Rehearsed Timings** to select or clear the check box to show the slide show without or with control by timings.)

NOTE

To record and hear sounds, you must have a sound card, speakers, and microphone.

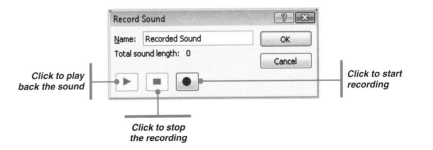

Record Sound

Name: Recorded Sound   OK

Total sound length: 0   Cancel

Click to play back the sound

Click to stop the recording

Click to start recording

CAUTION

If you have a recorded sound, such as a song in the background, and are recording a narrative over it, be sure the transition timings for both sounds are compatible. For instance, you'll want to set the background song to play over a given number of slides so that the transition to the next slide will not have to wait until the song has totally played, but will advance when your narration has finished, as set by Automatically After *recorded timing*.

3. Type a name for the recording:

- To begin the recording, click **Record**.
- To stop, click **Stop**.
- To play back the recording, click **Play**.

4. Click **OK** when you are done.

RECORD A NARRATIVE FOR YOUR PRESENTATION

You use the Slide Show menu to record a narrative for your presentation. The narrative will play as the slide show is presented. You can record and re-record to get the timings correct for each slide. You can record on selected slides or all slides. You use the timings to see how long your presentation will be, to judge the time you should spend on any given slide, and to perfect the message and the length of the presentation.

1. Select the slide on which you will begin the narration.

2. Click the **Slide Show** tab, and click **Record Narration**. The Record Narration dialog box appears.

3. **Click Set Microphone Level** to test your microphone volume and quality. Click **OK.**

4. When you are ready to start recording, click **OK**. (If the first slide is not selected, the Record Narrative dialog box will appear, asking whether you want to start recording on the current slide or the first slide. Select the appropriate one.)

5. The slide will be displayed on the screen in Slide Show view. Use these guidelines:

- Be sure the microphone is on. Speak into it. The narration for your slide show will be recorded as you speak.
- To move from one slide to the next, when you are finished recording on one, click the current slide, or right-click and click **Next**.
- To temporarily pause recording, right-click the slide and click **Pause Narration**.
- To continue recording, right-click the slide and click **Resume Narration**.

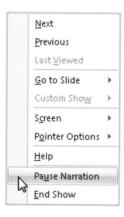

6. To end recording, right-click the slide and click **End Show**. You will see the message picture in the following illustration, prompting you to save timings. Click **Save** to save the slide timings with the narrations. Click **Don't Save** to discard the timings.

7. If you chose to save timings, and if it is not showing, click the **Slide Sorter** view to see the timings for each slide, as shown in Figure 9-8.

8. Refer to "Set Options for Sound Effects" earlier in the chapter to set up the directives for how your narrative will be played in the slide show. For example, if you want the slides to play automatically, all but the first can be set to Start After Previous. You may set the first to On Click.

Use Video Files in Your Presentation

As with sound files, you can insert video files and set options to vary the start, stop, timing, and other attributes of videos in your presentation. When you insert a video, you will see a picture of the beginning of the video rather than an icon.

INSERT A VIDEO

1. Select the slide that will contain the video.

2. Click the **Insert** tab, click the **Movie** down arrow in the Media Clips group, and, from the popup menu, click the source of your video file:

   - Click **Movie From File** to insert a video file from your own collections, not from part of the Clip Organizer collection.

   - Click **Movie From Clip Organizer** to insert a video clip from the Clip Organizer.

3. Find your video file, and insert it into the selected slide.

4. You will see a message asking how to start the movie, as shown in Figure 9-9:

   - Click **Automatically** to start the movie when the slide displays.

   - Click **When Clicked** to start the movie when the mouse button is clicked.

5. To preview the video on this slide, double-click the video picture, or click the **Slide Show** icon on the View mini-toolbar. To see the whole slide show, select a slide and press **F5**.

If there is a recorded sound on the same slide as the video and both are set to start automatically, the sound generally overrides the video.

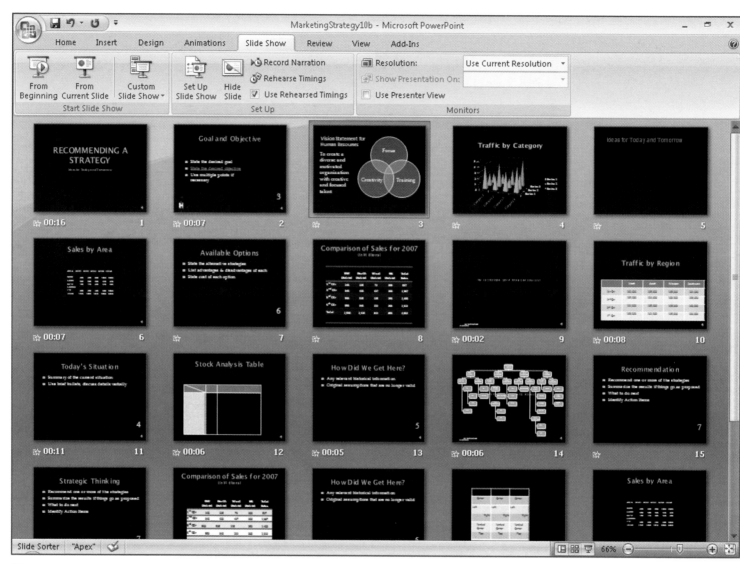

Figure 9-8: *The Slide Sorter view shows narrative timings.*

CHANGING VIDEO OPTIONS

These options, set on the slide, determine how the video portion of your slide show will run. The Movie Options group is accessed from the Options tab in the Movie Tools upper-level tab, which appears when the movie is clicked or selected.

Slide Show Volume ▾ | ☑ Play Movie: Automatically ▾ | ☐ Loop Until Stopped
☐ Hide During Show | ☐ Rewind Movie After Playing
☐ Play Full Screen

Movie Options

LOOP OR REWIND A MOVIE

To cause a movie to play repeatedly or to rewind, click the movie to select it, then click the **Movie Tools Options** tab. In the Movie Options group:

- Click the **Loop Until Stopped** check box to cause the movie to repeat.

- Click the **Rewind Movie After Playing** check box to return to the beginning of the movie.

FILL THE SCREEN WITH THE MOVIE

To run the movie at full-screen size, click the **Movie Tools Options** tab, and click the **Play Full Screen** check box in the Movie Options group.

RESIZE THE MOVIE

Occasionally, a video may look fuzzy at full-screen size. To fix this, you can resize the movie so that it plays in a smaller screen area during the slide show. To resize a movie, making it larger or smaller, select the movie and drag the sizing handles of the picture to the size you want.

–Or–

Set the size you want in the Size group on the Movie Tools Options tab.

Continued . . .

CHANGE START OR PLAY TIMES

You can delay the start of the video until a certain time after a slide has been displayed, or after a certain click sequence:

1. To display the Custom Animation task pane, click the **Animations** tab, and click **Custom Animation** on the Animations group.

2. In the Effects list of the task pane, select the play effect for the video. (If a play effect does not exist in the Effects list for the video, you must insert one. See Chapter 8 for instructions on how to do that.)

*Figure 9-9: **You can insert a movie into your slide that starts automatically or when you click the mouse.***

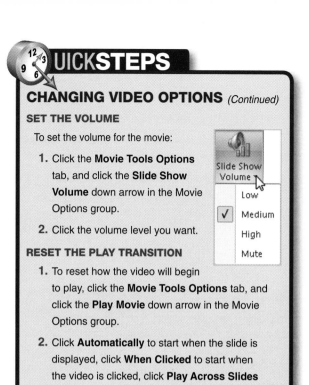

CHANGING VIDEO OPTIONS *(Continued)*

SET THE VOLUME

To set the volume for the movie:

1. Click the **Movie Tools Options** tab, and click the **Slide Show Volume** down arrow in the Movie Options group.

2. Click the volume level you want.

RESET THE PLAY TRANSITION

1. To reset how the video will begin to play, click the **Movie Tools Options** tab, and click the **Play Movie** down arrow in the Movie Options group.

2. Click **Automatically** to start when the slide is displayed, click **When Clicked** to start when the video is clicked, click **Play Across Slides** to have the video play as the slides advance independently beneath the video.

3. Open the Effects menu by clicking the down arrow. Select **Timing**. The Effect Options dialog box is displayed with the Timing tab open.

- Click the Delay spinners to set the amount of time before the video is to start.

- To play the video in the normal sequence of click events, click **Triggers**, and click **Animate As Part Of Click Sequence**. To delay the video until something on the screen is clicked, click **Start Effect On Click Of,** click the down arrow, and click the click-event that will start the video.

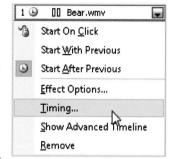

INSERT ACTION BUTTONS

Action buttons can be inserted on the beginning slide of a video to act as triggers for starting, pausing, and stopping the video. These replace the mouse clicks normally used to start, pause, and stop it. To insert an action button:

1. Click the slide containing the movie.

2. Add the buttons to the slide. To do this, click the **Insert** tab, click **Shapes**, and select a button that fits your video scheme under the Action Buttons list, at the bottom of the popup menu (such as the Action Button: Movie 🖭):

- Your pointer will become a cross. Drag it on the slide where you want the button shape. When you release the mouse, the Action Settings dialog box will appear.

- On the Action Settings dialog box, under Action On Click, click **None**. Then click **OK**.

3. Open the Custom Animation task pane. Select the movie on your slide.

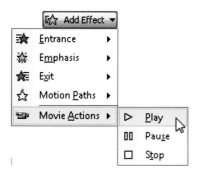

4. Add the play effects to the movie. To do this, on the task pane, click **Add Effect**, select **Movie Actions**, and click the effect you want, for instance, **Play**. Repeat this for each action you want for the buttons.

5. Make the buttons the trigger for the actions. To do this:

   ● In the Effects list on the task pane, select each effect to be triggered by the button.

   ● Click its down arrow, and select **Timing**.

   ● Click **Triggers**, click **Start Effect On Click Of**, and click the action button you want.

Package Presentation Files

You can copy all the presentation files to a folder or burn them on a CD (or DVD) in order to easily transport them to another computer to show a presentation. This is called packaging.

1. Open the presentation to be packaged.

2. Click the **Office Button**, click **Publish**, and select **Package For CD.** The Package For CD dialog box will appear. You may see a message that some of the files will be upgraded to compatible file formats for PowerPoint Viewer.

3. Type a name in the **Name The CD** text box.

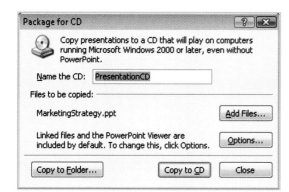

4. Click **Add Files** if you need to add files other than those which are listed under Files To Be Copied (linked files and the PowerPoint Viewer are included by default, so they don't need to be added). The Add Files dialog box will appear. Find the files you want to include, and click **Add**. They will be added to the list of files to be copied.

5. Click **Options** to specify whether PowerPoint Viewer will be used to view the slide show (the recipient may not have PowerPoint), which presentations to include and in which order, and whether to include linked or embedded TrueType fonts and to protect the PowerPoint files with a password. Click **OK** to close the Options dialog box.

   Click **Copy To Folder** to copy the files to a unique folder. After setting these options, click **OK**.

   –Or–

Click **Copy To CD** to burn the files to a CD. If you have linked files, you will be asked if you want to include them in the package. Then you will be asked to insert a CD. A message will ask if you want to continue if comments and annotations are included in the slides. If you do, click **Yes.**

6. The files will be copied. If you want to copy the files to another folder or CD, click **Yes**.

7. Click **Close** to close the Package For CD dialog box.

Use the Internet with Your Presentations

You can use the Internet in several ways. You can insert a hyperlink to a Web page that is embedded in your presentation. You can save your presentation to an FTP (File Transfer Protocol) location. You can save your presentation as a Web page on a local computer, an intranet, or the Internet. Others can then view your presentation with a Web browser.

Connect to Web Pages with Hyperlinks

PowerPoint makes it easy to incorporate information stored on Web sites as part of your slide show. A slide show can be published on the Internet or can provide the speaker access to Web pages when making the presentation. You can connect to a Web page by inserting a hyperlink directly into the presentation or by placing an action button in your slide, which connects to the Web page when clicked.

INSERT A HYPERLINK

To place a hyperlink directly on a slide:

1. Display the slide you want to contain the hyperlink in Normal view.

2. Type the text you want to become a hyperlink:

   - If the text is the URL (Uniform Resource Locator) of a Web page, press **ENTER** or **SPACEBAR**, and the text will be recognized as a hyperlink, as shown below. Your task is done.

     www.cofinances.org

NOTE

Hyperlinks normally only work during a slide show. However, for testing purposes, you can right-click a hyperlink in Normal view, and click **Open Hyperlink** to make sure it works. Using hyperlinks, you can create links to additional information for the presentation on the Internet, intranet Web pages, Web pages on your own computer, e-mail messages, or other files, such as spreadsheets or Microsoft Word documents.

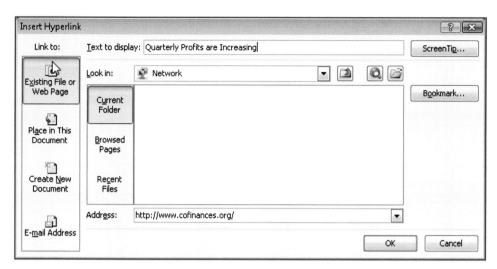

Figure 9-10: *To insert a hyperlink in your presentation, you need to identify the text that will be the hyperlink and the address to which it will be linked.*

- If you want the hyperlink to be part of the text of the presentation, select the text by highlighting it to prepare for the next step.

3. Click the **Insert** tab, and click **Hyperlink**. The Insert Hyperlink dialog box will appear:

   - In the Address, type or find the URL of the Web site, either Internet- or intranet-based, that will be linked to the selected text, as shown in Figure 9-10.

   - Click **Existing File Or Web Page** to find a file on your computer, on an intranet, or on the Internet.

   - Click **Place In This Document** to enter a hyperlink to another slide in the presentation.

   - Click **Create New Document** to enter a hyperlink to a new document yet to be created (you can edit the new document now or later).

   - Click **E-mail Address** to enter a link to an e-mail address. Enter the address and subject.

4. Click **OK**. The text will be colored and underlined to show that it is a hyperlink, such as:

USE ACTION BUTTONS TO CONNECT TO A WEB PAGE

You can insert a hyperlink in the form of an action button on a slide that, when clicked, connects to a Web page.

1. In Normal view, display the slide that you want to contain the action button.

2. Click the **Insert** tab, and click **Shapes** in the Illustrations group. A popup menu will be displayed.

3. Click an action button shape from the bottom of the menu. The pointer will become a cross, which you drag diagonally across the slide to form a button shape. When you release the pointer, the Action Settings dialog box will appear.

4. Click **Hyperlink To.**

5. Open the drop-down list box, and click the hyperlink connection. For a Web site, click **URL**.

6. In the Hyperlink To URL dialog box, type the URL address, as shown in Figure 9-11 (you don't need to type http://), and click **OK**. Click **OK** again to close the Action Settings dialog box. The hyperlink is now attached to the action button.

*Figure 9-11: **The Action Settings dialog box allows you to connect a Web site from an action button on your slide.***

NOTE

You only see the file extensions if you chose to not hide them in Windows Explorer. Click **Organize** in the Windows Explorer window, click **Folder And Search Options**, and click the **View** tab. Then clear the **Hide Extensions For Known File Types** check box.

MANAGING AND SUPPORTING A LINKED FILE DURING A SAVE

To manage and pull together the most recent files:

1. Click the **Files** tab.

2. To pull together the supporting files of the presentation, click the **Organize Supporting Files In A Folder** check box. This will make sure that all the sound and media files are together with the presentation.

3. To get the most recent updates of linked files, click the **Update Links On Save** check box.

4. Click **OK**.

SET DEFAULT FONTS

To set the default fonts for the saved presentation:

1. Click the **Fonts** tab.

2. Under **Character Set**, click the language to use for the presentation.

3. Click the **Proportional Font** down arrow, and click the font to use on the saved file. Click **Size** to the change the size of the font.

4. Set the fixed-width font and its size, if needed.

5. Click **OK**.

7. Format the button as needed (Figure 9-12 shows an example of a slide with an action button connecting to a Web page.):

- In the Drawing Tools Format tab, click **Shape Effects** in the Shape Styles group to create a custom shape, such as a bevel.

- Use the sizing handles to make the button the size you want.

- Click the **Insert** tab, click **Text Box** button, drag it to create the text box. Type the words you want to appear on it. Resize and position it on the action button as needed.

- Drag the button to where you want it placed on the slide. (You may want to combine the text box and the action button into one item. Select both objects and click the **Group** button on the Drawing Tools Format tab.)

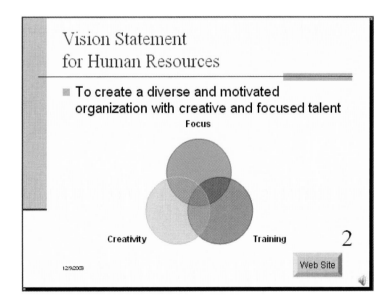

*Figure 9-12: **The action button can be used to connect to a web page on the Internet or intranet while you are giving a presentation.***

To update a slide show that has been published in a Web page format, simply make changes to the original presentation, not the published one, and go through the steps to republish it as a Web page.

To find the location of the presentation, click the **Office Button**, click **Prepare**, and then click **Properties**. The path to the file is on the General tab.

Publish Your Presentation as a Web Page

You can publish your presentation as an HTML (Hypertext Markup Language) file, or a Web page. This enables viewers who do not have PowerPoint to view the presentation with a browser. Using this technique preserves the links, color schemes, and other design elements created with PowerPoint. The file and all the supporting objects are saved to a Web page and an associated common folder. You can save the file to a local computer, to an intranet server, or to an Internet server.

1. Open the presentation that you want to save as a Web page, click the **Office Button**, and click **Save As**. The Save As dialog box will appear.

2. Enter a file name.

3. Click the **Save As Type** down arrow, and click **Web Page**, as shown in Figure 9-13.

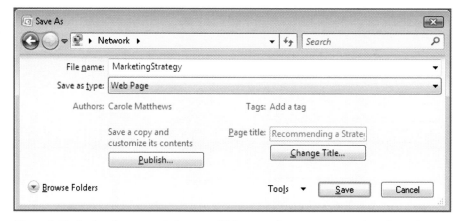

Figure 9-13: *Saving the presentation as a Web page allows you to post it online, where others can view it.*

NOTE

When you "save" a file using Save As, you are creating a copy of the file that replaces the presentation currently on your screen with the copy. To update the copy, you make changes directly to it. The original and the copy go their separate ways. When you "publish" a file using Save As, you are creating an .htm file that can be viewed by a browser. Your original file remains on the screen. If you want to update the published file, you make changes to the original and publish it again.

TIP

If you use a browser other than the default browser to view the saved Web pages, the slide show may not automatically start. In the nondefault browser, click the **File** menu, and click **Open**. In the Open dialog box, select the saved file. Click **Open**. Use the Navigation pane to go through the slide show.

4. To change the title that will appear in the title bar of the browser, click **Change Title**, and, in the Set Page Title dialog box, type a new page title. Click **OK**.

5. Click **Publish**, and the Publish As Web Page dialog box, shown in Figure 9-14, will appear:

- Under Publish What?, click **Complete Presentation** to save all slides; or, click **Slide Number** and click the spinners to set the beginning and ending slide numbers.

- To display the speaker notes with the presentation, click the **Display Speaker Notes** check box. Clear the check box to hide the notes.

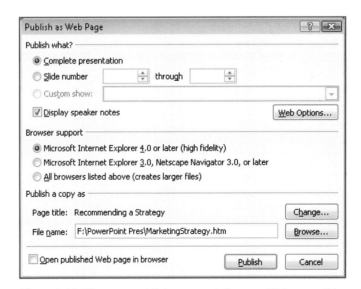

Figure 9-14: When you publish a presentation as a Web page, this dialog box helps to establish exactly what is saved and how it will be supported.

- See "Changing Web Options" QuickSteps for information on changing the most commonly used Web options.

- Under Browser Support, select the relevant check boxes for the browsers that are supported in viewing the presentation.

- Under Publish A Copy As, click **Change** to change the page title. Click **Browse** to locate the file, or type the path and name of the saved file, if it is not already listed.

- Click the **Open Published Web Page In Browser** check box to have the saved Web page open automatically when the publishing action is complete.

6. Click **Publish** to save the presentation as a Web page. A file and folder are created using the same file name. The folder contains all the slides and objects as .gif and other file types. You need both the file and folder if moving or copying the presentation.

Changing Web Options

Most of the options in this QuickSteps will use the same Web Options dialog box shown in Figure 9-15.

ACCESS THE WEB OPTIONS DIALOG BOX

To display the Web Options dialog box, follow steps 1–5 in "Publish Your Presentation as a Web Page." Then click Web Options.

–Or–

You can click the **Office Button**, click **Save As**, click the **Tools** button, and then click **Web Options**. Figure 9-15 shows the Web Options dialog box.

SET WEB COLORS FOR NAVIGATIONAL CONTROLS

To set the way color is handled in the navigational controls displayed by the saved Web page:

1. Click the **General** tab.

2. Click the **Add Slide Navigation Controls** check box.

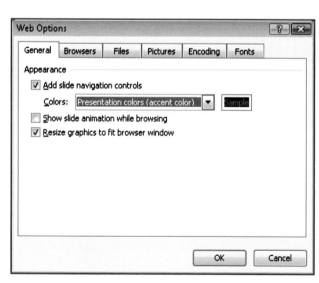

Figure 9-15: *The Web Options dialog box allows you to set various web options.*

3. Click the **Colors** down arrow, and select the way color will be displayed on the navigation controls buttons. You will see a preview in the Sample box.

4. Click **OK**.

SHOW ANIMATION WITH BROWSER

To show animation while the presentation is being viewed in the browser:

1. Click the **General** tab.

2. Click the **Show Slide Animation While Browsing** check box.

3. Click **OK**.

SELECT ADDITIONAL BROWSER CONTROLS

To specify additional browsers that may be used and to give additional specifications on saving the Web page:

1. Click the **Browsers** tab. Under Target Browsers, click the **People Who View This Web Page Will Be Using** down arrow. Click the oldest browser that can be expected. Note the warning that the older choices display progressively smaller Web pages.

2. Under Options:

   - Click **Allow PNG As A Graphics Format** to save the file in a more compressed file format, making file size smaller and the files faster to load. To use PNG (Portable Networks Graphics) file format, the browser must be a more recent one, at least Microsoft Internet Explorer 5.0 or later.

   - Click **Rely On VML** (Vector Markup Language) **For Displaying Graphics In Browsers** to generate vector-based images on-the-fly using simple XML (Extensible Markup Language).

   - Click **Save An Additional Version Of The Presentation For Older Browsers** to save a copy for use with the older browsers. This is useful if you chose the PNG format.

   - Click **Save New Web Pages As Single File Web Pages** to encapsulate all the supporting presentation files into one file instead of a file-and-folder combination.

3. Click **OK**.

Chapter 10

Printing and Running a Slide Show

This last chapter addresses how to display the output of a PowerPoint presentation. You may wish to present it as a slide show projected before an audience, on another monitor controlled by your laptop computer, or as a slide show running by itself on a standalone computer or kiosk. You may print it as transparencies, as a PostScript file for 35-mm slides, or simply as a printed handout. PowerPoint gives you a great deal of flexibility in how you offer your presentation.

Run a Slide Show

How you run your presentation depends, of course, on the circumstances around your need for creating it. Designing a show to run by itself is often useful for trade shows or other places where you want a presentation to automatically run repeatedly with no presenter. The viewer watches, with

limited or no ability to intervene with the presentation. The presentation may entice hundreds of people to stop as they stroll through, and watch it for a few minutes or through the whole slide show. In contrast, the presenter has total control over a "manned" presentation given before an audience varying from thousands to a small group, before a full auditorium of listeners, a classroom, a meeting, or a family gathering.

Automate a Slide Show

In order to run a slide show automatically, without any intervention from either the presenter or the viewer:

1. Open your presentation and click a slide to select it.

2. Click the **Animations** tab, and then, in the Transition To This Slide group, click the **Automatically After** spinners to set the number of seconds; or you can select the displayed time, and type the time you want.

3. In the Transition To This Slide group, click **Apply To All**.

4. To allow the viewer to manipulate the slide show, click the **Slide Show** tab, and click **Set Up Slide Show** in the Set Up group. The Set Up Show dialog box appears.

    - Click **Browsed At A Kiosk (Full Screen).**

      –Or–

    - Click **Browsed By An Individual (Window)** and click **Loop Continuously Until 'Esc'** To have the slide show automatically repeat and to prevent the viewer from manipulating it, as you would at a trade show

5. Click **OK** to close the Set Up Show dialog box.

Use a Laptop to Control the Presentation

When you connect a laptop to a projector or monitor, you may need to fine-tune the resolution and audio before you can run the presentation from your laptop as you normally would.

NOTE

You'll notice as you change the resolution that the size of the monitor images, noted as 1 and 2, change size relative to each other. The changes also depend on which monitor is selected.

QUICK**FACTS**

CLARIFYING KIOSK OPTIONS

In the Set Up Show dialog box (click the **Slide Show** tab, and then click **Set Up Slide Show**), you'll find that the Loop Continuously and Browsed At A Kiosk options are mutually exclusive. With Browsed At A Kiosk, the user is able to manipulate the show to see whatever he or she wants, moving as desired through the slide show. You can't do that *and* have the show loop continuously. If you choose Browsed At A Kiosk, the option Loop Continuously is dimmed (unavailable); if you choose Loop Continuously and then select Kiosk, the Kiosk option will now be selected but Loop Continuously will be dimmed. If you change your mind and want the presentation to loop, select Browsed By An Individual (Window), and Loop Continuously will again be available.

SET RESOLUTION AND VOLUME

1. Connect the cables from the projector or monitor to the laptop and the audio cables from the speakers to the laptop, according to your laptop documentation.

2. To set the resolution on your laptop computer, right-click the **Desktop** and click **Personalize** (in Microsoft Window Vista) or **Properties** (in Windows XP).

3. Click **Display Settings** in the Windows Vista Appearance And Personalization window, or click the **Settings** tab in Windows XP Display Properties dialog box.

4. Under Resolution, shown in Figure 10-1, drag the slider to the resolution that is common with the projector system (use 800 × 600 if you are unsure). You can flip back and forth between the monitor boxes shown in the dialog box to adjust the settings for both.

5. To set the volume, click the **Volume** icon 🔊 on the taskbar. Start the presentation.

6. Drag the volume slider where you want it.

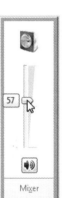

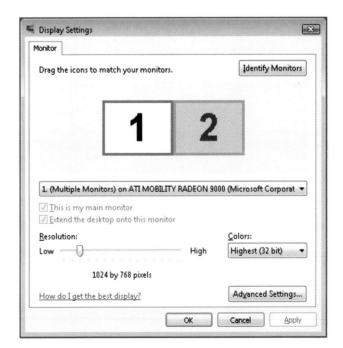

Figure 10-1: Adjust the resolution using the Display Settings dialog box.

NOTE

If you use PowerPoint Viewer (which you might if you don't have PowerPoint installed), you will not be able to edit the presentation.

NOTE

PowerPoint supports only two monitors for a slide show. Even if your computer has the ability to use more than two monitors, PowerPoint will use only the primary and secondary monitors.

CAUTION

If you have set any animations to occur, they may also be included in the timing. For instance, if you have the automatic timing set for ten seconds and also have a heading that will be displayed, the slide will be displayed first, the heading will be displayed after ten seconds, and the next slide will appear ten seconds after that. If the animation does not advance the way you expect, it may be set for "on click," and you may have to click the mouse to start the animation.

START THE PRESENTATION WITH POWERPOINT

Start the presentation exactly as you would on your own computer.

1. Start PowerPoint and open your presentation.

2. Press **F5** to start the slide show from the beginning.

START THE PRESENTATION WITH POWERPOINT VIEWER

If your packaged presentation runs from a CD/DVD (see Chapter 9 for information on packaging PowerPoint files), you might have chosen to install the PowerPoint Viewer as part of the packaging process. If you don't have PowerPoint and want to view slide shows, you can install the PowerPoint Viewer from the Microsoft Office Online Web site. (To find out how, click the **Microsoft Office PowerPoint Help** icon ⓐ, type <u>PowerPoint Viewer</u> in the search text box, and click **Search**.)

When you use PowerPoint Viewer for the first time, you will need to go through the initial screens to accept the end user license agreement for Microsoft software. After that, the presentation may start automatically without you doing anything more. If it does not:

- To start PowerPoint Viewer with a packaged CD presentation, use Windows Explorer to find the packaged presentation, and double-click the PowerPoint Viewer file, **pptview.exe**. Find the presentation you want to run (use Browse if necessary), and select it. Then click **Open.**

  –Or–

- If you have installed PowerPoint Viewer from the Microsoft Office Online Web site, click **Start**, select **All Programs**, and click **Microsoft Office PowerPoint Viewer 2007**. Find the presentation you want to run (use Browse if necessary), and select it. Then click **Open**.

Present a Dual-Monitor Slide Show

If you have a dual-monitor display card installed in your computer and are using a later version of Windows (XP or Vista), you can have different images of the slide show displayed on your primary monitor (perhaps a laptop) and on a projector or secondary monitor. For instance, your primary monitor can be

QUICKSTEPS

SETTING UP A SLIDE SHOW

All the topics in this QuickSteps require that the Set Up Slide Show dialog box be displayed. To do so, click the **Slide Show** tab, and click **Set Up Slide Show**. Figure 10-2 shows the Set Up Slide Show dialog box. (The Multiple Monitors section of the dialog box is covered in "Present a Dual-Monitor Slide Show.")

SHOW SELECTED SLIDES

The default for a slide show is to show all slides in the presentation. To show a range of slides, under Show Slides, click the **From** and **To** spinners to set the range.

DETERMINE THE TYPE OF PRESENTATION

To determine the type of presentation and how it will be run, select among these choices:

- Click **Presented By A Speaker (Full Screen)** to display a full-screen slide show that will have a speaker controlling the slide display.

- Click **Browsed By An Individual (Window)** if the slide show will be run by the viewer. Click **Show Scrollbar** if the scroll bar will be displayed for the viewer to use.

- Click **Browsed At A Kiosk (Full Screen)** if the slide show is to run automatically with no intervention by the viewer.

USE TIMINGS TO ADVANCE SLIDES

To advance from one slide to the next using previously set timings (rather than advancing the slides manually), click **Using Timings, If Present**.

Continued . . .

Figure 10-2: The Set Up Slide Show dialog box controls many aspects of how a slide show is run.

showing speaker notes, the presentation outline, and scroll bars and buttons, while these are hidden on the projector or monitor, which sees only the full-screen display of the slide show.

There are two methods of viewing a slide show using two monitors. The first uses Presenter view. (See "Use Two Monitors with Presenter View.") This offers a structured way of controlling the slide show. What is seen on the secondary monitor is the full-screen slide show. On the primary monitor is a reduced slide show with tools, thumbnails of the slides, and speaker notes. The second method is more freeform. Both monitors see the full-screen slide show, but the presenter can use pen tools and other tools not available in Presenter view. (See "Use a Pen Tool.") In this second method, the presenter is actively working with the slides while showing them.

UICKSTEPS

SETTING UP A SLIDE SHOW (Continued)

LOOP CONTINUOUSLY THROUGH THE PRESENTATION

Under Show Options, click **Loop Continuously Until 'Esc'** to cause the presentation to repeat until **ESC** is pressed. This is used for a trade show, for instance.

HIDE THE NARRATION DURING A SLIDE SHOW

To avoid playing the narration during the slide show, under Show Options, click **Show Without Narration**.

HIDE THE ANIMATION DURING A SLIDE SHOW

To hide any animation in the presentation, under Show Options, click **Show Without Animation**. This can make the slide show faster and easier to control. You do not have to click the mouse repeatedly to initiate various animations as well as to advance the slide show or wait for the animations to occur before continuing with the presentation.

SET THE SLIDE SHOW RESOLUTION

To set the resolution, click the **Slide Show Resolution** down arrow, and click a setting.

Slide show resolution:	Use Current Resolution
	640x480 (Fastest, Lowest Fidelity)
	800x600
	1024x768 (Slowest, Highest Fidelity)
	Use Current Resolution

SET UP MULTIPLE MONITOR SUPPORT

First, you must enable one computer to echo its images on a secondary monitor device.

1. To open the Display Settings dialog box, right-click the desktop for Windows Vista, and click **Personalize**. On the Appearance And Personalization dialog box, click **Display Settings**. The Display Settings dialog box is displayed. For Windows XP, right-click the desktop, click **Properties**, and click the **Settings** tab on the Display Properties dialog box.

2. On the Display Settings dialog box, click the monitor that represents the primary monitor, usually **1**.

3. Click the **This Is My Main Monitor** check box. If the option is unavailable but is selected, that option is set by default.

☑ This is my main monitor
☑ Extend the desktop onto this monitor

4. Click the secondary monitor, usually **2**.

5. If you are using Presenter view, click the **Extend The Desktop Onto This Monitor** check box, as shown in Figure 10-3. If you are using the full-screen slide show on both monitors, do not select this.

6. If needed, adjust the screen resolution and color quality to match the primary monitor.

7. Click **OK**.

USE TWO MONITORS WITH PRESENTER VIEW

After you have enabled the dual-monitor support, you can open your presentation. Presenter view offers some tools for navigating through the slides and for viewing speaker notes.

1. Open your presentation in PowerPoint.

2. Click the **Slide Show** tab, and click **Set Up Slide Show** in the Set Up group.

3. Under Multiple Monitors, click the **Display Slide Show On** down arrow, and click the monitor you want to be the one on which the presentation will be full-screen, usually **Monitor 2 Generic PnP Monitor**.

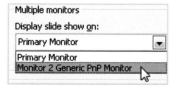

TIP

When using a laptop and another monitor, you have a few different ways to control the secondary device. On a Dell, use the **FN** key with **F8**. After you have the laptop connected to a monitor or projector, press the keys appropriate to your computer (in the case of Dell, **FN + F8** or **CRT/LCD**) a few times to cycle through the choices, for example, just laptop, laptop and secondary synched, just secondary, back to laptop only.

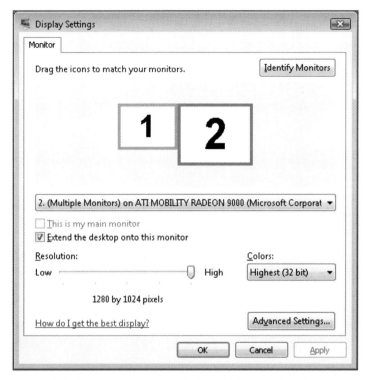

Figure 10-3: Set up your computer to handle dual-monitor display.

4. Click the **Show Presenter View** check box to make the Presenter view tools available to you on the primary monitor.

5. Click **OK**.

6. Click **Slide Show** to test the display; or you can press **F5** to start the presentation from the beginning.

RUN A SLIDE SHOW IN PRESENTER VIEW WITH DUAL MONITORS

When the support for the dual monitors has been established and you start the presentation, you have different screens available on the primary and secondary monitors. Figure 10-4 shows what the primary monitor looks like and the Presenter view tools for helping the presenter walk through the slide show.

TIP

To review slide show navigation options, right-click the show and click **Help**.

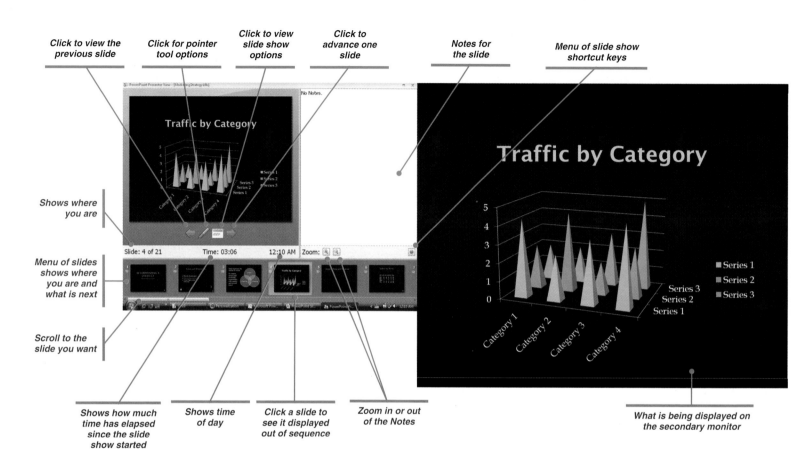

Click to view the previous slide

Click for pointer tool options

Click to view slide show options

Click to advance one slide

Notes for the slide

Menu of slide show shortcut keys

Shows where you are

Menu of slides shows where you are and what is next

Scroll to the slide you want

Shows how much time has elapsed since the slide show started

Shows time of day

Click a slide to see it displayed out of sequence

Zoom in or out of the Notes

What is being displayed on the secondary monitor

Figure 10-4: The primary monitor controls the presentation using the Presenter view.

RUN A FULL-SCREEN SLIDE SHOW WITH DUAL MONITORS

If you prefer to see a full-screen slide show and use the pen or other tools that are available with the right-click menu rather than the tools available with Presenter view (shown in Figure 10-4), do not select the Show Presenter View check box under Multiple Monitors in the Set Up Show dialog box. With that disabled, you will see the same display on both screens. You will also have the navigational buttons on the lower-left area of the screen and the slide show menu available when you right-click the screen, as seen in Figure 10-5.

10

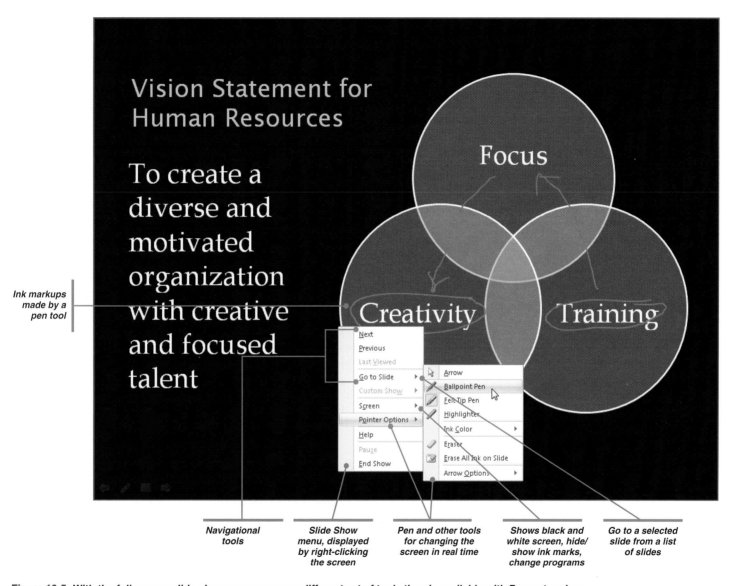

Figure 10-5: *With the full-screen slide show, you can use a different set of tools than is available with Presenter view.*

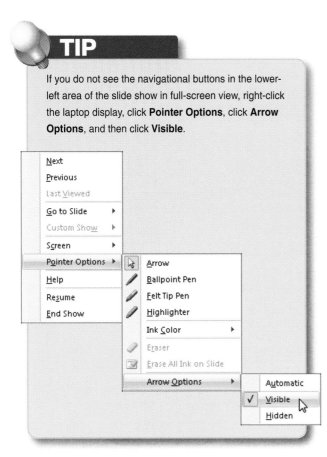

Use a Pen Tool

If you are not using Presenter view during a slide show, you can use a pen tool or highlighter to emphasize points, draw connecting lines, circle text you want to discuss, and more, as illustrated in Figure 10-6. Your marks will not be saved until you signal PowerPoint to do so. You must be in Slide Show view to do this.

1. With your presentation in Slide Show view, right-click the slide and click **Pointer Options**. (Or press **CTRL+P** to display the pen tool immediately.)

2. From the subsidiary menu, click the kind of pen you want:

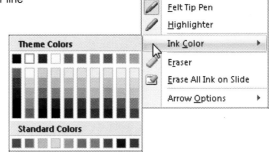

- **Ballpoint** creates a thinner line

- **Felt Tip Pen** creates a thicker line

- **Highlighter** creates a broader highlighter effect

3. To select a different color, right-click the screen, select **Ink Color**, and click the color you want.

4. When the slide show is over, you will be asked if you want to keep your ink annotations. Click **Keep** to save the markings. Click **Discard** to do away with them.

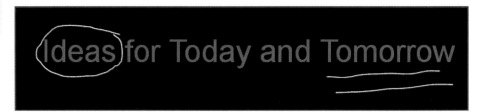

Figure 10-6: You can use a pen tool to emphasize points during your presentation.

TIP

Try these tricks to speed up your presentation: reduce the screen resolution; use graphic hardware acceleration if it is available on your computer; reduce animation of individual objects and bullets or the size of animated pictures on a slide; simplify the animations you have; and avoid using background special effects, such as gradient, textured, or transparency enhanced backgrounds.

QUICKSTEPS

NAVIGATING A SLIDE SHOW

If your slide show is not run automatically, you can use the following methods to navigate through your slide show.

START A SLIDE SHOW

From within PowerPoint, click **Slide Show** 🖵 to start at the current slide:

- Click the **Slide Show** tab, and click **From Beginning** in the Start Slide Show group to view the presentation from the beginning, or click **From Current Slide** to view the presentation from the current slide on.

From Beginning | From Current Slide | Custom Slide Show ▾
Start Slide Show

–Or–

- Press **F5**.

–Or–

- In My Computer or Windows Explorer, find the .pptx file and double-click it.

–Or–

Continued . . .

Rehearse Your Timing

You can rehearse the length of time it takes you to present your slide show.

1. With your presentation in Normal or Slide Sorter view, click the **Slide Show** tab, and click **Rehearse Timings** in the Set Up group.   ⏱️ Rehearse Timings

2. The presentation will begin with a full-screen slide show and a timer in the upper-left corner of the screen.

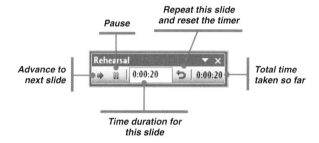

3. Go through your slide show as you expect to actually present it.

4. Click the **Next** arrow on the Rehearsal dialog box to move to the next slide, or press **PAGE DOWN**. If you need to try a slide again, click **Repeat** and do it over. If you need to stop for a time, click **Pause**.

5. When you are done, PowerPoint will display a message stating the time you have taken and asking whether you want to record the slide timings for use in timing the display of the slides during the actual presentation.

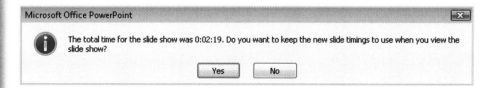

6. Click **Yes** to record the timings and create a timed presentation. The timings will appear on the bottom of the slides in Slide Sorter view. Click **No** to discard the timings.

Display a Blank Screen

As you are making a presentation, you may want to pause for a moment and hide the slide being displayed. You cannot be in Presenter view to do this.

1. For a white screen, press **W**; for a black screen, press **B**.

    –Or–

    In Slide Show view, press **SHIFT + F10** or right-click the slide. A menu will be displayed. Click **Screen** and select from these choices:

    - Click **White Screen** to display a totally white screen.
    - Click **Black Screen** to display a totally black screen.

2. When you are ready to continue, click **ESC**.

Create a Custom Slide Show

You can create a custom show from your current presentation by adding, removing, or shuffling the slides. Your new custom presentation is a subset of the current one.

1. Click the **Slide Show** tab, and click **Custom Slide Show** in the Start Slide Show group. Click **Custom Shows**. The Custom Show dialog box will appear.

2. Click **New** to create a new presentation. The Define Custom Show dialog box will appear, as shown in Figure 10-7.

3. Type a name in the **Slide Show Name** text box.

4. Select the titles of the slides you want from the Slides In Presentation list, and click **Add**.

5. To re-order the slides, select a slide in the Slides In Custom Show list, and click the up and down arrows on the right of the dialog box.

6. To delete slides from the new slide show, select the slide from Slides In Custom Show, and click **Remove**.

7. When you are finished, click **OK**.

UICKSTEPS

NAVIGATING A SLIDE SHOW (Continued)

- To go to a specific slide number, right-click the current slide, click **Go To Slide**, and click the slide you want.

–Or–

- Type the number of the slide, and press **ENTER**.

EXIT THE SLIDE SHOW

To exit a slide show, press **ESC**.

UICKSTEPS

SETTING PRINT OPTIONS

Print options can be set in the Print dialog box, which is displayed by clicking the **Office Button** and clicking **Print**.

OPEN PRINT PREVIEW

To quickly preview the presentation before you print it, click the **Preview** button.

PRINT SELECTED SLIDES

To select some of the slides, but not all, to be printed:

1. Click **Slides**.

- To enter a range of slides, type the first slide number, a hyphen, and the last slide number (for example, 5-15).

- To print individual slides, type the slide numbers separated by a comma (for example, 1,3,6). Combine ranges and individual slides with a comma (for example, 1,3,5-10,20-22).

⦿ Slides: 1-3,5,15|

Continued . . .

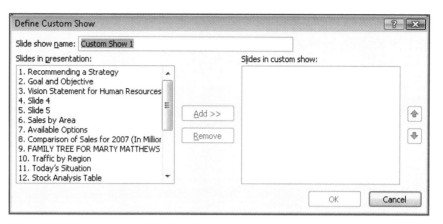

Figure 10-7: Create a new slide show from a current one by modifying the slides used and their order.

8. To review the new presentation, click **Show**; or to finish without viewing the slide show, click **Close**.

9. You can run the custom show in the future by clicking its name on the Custom Slide Show menu.

Place a Presentation Shortcut on Your Desktop

To place a shortcut to your presentation on the desktop:

1. Find the file using Windows Explorer.

2. Drag the file to the desktop with the right mouse button held down.

3. Release the button and click **Create Shortcut Here**.

Print Presentations in Various Ways

A presentation can be printed to paper (in color or grayscale), to transparencies, or to a file for transfer to a 35-mm slide-service bureau or for high-resolution

10

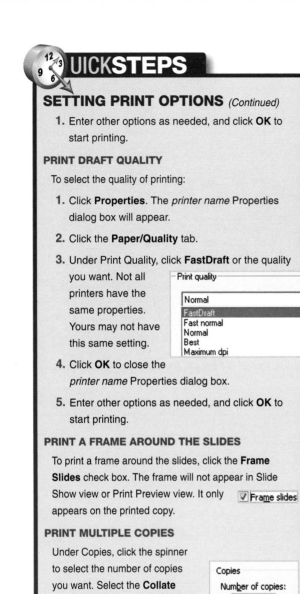

SETTING PRINT OPTIONS *(Continued)*

1. Enter other options as needed, and click **OK** to start printing.

PRINT DRAFT QUALITY

To select the quality of printing:

1. Click **Properties**. The *printer name* Properties dialog box will appear.

2. Click the **Paper/Quality** tab.

3. Under Print Quality, click **FastDraft** or the quality you want. Not all printers have the same properties. Yours may not have this same setting.

4. Click **OK** to close the *printer name* Properties dialog box.

5. Enter other options as needed, and click **OK** to start printing.

PRINT A FRAME AROUND THE SLIDES

To print a frame around the slides, click the **Frame Slides** check box. The frame will not appear in Slide Show view or Print Preview view. It only appears on the printed copy.

PRINT MULTIPLE COPIES

Under Copies, click the spinner to select the number of copies you want. Select the **Collate** check box if you want the copies to be printed so that pages are automatically separated into complete, sequenced sets. (This is the default option.)

---

printing. In this section, you will learn how to print to a printer or file to produce these types of output.

Preview Slides Before Printing

As part of the print process, you can quickly preview your slides before printing them, as seen in Figure 10-8.

1. Click the **Office Button**, point to **Print**, and then click **Print Preview** in the popup menu.

2. At the top of the window, under **Print What?,** click the **Slides** down arrow. See Chapter 4 for further information on previewing notes, outline pages, and handouts.

3. The pointer will initially be a **Zoom** icon. You can click to zoom up and click again to zoom down. To be more precise in the magnification, click the **Zoom** button, and select a magnification. You can toggle back and forth between a selected magnification and the last one used by clicking the magnifying glass that the pointer morphs into.

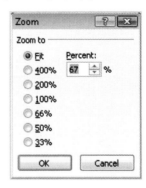

4. To advance to the next page, click **Next Page** in the Preview group, click the scroll bar, or press **PAGE DOWN**. Click **Previous Page**, click the scroll bar, or press **PAGE UP** to return to a previous slide.

5. If you decide to print the previewed slides, click **Print**.

6. Click **Close Print Preview** to return to the regular slide display.

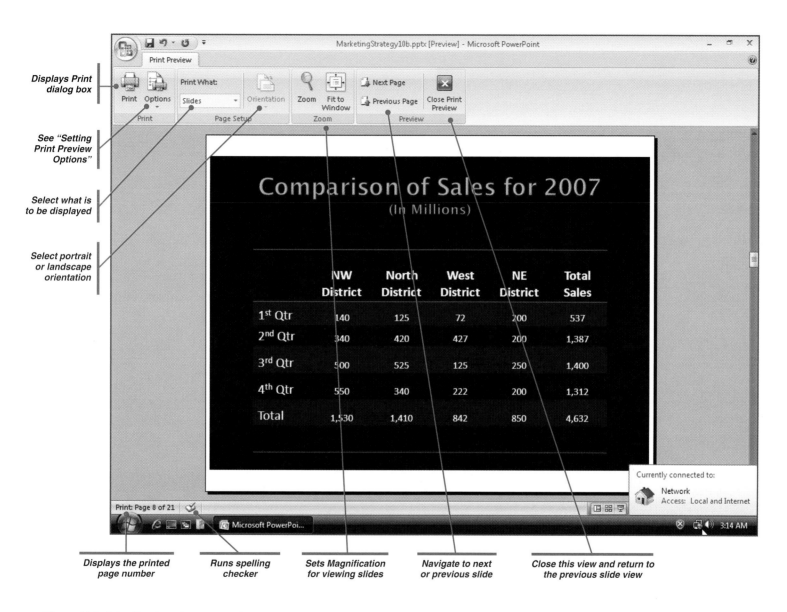

Displays Print dialog box

See "Setting Print Preview Options"

Select what is to be displayed

Select portrait or landscape orientation

Displays the printed page number

Runs spelling checker

Sets Magnification for viewing slides

Navigate to next or previous slide

Close this view and return to the previous slide view

Figure 10-8: Print Preview gives you a chance to spot any changes you want to make before printing.

NOTE

These print options are also available in the Print dialog box.

QUICKSTEPS

SETTING PRINT PREVIEW OPTIONS

You can set some of the printer options in the Print Preview screen. You might want to do this here instead of in the Print dialog box in order to preview the effects of the options. Figure 10-9 shows the Options menu. Click **Print Preview** to display the Print Preview screen, and click **Options**.

ESTABLISH PRINT COLOR

To designate the color in which the slides will be previewed and printed:

1. Click **Options** in the Print group, and click **Color/ Grayscale** to open the subsidiary menu.

2. Click one of these options:

   - **Color** for color slides (requires a color printer)

     1st Qtr
     2nd Qtr

   - **Grayscale** for grayscale slides

     1st Qtr
     2nd Qtr

   - **Pure Black And White** for no gray tones

     1st Qtr
     2nd Qtr

HIDE OR PRINT COMMENTS, MARKINGS, AND HIDDEN SLIDES

Click **Options** in the Print group. You can toggle Print Hidden Slides and Print Comments And Ink Markup.

Continued . . .

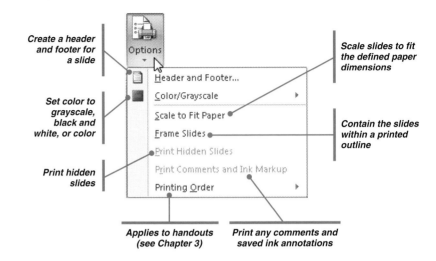

Create a header and footer for a slide

Set color to grayscale, black and white, or color

Print hidden slides

Scale slides to fit the defined paper dimensions

Contain the slides within a printed outline

Applies to handouts (see Chapter 3)

Print any comments and saved ink annotations

Figure 10-9: The Print Preview Options dialog box allows you to set various options and then preview them.

Configure Page Setup

Set up the slide width and height, page size, slide orientation, and the beginning slide number by using the Page Setup dialog box.

1. Click the **Design** tab, and click **Page Setup** in the Page Setup group. The Page Setup dialog box will appear, as shown in Figure 10-10.

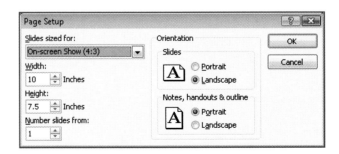

Figure 10-10: The Page Setup dialog box displays options for varying your slide printout.

SETTING PRINT PREVIEW OPTIONS

(Continued)

A check mark beside the options means that hidden slides, comments, and ink markups will appear in the preview and be printed. To deselect the options, click the check marks to remove them. (If Print Hidden Slides or Print Comments And Ink Markup is dimmed, it means these are not in the presentation.)

INSERT HEADERS AND FOOTERS

To insert a header or footer on a slide or on all slides, click **Options** in the Print group, and click **Header And Footer**. The Header And Footer dialog box will appear.

1. Select the **Date And Time** check box to include the date and time on the slide:

   - Click **Update Automatically** and click the down arrow to choose a style in which the current date and time should appear when automatically updated.

   –Or–

   - Click **Fixed** and type a date and time (or other text) that you want to appear on the slide without being updated.

2. Click the **Slide Number** check box to have the slide number appear on the slide.

3. Click the **Footer** check box, and type the footer text in the text box.

Continued . . .

2. Select among these options:

   - To select a page size, click the **Slides Sized For** down arrow, and click an option.

   - To precisely enter the slide size, use the spinners to set the width and height.

   - To set a starting slide number other than 1, click the **Number Slides From** spinner.

   - Under Slide Orientation, click **Portrait** to set the slide orientation to tall. Click **Landscape** to set the slide orientation to wide.

3. Click **OK** to close the Page Setup dialog box.

Print Transparencies

You may want to print your slides on transparencies to present the slide show with an overhead projector. Use the Page Setup dialog box to set the type of output media. (Not all printers have a specified software option for printing transparencies. If yours doesn't, see your printer's manual for instruction on how to print transparencies.) PowerPoint will optimize your slides for the black-and-white or color printer that you choose.

1. Click the **Design** tab, and click **Page Setup**.

2. Click the **Slides Sized For** down arrow, and click **Overhead**.

3. Set the orientation and other options as needed.

4. Click **OK** to close the dialog box.

5. Print the slides as usual.

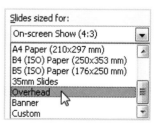

SETTING PRINT PREVIEW OPTIONS

(Continued)

4. Click the **Don't Show On Title Slide** check box to prevent the selected information from being displayed on the first or title slide.

5. Click **Apply** to apply the options to only the selected slide or click **Apply To All** to apply the options to all slides.

See Chapter 3 for information about headers and footers for notes and handouts.

SCALE SLIDES TO FIT PAPER

Since you can print the slides on a variety of paper sizes, you can scale the slides to fit the size, whatever it may be. To do so, click **Options** in the Print group, and place a check mark next to **Scale To Fit Paper**.

NOTE

If you do not have the required PostScript driver, get one from your source for 35-mm slides. Install it in Windows Vista by clicking **Start**, clicking **Hardware And Sound**, and, under Printers clicking **Add A Printer**. In Windows XP, click **Start**, click **Printers And Faxes** (your path to the Printers and Faxes Control Panel feature may vary, depending on your operating system), and click **Add A Printer**.

TIP

Since Windows adds a .prn file extension to the saved file, you may want to change it to .ps, for PostScript.

Print a PostScript File for 35-mm Slides

You cannot print 35-mm slides using PowerPoint. However, you can create a PostScript file to take to a business that can then create 35-mm slides from that. To create PostScript files, you must have a color PostScript driver installed on your computer. Many come with the Windows operating system, but your source for creating 35-mm slides may have specific file types that you need to produce. After receiving those specifications, you may print a PostScript file.

1. First, click the **Design** tab, and click **Page Setup** in the Page Setup group. The Page Setup dialog box will appear.

2. Click the **Slides Sized For** down arrow, and click **35mm Slides**.

Slides sized for:
Overhead ▼
A4 Paper (210x297 mm)
B4 (ISO) Paper (250x353 mm)
B5 (ISO) Paper (176x250 mm)
35mm Slides
Overhead
Banner
Custom

3. Click **OK** to close the dialog box.

4. Click the **Office Button**, and click **Print**. The Print dialog box will appear.

5. Click the **Name** down arrow, and click the name of your PostScript printer driver.

6. Click the options you want:

   - Select **Slides** in Print What?.
   - Select **Color** in the Color/Grayscale drop-down list box.
   - Clear the **Print Comments And Ink Markup** check box.
   - Click the **Print Hidden Slides** check box.
   - Select any other options you want.

7. Click the **Print To File** check box.

8. Click **OK** to start the printing to a file. The Print To dialog box will appear.

9. In the Print To File dialog box, type your file name and location where it is to be saved. Click **Save**.

Stop Printing

To halt the printing of the slides while printing is in progress:

1. Double-click the **Printer** icon in the taskbar. A dialog box for your printer will appear.

2. Click the presentation name to select it.

3. Click **Document** and click **Cancel**.

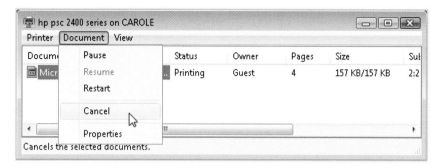

4. Click **Yes** to confirm that you want to cancel the print job.

5. Click **Close** to close the dialog box.

Change Printers

To print to a printer other than the default one for your computer:

1. Click the **Office Button**, and click **Print**. The Print dialog box will appear.

2. Click the **Name** down arrow, and click the printer you want to use:

   ● If you are on an Active Directory domain and the printer is not there, click **Find Printers** and follow the directions on the dialog box to search for and find the printer.

   ● If the printer is not on your computer or network, you must add it. Click **Start**, click **Control Panel** (your path to the Printer Control Panel feature may vary, depending on your operating system), click **Hardware And Sound**, and click **Printer**. Click the **Add A Printer** button. Follow the wizard or dialog box prompts to install the printer on your computer or network.

3. When the correct printer name is in the Print dialog box and you have selected the options you want, click **OK** to begin printing.

For more information on installing printers on the Windows Vista operating system, see *Windows Vista QuickSteps*, published by McGraw-Hill/Osborne.

Because the print queue fills so quickly, you may not be able to cancel the printing of all the slides. Also, if your presentation is short, the **Print** icon will be present on the taskbar for a short time. You may not be able to click it fast enough.

Use the Quick Print Feature

To print immediately using your default printer and options:

1. Click the **Office Button**.

2. Hold your pointer over the Print option, but do not click it.

3. On the context menu, click **Quick Print**.

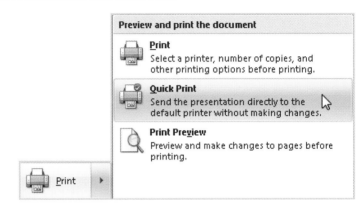

Numbers

Fill formatting option, using with charts, 138–139

First Column tool, using with tables, 101

Fit Slide to Current Window button, description of, 4

Fit Slide To Current Window feature, using, 43

Fit To Window feature, using, 43

flipping shapes, 173

folders
  adding clips to, 121
  adding to Clip Organizer, 121–122
  copying presentation files to, 189
  creating, 17

font color, changing, 65

Font dialog box, using, 77–78

Font group, using with tables, 97–98

fonts
  changing, 64–65
  changing for presentations, 46
  changing for themes, 44, 46
  creating sets of theme fonts, 46
  seeing effects of, 44
  setting defaults for saved presentations, 193, 195
  types of, 44

footers
  entering, 52
  hiding on title page, 52
  inserting on slides, 215–216
  removing, 52
  using on notes and handouts, 60–61
  using on slides, 51–52

Format Data Labels, displaying for charts, 136

Format dialog boxes, using with charts, 137, 139–140

Format elements dialog box
  closing, 140
  displaying, 137

Format Painter
  copying attributes with, 51–52
  using, 125

formatting
  copying with Format Painter, 80
  showing and hiding in outline text, 31

formatting toolbar, using, 98

formulas
  copying, 112
  entering, 111–112

frames, printing around slides, 212

Freeform tool, using, 168

G

gap depth and width, adjusting for charts, 143

Get Updates option, accessing, 13

Go To Microsoft Office Online option, accessing, 13

gradient backgrounds, creating for slides, 159–160

graphic attributes, copying between slides, 51

graphic effects, changing themed graphic effects, 47

graphic styles, changing in SmartArt, 128

graphic text, altering, 127

graphics
  adding shapes to, 127
  displaying layout options for, 127
  inserting, 27
  inserting SmartArt graphics, 126
  resetting in SmartArt, 128

graphs versus charts, 130

gridlines
  displaying to draw tables, 92
  formatting in charts, 147
  showing and hiding, 109

grids and guides
  aligning shapes with, 172
  displaying, 123–125

Group tool on Table Layout tab, description of, 109

groups
  of commands and tools, 5
  recombining after ungrouping, 169
  relationship to ribbon, 4

guides and grids
  aligning shapes with, 172
  displaying, 123–125

H

handout master, changing, 68–70

handout thumbnails, removing borders from, 61

handouts
  displaying slides on, 63
  including page numbers in, 61
  printing, 61
  using headers and footers on, 60–61

Header and Footer dialog box
  displaying, 51
  options on, 215
  specifying printing options on, 63

Header Row tool, using with tables, 101

headers
  including dates and times in, 61
  inserting on slides, 215–216
  removing, 52
  using on notes and handouts, 60–61

heading font, explanation of, 44

Height tool on Table Layout tab, description of, 108

Help system, accessing, 12–13

hidden slides, hiding and printing, 214–215

Hierarchy category in SmartArt, explanation of, 126

HTML outlines, using, 29

hyperlink color, changing, 53

hyperlinks
  inserting and removing, 52–53
  placing on slides, 190–191

I

identifying information, adding to presentations, 11–12

images
  creating mirror images for shapes, 169–170
  types of, 115

indenting with keyboard, 32

Ink Color option, using with pen tools, 208

Insert Hyperlink dialog box, opening, 191

Insert Sound dialog box, displaying, 178

Insert tools on Table Layout tab, descriptions of, 107

insertion point, being careful with, 42

Installed Templates presentation, choosing, 5

Installed Themes presentation, choosing, 5

Internet, searching for clip art on, 122–123

K

keyboard
  cutting and pasting text with, 80
  editing with, 79
  indenting with, 32
  starting PowerPoint from, 2

keyboard shortcuts
  accessing ribbon, 4
  blank screen, 210
  for copying information, 78
  copying slide contents, 46
  copying slides, 46
  creating new lines in outlines, 31
  dual monitors used with Dell laptops, 205
  entering bulleted text, 36
  indenting, 32
  inserting slides, 36, 46

inserting tabs in table cells, 98
moving pointer within text, 79
moving to placeholders, 36
navigating slides, 36
pen tools, 208
removing slides, 46
returning to arrow pointer, 208
for saving presentations, 15
selecting text, 79
for starting and ending slide
    shows, 36–37
starting PowerPoint, 2
for starting presentations, 46
starting slide shows, 8, 209
for switching from Slide Show to
    Normal view, 37
toggling ribbon size, 6
for undoing actions, 111
keywords
    adding to clips, 124
    deleting from clips, 124–125
    modifying, 125
Kiosk options, explanations of, 201

L

labels, adding to text boxes, 127
laptops
    setting resolution and volume
        on, 201
    starting presentations on, 202
    using as control devices for
        projectors or monitors, 200
    using with other monitors, 205
Last Column tool, using
    with tables, 101
layout masters, relationship to slide
    masters, 63
layout options, displaying for
    graphics, 127
layouts
    explanation of, 20
    inserting tables from, 90–91
    selecting, 25–26

leader lines, showing and hiding on
    pie charts, 135–136
legend entries, rearranging for Excel
    source data, 134
legends, formatting for charts,
    141–142
Line formatting option, using with
    charts, 138
line spacing, adjusting, 74
Line Style formatting option, using
    with charts, 138
lines, moving up and down, 32
linked files, managing, 181
List category in SmartArt,
    explanation of, 125
lists, using SmartArt graphics
    for, 77–78
Lock Aspect Ratio tool on Table
    Layout tab, description of, 108
Loop Continuously option, example
    of, 200
Loop Until Next Sound feature,
    using, 152

M

margins
    setting cell margins for
        tables, 98
    setting in text boxes, 73
markings, hiding and printing,
    214–215
master layouts, editing, 64–66
master slides, explanation of, 20
masters. See layout masters; slide
    masters
Matrix category in SmartArt,
    explanation of, 126
menus. See ribbon
Merge Cells tool on Table Layout tab,
    description of, 107
microphones, testing for recording
    sound files, 182–183

Microsoft Excel 2007 window,
    opening, 134
Microsoft Office drawings,
    converting clip art to, 126
Microsoft Office Online presentation,
    choosing, 6
Microsoft resources, accessing, 13
Microsoft Word, copying tables
    from, 94–95
Microsoft Word (.doc) outlines,
    using, 29
mini toolbar, displaying, 10–11
mirror images, creating for shapes,
    169–170
monitors. See also dual monitors
    options for using dual monitors, 203
    setting up multiple monitor
        support, 204
    using with laptops, 205
move split action, performing, 39
movies. See also videos
    filling screens with, 187
    looping and rewinding, 187
    resizing, 187
My Templates presentation,
    choosing, 5

N

narration, hiding during slide
    shows, 204
narrative timings, compatibility
    of, 184
narratives, recording for
    presentations, 184–185
navigational buttons, displaying, 208
New From Existing presentation,
    choosing, 6
Normal view
    editing custom themes in, 48
    getting back to, 8
    opening, 8
    switching to, 37

notes
    adding objects to, 56
    changing backgrounds of, 56
    creating in Notes Page, 59
    creating in Notes pane, 56
    including page numbers in, 61
    making global changes to, 67
    printing, 59
    printing speaker notes, 60
    using headers and footers on, 60–61
notes master, 67–68
Notes Page, opening, 56
Notes pane
    adding text placeholder to, 68
    description of, 4
    location of, 3
Number option, using with charts,
    138–139
numbering styles, changing, 77

O

objects
    copying attributes between, 125
    cropping, 117–118
    examples of, 125
    moving, 117
    re-ordering, 171
    resizing, 118, 173
    selecting, 117
Office Button
    description of, 4
    location of, 3
Office Clipboard. See Clipboard
Office drawings, converting clip art
    to, 126
Opening Page Default, setting, 7
Outline tab
    description of, 4
    expanding, 26
    location of, 3, 28
outline text
    moving up and down, 31

T

tab settings, changing, 74–76
table backgrounds, using special
    effects in, 103–105
table borders, defining, 93
table cells
    entering text in, 97
    inserting tabs in, 98
    merging and splitting, 112
    merging to enlarge pictures,
      104–105
    rotating text in, 100
    selecting, 109
    setting heights and widths of, 111
Table Layout tab, options on, 107–109
table outline, creating, 93
table styles
    enabling options for, 100
    removing formatting of, 102
Table Styles tool, using
    with tables, 101
tables
    adding effects to, 93
    adding text to, 93
    advisory about using Eraser tool
      with, 106
    basics of, 90
    changing border colors for, 106
    changing border style in, 105–106
    changing border weights for, 106
    copying from Word, 94–95
    deleting, 98
    determining selected status of, 93
    displaying and hiding border lines
      in, 105
    displaying formulas in, 111–112
    drawing, 91–93
    formatting text in, 97–98
    inserting, 27
    inserting from layouts, 90–91
    inserting from scratch, 91
    selecting, 110
    setting cell margins for, 98

using pictures in, 104
using preset styles with, 102
tabs, inserting in table cells, 98
tags, relationship to XML files, 14
templates
    choosing, 5
    contents of, 23
    creating, 23
    finding, 24
    saving, 23
    saving presentations as, 16
    for themes, 20
text
    adding to tables, 93
    aligning, 79–80, 97–98
    altering on graphics, 127
    centering, 97–98
    changing in WordArt images, 164
    cutting and pasting with
      keyboard, 80
    deleting, 79
    disabling word wrap for, 73
    entering in table cells, 97
    filling and outlining, 164
    fitting with AutoFit feature, 81–82
    formatting in charts, 146–147
    formatting in tables, 97–98
    moving and copying, 80
    moving pointer in, 79
    rotating in table cells, 100
    selecting, 79
    typing within shapes, 168
text attributes
    copying between slides, 51
    modifying, 26, 64–65
text boxes
    adding labels to, 127
    anchoring text in, 73
    changing fill color in, 74
    changing widths and heights
      of, 72
    copying, 73
    deleting, 72
    entering text in, 72

inserting, 71
moving, 72
positioning precisely, 74
rotating, 73
rotating text in, 73
setting margins in, 73
setting up columns in, 74
Text Direction tool on Table Layout
    tab, description of, 108
text effects, applying, 165
text layouts, using, 70–71
text placeholders, adding to Notes
    pane, 68
text selections, copying multiple
    selections, 80
textured backgrounds, creating for
    placeholders and shapes, 161
theme colors, customizing, 47–50
Theme Effects feature, accessing, 47
theme fonts
    changing, 44, 46
    creating sets of, 46
themed graphic effects, changing, 47
themes
    applying to all slides, 24
    applying to selected slides, 25
    changing colors of, 43–44
    creating presentations from, 22–23
    explanation of, 20
    finding, 24
    saving changes to, 50
    saving custom themes, 50–51
    setting default theme for future
      presentations, 25
    using multiple design themes, 42
tick mark types, specifying for axes
    in charts, 145
time
    displaying in Header and Footer
      dialog box, 51–52
    including in headers, 61
timing
    advancing slides with, 203
    rehearsing, 209

title masters, creating, 66–68
title page, hiding footers on, 52
titles
    adding to presentations, 25
    altering for charts, 141–142
    changing in browsers, 195
    removing AutoFit feature for, 82
tools, groups of, 5
tooltips, displaying for effects, 156
Total Row tool, using with
    tables, 101
transition timings, checking for
    sounds, 184
transitions
    application of, 152
    making between slides, 150–152
transparencies, printing, 215
Triggers option, using
    with videos, 189
.txt (Plain Text) outlines, using, 29

U

undoing actions, 111

V

vector image, explanation of, 115
video options, changing, 187–188
videos. *See also* movies
    changing start and play times of,
      187–188
    inserting, 185
    inserting action buttons in,
      188–189
    overriding with sounds, 185
    resetting play transitions for, 188
    setting volume of, 188
    starting, pausing, and stopping,
      188–189
View Gridlines tool on Table Layout
    tab, description of, 107
View toolbar, description of, 4

views
 opening, 8
 returning to, 9
volume
 setting for videos, 188
 setting on laptops, 201

W

Web, searching for clip art on,
 122–123
Web colors, setting for navigational
 controls, 196–197
Web Options dialog box, displaying,
 193, 196

Web pages
 connecting to, 192–193
 publishing presentations as, 194–196
 using browsers with, 195
white screens, displaying, 210
Width tool on Table Layout tab,
 description of, 108
windows
 cascading, 39, 41
 displaying separately, 39–40
 fitting slides in, 43
Word (.doc) outlines, using, 29
Word, copying tables from, 94–95
word wrap, disabling, 73
WordArt effects, applying, 164

WordArt images, changing
 text in, 164
WordArt Styles, using, 65
workbooks, viewing information
 about, 12

X

x in file extensions, meaning of, 14
x-axis in charts
 changing for Excel source data, 134
 determining in Excel, 135
 explanation of, 130
XML (eXtensible Markup Language)
 formats, overview of, 14–15

Y

y-axis in charts
 changing for Excel source data, 134
 determining in Excel, 135
 explanation of, 130

Z

z-axis in charts, explanation of, 130
zoom buttons, location of, 3
zoom feature, using, 42–43
Zoom slider
 description of, 4
 location of, 3
Zoom view, using, 173